MAN OF TASTE

FILM AND CULTURE

FILM AND CULTURE

A series of Columbia University Press

EDITED BY JOHN BELTON

The Cinema of Extractions: Film Materials and Their Forms, by Brian Jacobson

George Cukor's People, by Joseph McBride

Death by Laughter: Female Hysteria and Early Cinema, by Maggie Hennefeld

The Rebirth of Suspense: Slowness and Atmosphere in Cinema, by Rick Warner

Hollis Frampton: Navigating the Infinite Cinema, by Michael Zryd

Perplexing Plots: Popular Storytelling and the Poetics of Murder, by David Bordwell

Horror Film and Otherness, by Adam Lowenstein

Hollywood's Embassies: How Movie Theaters Projected American Power Around the World, by Ross Melnick

Music in Cinema, by Michel Chion

Bombay Hustle: Making Movies in a Colonial City, by Debashree Mukherjee

Absence in Cinema: The Art of Showing Nothing, by Justin Remes

Hollywood's Artists: The Directors Guild of America and the Construction of Authorship, by Virginia Wright Wexman

Film Studies, second edition, by Ed Sikov

For a complete list of books in the series, please see the Columbia University Press website.

MAN OF TASTE

The Erotic Cinema of Radley Metzger

ROB KING

Columbia University Press

New York

Columbia University Press
Publishers Since 1893
New York Chichester, West Sussex
cup.columbia.edu

Library of Congress Cataloging-in-Publication Data
Names: King, Rob, 1975– author.
Title: Man of taste : the erotic cinema of Radley Metzger / Rob King.
Description: New York : Columbia University Press, 2025. | Series: Film and culture | Includes bibliographical references and index.
Identifiers: LCCN 2024024927 (print) | LCCN 2024024928 (ebook) | ISBN 9780231214049 (hardback) | ISBN 9780231214056 (trade paperback) | ISBN 9780231560160 (ebook)
Subjects: LCSH: Metzger, Radley—Criticism and interpretation.
Classification: LCC PN1998.3.M4835 K56 2025 (print) | LCC PN1998.3.M4835 (ebook) | DDC 791.4302/33092—dc23/eng/20240724
LC record available at https://lccn.loc.gov/2024024927
LC ebook record available at https://lccn.loc.gov/2024024928

Printed in the United States of America

Cover design: Elliott S. Cairns
Cover image: Audubon Films

Simulation, then, is the crucial word. Too much reality is just too much. But when we can control its dosage—when we can write the script, hire the actors, and direct the performance—the field of excitement is prepared.

—Robert J. Stoller, *Observing the Erotic Imagination*

CONTENTS

MAN OF TASTE

INTRODUCTION

Radley Metzger, Man of Taste

Consider the man of taste: Radley Metzger, a forty-year-old bachelor-filmmaker, as profiled in the pages of a 1969 issue of *Gentlemen's Quarterly* (figure 0.1). His distinctions are many. He is handsome. "He looks younger, slenderer and handsomer than he photographs," we are told, "bearing a striking resemblance to the pre–New York Philharmonic Leonard Bernstein." He is fashionable: four photo illustrations show Metzger in different getups from his own wardrobe, personally tailored for him by Italian costume designer Enrico Sabbatini. ("My taste runs international," Metzger explains.) He is successful in his chosen business, having directed, produced, or distributed some twenty-eight films, which have "grossed for him anywhere from $1½ million to $3 million each." He is a devotee of the art of cinema, in particular of the studio-era Hollywood that preceded him: "The man knows—and loves—movies. You know it from the affectionate way he talks about them and not because he tells you he's seen 'Citizen Kane' 127 times."[1]

And he makes sex films.

One of these things is, of course, not like the others—which is actually the underlying point of the *GQ* piece. As the author notes: "Radley Metzger, according to stereotype, should be loud-mouthed, crude and lecherous, with fleshy face and fat cigar. Actually, he's more Prince Hamlet than King Leer." This sense of cognitive dissonance also lies at the heart of the present book, a critical study of a filmmaker whose career offers a kind of fun-house-mirror reflection of an era in which American film culture was transformed by a language of taste and distinction. The years in which Metzger flourished as a filmmaker—the late 1950s through the late 1970s—mark out the period when cinema's reputation as an art form was at its loftiest, thanks to the postwar popularization of new

I,
A FILM MAKER

AN INTERVIEW BY RON ALEXANDER

TO RADLEY METZGER, SEX IS A MONEY-SPLENDORED THING

"I, A Woman"
"Carmen, Baby"
"Therese and Isabelle"
"The Libertine"
"Camille 2000"

The motion pictures above are not necessarily the beginning of a satyr's decade-end ten-best list. What they do have in common is that they are five of 28 films either produced, directed or distributed by the same man, and they have grossed for him anywhere from \$1½ million to \$3 million each. Or, to quote Variety vernacular, "Metzger, Leighton and Sexcess Formula: Audubon's 28 Films All in Black."

Audubon is a 9-year-old film distributor; Leighton is Ava, its secretary-treasurer and sales manager ("the sole female sales manager in the business," according to an Audubon press release) and Metzger is Radley, its 40-year-old bachelor-director and, until last June when Audubon Films became a corporation, sole proprietor.

Even for an industry which exhibits constant astonishments, Radley Metzger is something of a phenomenon. Until he came on the scene, the so-called "sexploitation films," flaunting titles like "Olga's Girls" and "Always on Saturday," were banished, justifiably, to the shabbier open-till-4 a.m.-type movie houses in the, shall we say, less-desirable sections of some cities.

While Metzger can never be accused of having cleansed sex-stressing films, he most certainly did polish them and endow them with Class. He didn't so much bring underground films above ground as move them across the tracks to more respectable parts of town: from New York's West 42nd Street to East 57th; the equivalent of moving from Times Square Sam's Discount Store to Sex Fifth Avenue, as it were.

Even the ads for his films now display surprising propriety; whereas several years ago one of his first, "The Dirty Girls," was newspaper-advertised as "'The D—Girls'—call the theater for its real name!" the announcements for "Camille 2000" are absolutely elegant. Suggestive, but elegant. His films — perhaps sick, but certainly slick — are increasingly lavish. Technicolor, Panavision, handsome settings, chic (but revealing) clothes (when

continued on page 146

0.1 Radley Metzger in *Gentlemen's Quarterly* (Winter 1969–70). Photos by Zachary Freyman.

Source: Courtesy of the estate of Robert Kohler.

critical categories like the "foreign film," "art cinema," and the "auteur" director. Metzger was at once an active agent in these processes and somebody who sought to channel his own cinephile aspirations into the more questionable arena of adult film, first in the world of 1960s sexploitation cinema and then, the following decade, in hardcore pornography. Along the way, he would become the American sexual revolution's flagship example of what film scholar David Andrews has dubbed the "cult-art auteur": a filmmaker who achieves *subcultural* legitimacy—here, within the field of adult cinema—but lacks more general *cultural* legitimacy, or, to put it somewhat differently, a filmmaker who has legitimate *aspirations* but no legitimate *accomplishments*.[2]

How else to explain the career of a filmmaker who worked at Janus Films in the late 1950s cutting trailers for films that would immediately enter the art-house pantheon—Ingmar Bergman's *The Magician* (1958) and Andrzej Wajda's *Ashes and Diamonds* (1958), among others—but whose own attempts to incorporate art-house distinction into sexploitation fare were often dismissed as mere charlatanism? What to make of a director who once expressed his hope that "deep down," on his inside, an "Orson Welles is just sitting there" waiting to break out, but whose most uncontested achievement would be a pseudonymously directed hardcore film—*The Opening of Misty Beethoven*—that, six years after its 1976 release, was picked for the top spot in Jim Holliday's *The Top 100 X-Rated Films of All Time*?[3] Cult-art auteurs, notes Andrews, often have mixed feelings about the works for which they are most celebrated, since it is difficult for them to square the terms of their acclaim with their own aspirations. How much more so for Metzger, though, whose ambitions were channeled into films that were fêted among less reputable quarters for displaying "lots of tits, gorgeous broads, orgies, fucking; it's all there! (No cock or hair)."[4] Orson Welles never got a review like that.

This book uses Metzger's career to investigate what taste means and how it works when it is exercised within the sphere of what taste scorns. It tells the story of a filmmaker whose aestheticism took root in a soil well beyond the manicured lawns of cultural legitimacy, and of the curious forms into which his aestheticism flowered. It is a tale of bad faith and a journey to taste's end.[5]

Yet perhaps this territory is not as strange as first appearances imply. A common enough concept captures the veneer of legitimacy to which adult fare often aspires, namely, the ideal of "the erotic," of erotic*a* and erotic*ism*. This was in fact Metzger's favored terminology whenever he was asked to define his movies. "I tend to gravitate toward the word *erotic*," he once explained, although he immediately acknowledged his own uncertainty by adding: "I don't know if they're erotic movies or movies with a high content of eroticism."[6]

But what did "erotic" mean in Metzger's cagey usage? In the first instance, it surely meant *not pornography*, a label to which Metzger was much more resistant, at least until his hardcore turn in the mid-1970s made it impossible to deflect. A television interviewer posed the question bluntly in 1971: "What do you say when people . . . say 'Well you make pornographic films?' I'm sure you disagree with that, but what do you say to them?" "I don't know," Metzger replied. "I usually just say 'shucks' or something like that. . . . I've been trying to think of something clever to say for the last few years, and I haven't come up with anything."[7] Metzger seems to have found his clever response quickly, though, since he was far more eloquent in a newspaper article a few weeks later. "My pictures are erotic, not obscene," he explained. "The finished product is to me, more a work of art with a message to convey than just a picture accented by nudity."[8]

Erotica vs. pornography: like all aesthetic categories, these have two sides as both *descriptions* and *evaluations*, or, better, as evaluations that present themselves as descriptions.[9] To label something pornography, as Metzger was clearly aware, is not just to identify something as a particular *type* of thing, but to pass judgment on it as a particularly *bad* or immoral thing, whereas erotica implies an exculpatory emphasis on aesthetic pleasures over and above any masturbatory utility. What gives Metzger his particular salience, in this respect, is that his career took shape at the same time that this division was itself coming into being, making him arguably the first erotic artist of the American cinema—or at least the first to think of himself in this way. As Walter Kendrick argued in his classic study *The Secret Museum: Pornography in Modern Culture* (1987), the porn/erotica division did not gain currency until the middle of the twentieth century. The term "pornography," Kendrick argues, had been the invention of nineteenth-century efforts to define morally censorable material, but "erotica" entered the general vocabulary only in the 1950s and '60s. "A word was needed to designate the increasing number of books that, though they dealt with sex, somehow did so in a safe and classy way."[10] Works deemed "erotic" on this formula were those whose sexual content was redeemed by artistic value, whereas pornography admitted no such redemption. The two categories were also differently "classed" in terms of the different publics they imply, with pornography the "low-class" bad object and erotica the "safe and classy" option. And then there is the question of *permissibility*, as Metzger's slippage from "pornography" to the legal category of "obscenity" in the preceding quotes makes clear.

This last factor is in fact the determinative one. Kendrick suggests that pornography is best thought of not in terms of any specific content, but as a kind of structural marker for what any given social order seeks to regulate and exclude, that is, to render impermissible. Pornography, he writes, is "not a thing but a concept, a thought structure," in that it names "an imaginary scenario of danger and rescue" in which the public is to be protected from "obscene" representations.[11] Whatever else the pornography/erotica dyad may be taken to mean, then, it always implies a boundary between an illicit or taboo "pornography" and a tentatively permissible "erotica."

But "permissible" has two sides, too, both in terms of what is legally allowable and in terms of what is socially acceptable, each of which were fronts on which Metzger was compelled to take arms at different phases in his career. During his early years in the industry, for instance, much of Metzger's energies were expended in courtroom activism against state and local censorship. As we will see, changes in obscenity law in the postwar years had the effect of emboldening the publishers and distributors of all manner of explicit material, with the result that by the end of the 1960s the legal definition of obscenity was no longer an effective tool of regulation or containment. But once that battle had been won, the erotica/pornography dyad came to be measured more in terms social acceptability or the lack thereof, which admitted of much more fluid and contradictory assessments. Metzger's campaign, in this regard, was to recast explicit film as sophisticated "works of art" for well-heeled moviegoers, as distinct from the more bluntly pornographic appeal of the "picture accented by nudity." But others understood the distinction differently. For feminist activist Gloria Steinem in the 1970s, for instance, erotica designated a "safe" women's alternative to a chauvinist pornography. ("Erotica is about sexuality," Steinem famously claimed, "but pornography is about power and sex-as-weapon.")[12] What Metzger and Steinem each meant by erotica is drastically different, but they both used the division to draw a *cordon sanitaire* in support of their own determination of acceptability—which is one way in which bad faith enters the picture wherever erotica is concerned. As the truism goes, one person's erotica (usually mine) is another person's pornography (usually yours).

The other way in which bad faith enters the picture is in the suspicion that the erotica/porn division is itself a spurious one. Erotica, the reasoning goes here, cannot *not* be pornography—or, at least, can never fully disentangle from it—insofar as the former's frisson depends on the latter's proximity.[13] The cultural historian Steven Marcus, for instance, made this case in his landmark study of nineteenth-century literary pornography, *The Other Victorians* (1966), when he described erotica as a mere "euphemism," as though erotica's pretensions to artistry are a mere alibi for pornography's illicit thrills, porn in art's clothing.[14] This was a suspicion that Metzger could never entirely put to bed, and it surfaced in reviews of almost every film he made. "It seems to me that Mr. Metzger is far more interested in the voyeuristic aspects of his production than in any serious endeavor," critic Hollis Alpert wrote of Metzger's 1968 lesbian drama *Thérèse and Isabelle*.[15] The filmmaker's next release, *Camille 2000* (1969), an updating of Dumas fils's *La dame aux camélias* (1848), was "a thoroughly bad and dishonest film," according to the London *Observer's* George Melly.[16] And his Pirandelloesque *The Lickerish Quartet* (1970) provoked *Boston After Dark* to lambast at length the hypocrisy of the middle-class audiences to which Metzger's movies were addressed: "Metzger's films allow middle-class people who have been conditioned to abhor pornography, but who secretly crave it, to indulge their erotic fantasies with the firm conviction that what they are witnessing on the screen is somehow more 'serious,' more 'uplifting,' than the crudely made quickies designed for the proles. Whether there is anything *morally* wrong with all this it is difficult to say. That there is something *aesthetically* wrong is clear."[17] It was New York critic Rex Reed, though, who found the best putdown with which to blow the whistle on Metzger in a review of *Little Mother* (1972) that described the director as "a pernicious photographer who makes glossy porno films that look like airline commercials."[18] Pernicious, dishonest, and aesthetically wrong. How to account for the conundrums to which Metzger's aspirations eventually led?

One place to find answers is in biography. Born January 21, 1929, Radley was the second of two boys raised in the Bronx by parents Julius and Anne Metzger (née Nassberg).[19] Julius was of German Jewish descent and worked as a private investigator, his mother second-generation Russian Jewish and a housewife. At some point during Radley's preteen years the family relocated to Manhattan's Upper

0.2 Radley Metzger in Straubenmuller Textile High School's 1946 yearbook. Metzger is in the second row, fourth from the right.
Source: AncestryLibrary.com.

West Side at Seventy-Ninth Street, and by the early 1940s he was enrolled in the city's Straubenmuller Textile High School—presumably tracking toward a career in the garment industry, at the time a traditionally Jewish occupation.[20] Certainly, by his graduation in 1946, he had developed the natty sense of style that *GQ* would subsequently praise him for, already evident in yearbook photos of him in Straubenmuller's "Player's Club" afterschool group (figure 0.2). Cinema was another teenage obsession. In later years, he would jokingly attribute his adolescent cinephilia to seasonal allergies, which drove him to find respite in movie theaters in the days before home air-conditioning.[21] His favorite refuge was the Audubon Ballroom, a picture palace on 165th Street in Washington Heights (and the future site of Malcolm X's assassination). "I'd come here often," he later recalled. "I'd see double bills, triple bills, here day after day. It was where I discovered film. It was where I fell in love. It was where I found my vocation. It was where I felt at home."[22]

For the rest of his life Metzger's cinephilia would retain something of that enumerative tone ("double bills, triple bills, day after day"), a quality that sociologist Pierre Bourdieu associates above all with the tastes of the "naïve" enthusiast who,

0.3 The Audubon Ballroom, with police protection following the 1965 assassination of Malcolm X.

Source: Courtesy of the Associated Press.

unlike the "connoisseur," emphasizes quantity of cultural consumption rather than quality, knowledge over contemplation, and *askesis* (dedication) over *aesthesis* (feeling).[23] It would manifest in his tendency early in his career to repeatedly "prove" his cinephile credentials by listing the number of times he had seen a given film: *Citizen Kane* (1941) 127 times, *Treasure of the Sierra Madre* (1948) 103 times, Tay Garnett's World War II drama *The Cross of Lorraine* (1944) eleven times (a boast that he wryly elaborated by noting that "most Jewish people didn't see it more than three or four times").[24] And it would underwrite the sometimes glibly "citational" style of his filmscripts, in which characters often give passing callouts to studio-era movies and film stars, a tendency whose apex comes in the last feature film to bear Metzger's name, *The Princess and the Call Girl* (1983), in which two characters get each other off by saying the names of 1930s Hollywood stars to each other. Still, his experiences at the Audubon were deep enough that, over a decade later, he would name his distribution company Audubon Films in honor of the location that had nurtured his love of film (figure 0.3).

Washington Heights looms large in Metzger's development for other reasons, too. He took his bachelor's degree in dramatic arts there at City College, where he studied film with instructors Hans Richter and Lewis Jacobs, graduating in 1952.[25] Metzger next began an aborted master's degree in theater at nearby Columbia University, abruptly terminated when he was conscripted into the Air Force during the Korean War, although he was never deployed. Metzger's time in Washington Heights may even offer a clue as to the social roots of his drive for distinction. As a "man of taste," Metzger was in one sense a product of his time: nearly every historian studying mid-twentieth-century American culture has recognized the growing attention paid to cultural and aesthetic preference as status markers during the postwar years. (As a *Harper's Magazine* writer put it in 1949: "It isn't wealth or family that makes prestige these days. It's high thinking.")[26] But Metzger's time in the Heights may have influenced his own take on these processes. Back in the 1930s, the neighborhood had served as a typical area of second settlement for assimilated New York Jews with middle-class aspirations; yet over the course of that decade it also became a major center for German Jewish refugees from Hitler's Europe, spurring tensions between the settled German Jewish populations and the newly arrived, many of whom were from Germany's rural south and whose small-town values were out of step with the middle-class stature that earlier immigrants had achieved. Social historian Steven Lowenstein observes that these new arrivals were very much the "opposite pole" of the more celebrated émigrés who fled Nazi Germany to influence American intellectual and artistic life: "On the one hand, the presence of these conspicuous non-English speakers seemed to jeopardize the American status of the native Jews. On the other, the inability of the [newly arrived] Germans to speak Yiddish (indeed their ill-disguised contempt for the language) seemed to many American Jews to show how un-Jewish the refugees really were."[27]

It remains a mystery how, or even if, Metzger, a young man of German Jewish descent, navigated this aspect of the neighborhood during his formative years there. We do know, however, that these tensions—between the assimilated and the arriviste, between old ways and new world—would provide the thematic core of his very first film, *Dark Odyssey*, shot at intervals on the streets of Washington Heights over a two-year period between 1956 and 1958.

Metzger's move into filmmaking was hardly unprepared for. During his time at City College he had begun offering his services as a freelance film editor, in which capacity he was hired by RKO's New York offices in 1950 to remove suggestive material from the Italian neorealist import *Bitter Rice* (1949)—an almost too-perfect inversion of what would become his modus operandi at Audubon, when he often *added* erotic content into foreign films he picked up for distribution (figure 0.4). He also served as an editor during his time in the Air Force, which he later recalled as "a marvelous place to learn because they never kept track of materials." Following his return to civvies he again found work at RKO, this time at its Manhattan studios on 106th Street, where he supervised the English dubs of imports like the Spanish film *Miracle of Marcelino* (1955) and, a cinephile's dream, Jean Renoir's *French Cancan* (1955). ("I found it thrilling because I was able to hold in my hands, and run back and forth, a film by Jean Renoir—which for somebody who is devoted to films was a very profound experience.")[28]

It was around this time that Metzger teamed up with a fellow editor, William Kyriakis, to codirect the picture that would eventually become *Dark Odyssey*, about a young Greek sailor who enters a New York Greek community to carry out an honor killing for his sister's rape (figure 0.5). Metzger first met Kyriakis when he got a job as a gopher on an independent feature film about the Greek Civil War, *Guerrilla Girl* (1953), for which Kyriakis had worked on the screenplay. Set in Greece but shot in the hamlet town of Garrison, New York, *Guerrilla Girl* had been a low-budget oddity that passed largely unremarked. (Among its sparse reviews was a brief, three-paragraph pan in the *New York Times*, where Bosley Crowther declared it "an effort that can barely be considered in the category of professional films.")[29] Not so *Dark Odyssey*, however, which even before its release garnered attention in both the *Times* and *Variety* as an example of the unusual financing and production methods in New York City's then-burgeoning independent film scene. To finance the film the duo had set up an independent company, Era KM Productions, funded by money from friends, relatives, and the actors themselves, all of whom owned company stock. "We had no illusions

0.4 Radley Metzger's own copy of the *Bitter Rice* lobby card.
Source: Author's collection.

about turning out an art film," Metzger explained of his creative objectives to the *Times*. "We've simply tried to tell an interesting story, that of a primitive ethnic code applied to an urban center."[30]

That story likely resonated with Metzger's own encounters with the divided German Jewish community of Washington Heights; certainly it must have for Kyriakis, whose upbringing as the child of Greek immigrants evidently sourced his preoccupation with Greek themes. The film's plot is nothing if not schematic in this respect, overlaying upon the *dramatis personae* of a family melodrama a range of different immigrant identifications. There is Yianni, the violent sailor from a Greek village, who serves as the film's emblem of "ethnic primitivism" (to paraphrase Metzger). There is Niki, the second-generation daughter of Greek immigrants, who becomes Yianni's love interest. And there is Helen, Niki's sister, who hides her American boyfriend, George, from her parents, who want her to date a nice Greek boy. Within this configuration, the two sets of first-generation characters, Yianni and the parents, stand for different aspects of their immigrant

0.5 Radley Metzger (*left*) and William Kyriakis, filming on the rooftops in Washington Heights, New York City.
Source: Courtesy of Joe Grispino.

heritage—on the parents' part a nostalgic investment in Greek communality, on Yianni's the "primitivism" which that nostalgia masks—while the second-generation sisters represent different responses to the pressures of assimilation.

Much of this plays out in heavy-handed fashion in the screenplay, as when Helen invites Yianni to listen to "some American jazz records" or when later he is told, "You can get away with that in your mountains, but here we have laws." But there is also evidence of a more native cinematic intelligence at work at the level of film form. For instance, during a traditional "sword dance" that Yianni performs at a party, Metzger and Kyriakis use editing to juxtapose the partygoers' smiles and applause with the psychological violence that Yianni experiences while performing (figure 0.6a–e). An accelerating montage of Yianni's flying limbs is gradually punctuated by flashback memories of previous moments of violent action or intent—a close-up of a gun hidden in his pants waist and, repeatedly, a shot of him slapping Niki in an earlier argument (figure 0.6f–l). The process of the film's montage is to extract Yianni's dance from the nostalgic pleasure it offers to the Greek immigrants who behold it and bring to the surface the "primitive" violence that serves as the dance's kernel. Homeland, as a term of immigrant experience, is here something that must be kept proximate but deferred—aestheticized as dance, sugarcoated as nostalgia. In contrasting the partygoers' enjoyment with Yianni's inner turmoil, Kyriakis and Metzger find cinematic form for the paradox of Yianni's relation to the immigrant community that both reveres and must reject what he represents.

Is it overreaching to find in this an analogy with the dynamics of eroticism that would animate Metzger's subsequent career?[31] That is, to see the immigrant experience of homeland as similarly structured in relation to a taboo—here premodern violence; for eroticism, pornography—that must be held at bay? The point is not, absurdly, to suggest any proximity between eroticism and the immigrant experience. Rather, it is simply to note how *Dark Odyssey*'s understanding of the immigrant's relation to the homeland already contains the animating structure that would inform Metzger's subsequent filmmaking. But *Dark Odyssey* also had more practical significance in that it redirected the future trajectory of Metzger's career. He often liked to boast of his directorial debut that it held the record for the lowest gross of all time in the theaters in which it played, which is a tall tale. What is certain, though, is that Metzger and Kyriakis struggled for three years to get any distributors or exhibitors interested in the film, during which time Metzger had to take on a variety of editing jobs to support himself (one of which, strangely enough, was on the sole directorial credit of actor Walter Matthau, the 1959 *Gangster Story*).[32] Eventually they managed to get a playdate for *Dark Odyssey* in the spring of 1961 at future porn entrepreneur Chelly Wilson's Cameo theater at Forty-Fourth Street and Eighth Avenue, on condition that they prepare a Greek-language dub for the neighborhood audience.[33] It was under those circumstances, with Greek- and English-language versions alternating one after the other, that the film opened to a surprisingly positive review by Howard Thompson of the *New York Times*, who described *Dark Odyssey* as a "thoughtful, unpretentious, creatively turned little drama" and offered the filmmakers "a warm welcome to the movie fold."[34] But, again, that was in 1961, almost three years after the film had first been readied for release, and five years since filming first began. In that delay was the lesson that would set Metzger on the trajectory that made his name. "It occurred to us that, if you didn't want that difficulty in distribution, you'd do well to put either horror or an erotic component in whatever you were doing."[35] Metzger opted for the erotic component.

0.6 Yianni (Athan Karras) performs a sword dance, punctuated by quick cuts to the assembled partygoers (*B*, *D*) and earlier scenes of violence (*F*, *I*, *J*, *K*). Screenshots from *Dark Odyssey*.

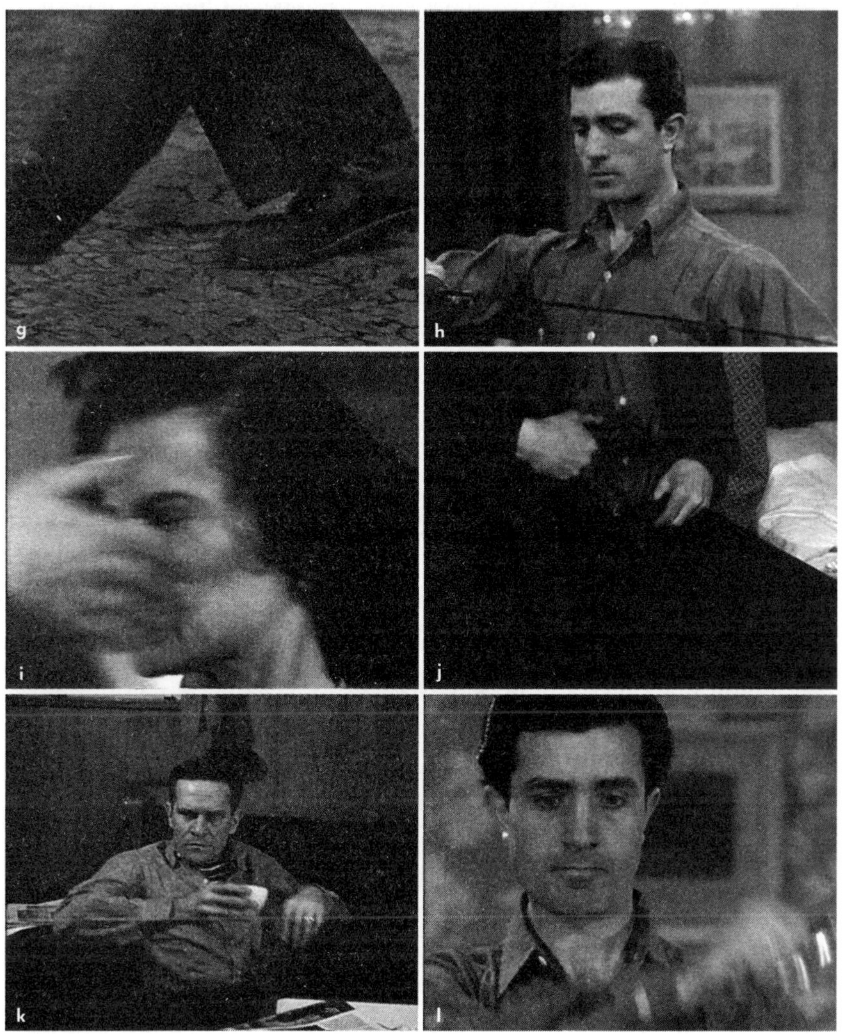

o.6 *(continued)*

The decision might seem an odd one given the kind of films and filmmakers that Metzger admired. But it makes sense in the light of a pattern noted by literary historian Josh Lambert: namely, that sexual material confers its *own* kind of prestige—what Michel Foucault calls a "speaker's benefit"—to the individual who disseminates it.[36] As Lambert argues in connection with midcentury Jewish publishers like Horace Liveright and Samuel Roth, sexually explicit or obscene material has historically offered a path for the those with scant financial resources and/or who are socially marginal to secure a type of distinction, even if of an unconventional variety. That's not to imply some kind of natural predilection for obscenity on the part of such groups, simply a practical reality—and a strategy that Metzger, burned by his attempt to make a serious film drama, chose to adopt.

The chapters to come will follow the implications of that decision. For now, however, I want to lay my cards on the table with a few words about the assumptions that inform this book, first as these relate to the concepts of erotica and the erotic. These might seem like shaky foundations on which to build an argument, for any of the reasons tracked earlier (erotica as bad faith, as euphemism, and so on). Yet, even granting that, it is surely the case that erotic euphemisms are just as real as pornographic plain speech and, as such, deserve examination in their own right. Nor does the vagueness with which the erotic is often charged preclude an analysis of its forms within the work of a filmmaker who routinely invoked the term.

It may be helpful, by way of first principles, to circle back to Walter Kendrick. If we follow him in thinking of pornography as a "thought structure," then the same necessarily applies to erotica, insofar as the latter concept is derivative of the former. Further, if the particular thought structure of pornography marks off certain representations *as taboo*, then it also follows that erotica (and its particular appeal) is a matter of *proximity to* those taboo things. It is a boundary phenomenon whose frisson could be likened to a kind of edging, to the excitation that accrues from lingering at—but never crossing—the threshold of what is forbidden. The pioneering sexologist Robert J. Stoller described the process well in *Observing the Erotic Imagination* (1985), where he assessed erotic pleasure as a practice of willful disavowal: "A necessary aspect of erotic excitement is that one must keep oneself from knowing too much, from knowing what is going on, from knowing one's reasons, from knowing one's intentions, from knowing one's desires. The old trick of eating your cake and having it: how to keep your knowledge working for you and yet to turn your eyes away, to blur your awareness." "How intricate," he concluded, "and how much a matter of aesthetics."[37] Put another way, the experience of the erotic attaches more to the trajectory of desire's approach than to the point of its fulfillment or satisfaction. It is an exercise of taste that flirts with what "good taste" has outlawed.

What can it mean, though, to describe what are usually thought of as genres of representation (pornography, erotica) as "thought structures?" For one thing, it acknowledges the obvious subjectivity of these classifications—the "I know it when I see it" conundrum famously articulated by Justice Potter Stewart describing his criterion for obscenity in *Jacobellis v. Ohio* (1964). Viewing pornography and erotica as thought structures means they should be understood primarily as evaluations of content in relation to the idea of taboo, and only secondarily in terms of the specific content itself.[38] The evaluations themselves may well change from person to person, across different historical time periods, and among various cultures (which is, of course, exactly why only "I" would know it only when "I" see it); what remains constant is the line in the sand that all such evaluations imply. But this in turn suggests an approach that would center the act of classification itself. The study of pornography, from a "thought structures" perspective, is essentially the study of how and why representations get classified across the line of taboo; erotica, meanwhile, can then similarly be approached in terms of the various strategies for keeping taboo at a distance and the ways in which that distance gets measured. Extending this logic, the book proposes three theses for modeling the category of erotica. First, as already noted, the field of the erotic refers to a category of representation closely related to pornography, yet that seeks to interrupt or defer pornography's taboo aspects. Second: instead of halting desire, the interruption is a productive or constitutive one that shifts desire toward alternative or compensatory sources of enjoyment (often, but not always, aesthetic ones). And third: the nature of the erotic varies based on the type of pornographic taboo it reacts against. The field of the erotic is more than just a derivative of pornography; it actively carves out unique domains that keep taboos at arm's length. This, for instance, is why Steinem's condemnation of "masculinist" pornography produces, as its alternative, an erotica that is redeemed by the purportedly "feminine" pleasures of softness and sensuality.

And it is why Metzger's desire to differentiate his work from "obscene" films that sought only to arouse ("just a picture accented by nudity") led him to invest in the more additive notion of an erotic "art" with a "message to convey." If the erotic is a boundary phenomenon, then it can take as many forms as there are means of keeping the taboo at bay.

The book's first three chapters accordingly use different phases of Metzger's career to explore erotica's productivity in relation to a number of discrete fields: the social, the aesthetic, and the psychosexual, the focus of chapters 1, 2, and 3, respectively. Each of these chapters is, in a sense, an essay on the workings of taste and distinction in relation to various formulations of taboo. In social terms, we will see, the erotic sensibility associates the pornographic taboo with the tastes of a social group (the lower classes, dirty old men, and so on) from which the erotic artist distances both their intended public and themselves (chapter 1). In aesthetic terms, erotica generates strategies of artistic transformation when the taboo thing is associated with certain properties of the medium of expression itself, necessitating a creative investment in alternate uses of the medium (chapter 2). And in psychosexual terms, erotica explores the dynamics of desire in the face of sexual taboos whose authority is at once feared and infringed upon (chapter 3). For all these reasons, the field of the erotic will emerge from these pages as no stable thing, but rather as a range of representations that emerge out of taboo's simultaneous evocation and deferral. Our working assumption will be that eroticism operates in the gap that produces effects of social difference, sexual desire, and aesthetic ornamentation as its consequences.[39]

The book's final two chapters necessarily take a somewhat different tack, since their focus falls on Metzger's work in hardcore porn in the 1970s, when he worked under the pseudonym "Henry Paris." Here Metzger's characteristic concern with distinction is explored in relation to the sexual fantasy worlds that his hardcore films construct (chapter 4) and the challenges he faced in rehabilitating his career in the years that followed (chapter 5). What becomes more prominent in these sections is a second overarching framework for the book; namely, the issue of authorship and Metzger's vexed relation to the stature of "auteur director." Whatever else it was, Metzger's identity as an "auteur of the erotic," to quote a 1971 career overview by *Today's Filmmaker*, ultimately became a trap of his own making, since it defined him in terms of a sensibility that the booming hardcore market of the 1970s required him to transgress.[40] In a very real sense, Metzger's own *name* now became his films' organizing taboo, an identity to be covered up by a welter of pseudonyms that would come to haunt and derail his later attempts to restore his authorial self. The man of taste, who staked his reputation on the operations of distinction, would in this way end up their victim.

The Metzger that emerges in the chapters to come will be a somewhat different figure than the Metzger discussed in existing scholarship on adult film, where he tends to crop up as a case study rather than the whole dish. Unfortunately, this case-study approach has had the effect of absorbing Metzger's career and output into the broader patterns and trajectories that scholars have called upon him to exemplify. Although his bid for art-house *distinctiveness* is widely acknowledged, Metzger's films have come to be treated as instead particularly *representative* of the genres of adult film: the "Henry Paris" titles become models of hardcore, as in Linda Williams's foundational *Hard Core*, while the "Radley Metzger" films are considered exemplars of softcore, as in David Andrews's *Soft in the Middle*.[41] Even Elena Gorfinkel's superbly contextualized history of 1960s sexploitation, *Lewd Looks*, doesn't quite escape this trap in a chapter that pairs Radley Metzger and fellow adult filmmaker Russ Meyer as *representing* "the bifurcated impulses of sexploitation film more broadly."[42] In the process, the borders between genre and author—that is, between the generic formulas of adult cinema and Metzger's relation to them—have become somewhat confused, perhaps understandably given Metzger's prominence within the field. If, as film historian Michael Bowen notes, "Radley Metzger and high-class erotica were virtually synonymous by the early 1970s," then it indeed becomes an open question whether the category of "high-class erotica" was more a matter of Metzger's style than an actual genre.[43] Which is the cart here and which the horse?

Things look rather different, though, if we begin not with the *categories* of adult film within which Metzger's career can be mapped (hardcore, sexploitation, and so on) but instead follow the career itself, its moments of success and of impasse, of profit and penury. Viewed thus, Metzger's contributions to the field of explicit film begin to appear more opportunistic than representative, a matter of sifting for possibilities within fields of filmmaking pioneered by others. As we will see, Metzger's aspiration to bring art-house aesthetics to adult film really solidified only after Audubon's successful release of the Swedish-Danish coproduction *I, a Woman* (1966) showed him the way, much as his turn to hardcore occurred only after Gerard Damiano's *Deep Throat* (1972) demonstrated the market viability of explicit sex films.[44]

An uncharitable perspective would view Metzger an exhibit A for media theorist Marshall McLuhan's famous dictum, "Good taste is the first refuge of the noncreative."[45] But McLuhan's quip works only if one overlooks the extent to which taste itself can be a type of creativity or authorship, which is one of the lessons to be drawn from Metzger's work. A second lesson, though, would be that taste also has negative valence as a way of closing things off, as another bon mot, this time Pierre Bourdieu's, has it: "Taste is first and foremost distaste, disgust and visceral intolerance of the taste of others."[46] The man of taste may well find himself faced with diminishing options as he attempts to defend the border that distinguishes his own acts of creativity from those of others, which is exactly the trap in which Metzger found himself in the later phases of his career. Perhaps it is all to the better, then, that the paradigm of the person of taste is no longer one that much exercises our present culture, as this book's final pages will address. But this does not mean that Metzger waged ignorant or pointless battles in his quest to place explicit film on a higher cultural plane. It simply means that the time for those battles has passed. To seek high-art value within traditionally illegitimate fields of creativity, as Metzger did in the sphere of explicit film, is to relativize and thereby undermine the very hierarchies that those terms and distinctions were originally designed to create. So if Radley Metzger was a harbinger of anything, it was perhaps not the standards of taste that he stood for but their dissolution.

CHAPTER 1

"TO CREATE THE KIND OF FILMS HE HAD FORMERLY ONLY PURCHASED"

The Distributor as Auteur

We do not know the exact date, but one day in 1959 a thirty-year-old Radley Metzger decided to roll the dice and head to New York City's 55th Street Playhouse, homebase of Janus Films. The plan was to approach the outfit as a potential distributor for *Dark Odyssey*. What he got instead was a job cutting trailers. There he had two encounters that catalyzed the creation of Audubon Films. One was with Janus's vice president, Ava Leighton, like him a second-generation Jewish immigrant—albeit of Russian, not German descent—with whom Metzger entered into a business relationship that would last until the end of her life in 1987 (figure 1.1).[1] The other was with a French film that Janus picked up while Metzger was working there, *Péché de jeunesse* (1959), which starred Agnès Laurent, one of several "sex kitten" starlets to have emerged in Brigitte Bardot's wake. Out of this alignment of coincidences, and desperate to pay off his debts from *Dark Odyssey*, Metzger took the opportunity to test his intuition about films with an "erotic component." Some years earlier Metzger had worked on the dubbing of Bardot's breakout film, *And God Created Woman* (1956), and he seems to have seen in the relatively unknown Laurent an opportunity to make a similar splash.[2] So he purchased an earlier Laurent title that no other distributors had wanted, the René Thevenet sex comedy *Mademoiselle Strip-Tease* (1957) and, teaming up with Leighton, who quit her position at Janus, created Audubon Films to distribute the picture under the new title *The Nude Set* (alternate title: *The Fast Set*, for more conservative jurisdictions).[3] "It was really a shock to me," Metzger recalled of the film's modest success, "because at the time I thought films only made you poor."[4] His debts paid, Metzger used the profits to pick up another Thevenet-Laurent film, *Les collégiennes* (1957), which he renamed *The Twilight Girls* (perhaps stealing from

1.1 Radley Metzger and Ava Leighton.
Source: Courtesy of Joe Grispino.

Della Martin's 1961 queer pulp novel, *Twilight Girl*). This time, however, he took more creative license by inserting a topless scene that he shot with stage actress Shelley Graham—who, under the pseudonym Georgina Spelvin, would go on to become a major figure in adult cinema of the 1970s in her own right.[5] "We integrated [the footage] so well that not even the laboratory could tell the difference," Metzger boasted. "In a strange way, it built up my confidence that I could shoot films that people would sit through."[6] Just two pictures in, Metzger had hit upon the practice that would define Audubon's first half decade: acquire a European sex film, retitle, reedit, and release.

Flash forward around a dozen years to 1973. In a midcareer overview titled "Aristocrat of the Erotic," *Film Comment* critic Richard Corliss took summary of the eight films that Metzger had directed to that point to argue that the filmmaker was on the cusp of "complete auteur status." But Corliss then immediately complicated his claim by changing the meaning of "auteur" as it applied to Metzger. If, in film-critical circles of the 1960s, the then-voguish notion of the "auteur" referred to the creative labor of a film's *director*, Metzger was in Corliss's eyes the odd case of a filmmaker whose auteurist stamp was initially defined by his work as a *distributor.* "It may be said that Metzger-the-distributor is as much an auteur as Metzger-the-director."[7] Which is to say that Metzger's authorship also, paradoxically, encompassed films directed by *other people*. There has, in fact, always been this sense in the commentary on Metzger that his authorial identity was first conjured through his curatorial practice, as though Metzger used the work of others to establish a creative identity that he then stepped into. When, for example, the Museum of Modern Art acquired and screened a number of his self-directed films in 1971, the program notes for the occasion described how Metzger's success as a distributor "allowed him finally to meld ambition with obsession, by creating the kind of pendulous, languid, aristocratic film he had formerly only purchased and re-edited."[8] Critics would also routinely conflate the broader Audubon brand with Metzger's directorial signature, as for example with Audubon's 1970 release of *The Laughing Woman*, an Italian film that Kevin Thomas at the *Los Angeles Times* described simply as the "new Radley Metzger film," with nary a mention of the film's actual director, Piero Schivazappa, or when *Playboy* magazine described the previous year's *The Libertine*, directed by Pasquale Festa Campanile, as "Radley Metzger's Italian-made" production.[9] It is in this sense that film scholar Elena Gorfinkel has recently discussed Metzger through the notion of "curatorial authorship," a term that neatly captures the way in which Metzger's "direction" encompassed both filmmaking and distribution as mutually reinforcing components of Audubon's overall brand.[10]

The notion of the film director as auteur is of course a long-standing, if fraught, *topos* of film studies; the role of the film distributor is, by contrast, one of the most undertheorized aspects of film culture. In tracing the formation of Audubon's brand identity, this chapter first locates Metzger's curatorial project within the rules and logics of exchange in the market for what has come to be called "cultural capital," that is, cultural prestige and value. In its first two sections, it considers how the distribution practices that Metzger and Leighton deployed at Audubon created new configurations of prestige that built upon what we might call the "erotic capital" of foreign films, and how the company established its reputation as the premier American disseminator of European and Scandinavian sex films.[11] The chapter then turns, in its third and fourth sections, to examine how Metzger's practice as a distributor also established the terrain upon which his particular stamp as a director took root. As literary scholar James English notes, most cultural criticism and history neglects the "middle space between acts of inspired artistic creation on the one hand and acts of discerning consumption on the other." In his role as a distributor, Metzger occupied that middle space, playing a role as an "administrator of culture" (the term is English's) in creating perceptions of value and discernment within the lowly sphere of sexploitation.[12] But in his role as a director, Metzger worked to shore up those self-same perceptions by making films that corresponded to them. Once we think of Metzger's creativity in terms of *value*-creation, we have an optic for assessing how both his choices as a distributor and his craft as a director were effectively twin aspects of a single endeavor. The way in which Metzger parlayed "perceptions of value" into "acts of artistic creation" is the story of this chapter.

"WE HAD TO GO IN WITH A HAMMER AND CHISEL": BUILDING A BRAND, PART 1

By what, then, was the value of the sex film to be measured? The answer, at the start of the 1960s, was simply *sex*—or at least the promise thereof. When Audubon entered the scene in 1961, the nascent sexploitation market was largely dominated by cheesecake pictures known as "nudie cuties" with titles like *The Immoral Mr. Teas* (1959), *Eve and the Handyman* (1961), and *The Adventures of Lucky Pierre* (1961) and taglines promising "You'll NEVER See This on TV!" and "Delightful, Delectable, Desirable, Delicious Damsels Devoid of Any and All Inhibitions." These were soon joined by a new crop of nudist camp epics like *Daughter of the Sun* (1962) and *World Without Shame* (1962) and—Audubon's distinctive contribution—foreign dramas goosed up with additional inserts of nudity and suggestive sequences. Promotion for these later categories differed slightly from the straightforwardly voyeuristic appeal of the nudie cuties: as Eric Schaefer notes, foreign imports were often marketed with more of a slant toward emotional drama and psychology (for example, "No longer children . . . not yet women . . . caught in the turmoil of their unformed emotions!" for Audubon's *The Twilight Girls*). But such distinctions likely owed more to the vanity of small differences, given that these various subgenres were, in Schaefer's words, largely "aligned in the public's imagination as often indistinguishable dirty movies."[13]

Foreign imports did, however, have the advantage of a certain opacity in this respect, since expectations of their greater sexual frankness vis-à-vis American films were often qualified by presumptions of more complex artistic ambitions. As has frequently been observed, the idea of "foreign films" was at the time an ambiguous category for which the allure of genuine artistry was inseparable from what critic Andrew Sarris referred to as their "ooh-la-la factor."[14] If, as Barbara Wilinsky avers, postwar art films were defined primarily in terms of their *difference* from the mainstream, then two key aspects of that difference were sex and foreignness.[15] Many films that have since been enshrined as prototypical examples of postwar art cinema were in fact promoted in terms of their risqué appeal. Schaefer has himself noted how censor-baiting imports like the 1933 Czech film *Exstase* already had a prewar history on alternative distribution circuits, where they were often "wrapped in the lurid garments of exploitation."[16] But this only intensified after the war as Hollywood's slowing production output sparked a surge of foreign imports (a rise of some 132 percent in the years between 1946 and 1956), resulting in a situation in which films like *Rome, Open City* (1945) could be advertised as "Sexier than Hollywood ever dared to be!" and Ingmar Bergman's *Summer with Monika* (1953), retitled *Monika, Story of a Bad Girl*.[17] Sexploitation film magazines like *Adam Film Quarterly* (launched 1966, renamed *Adam Film World* in 1969) meanwhile devoted their energies not just to homegrown sexploitation but also to art films and the work of foreign auteur directors, all of which they subjected to the same critical lens (which is why, for instance, Ingmar Bergman was profiled in *Adam Film Quarterly* as the "Cinema Sultan of Sex Shockers.")[18]

By the time Audubon was founded, in other words, explicit sexuality had come to be expected of foreign films to such an extent that the terms "foreign film," "art film," and "sex film" were for several years almost synonyms. Yet it is not at all clear that Metzger meaningfully exploited that ambiguity in his initial acquisitions for Audubon. Despite Metzger's reputation today as a filmmaker who, in Gorfinkel's words, "took advantage of the slippages . . . and overlaps between the grind-house and the art-house" to create a new kind of "art-porn hybrid," his early distribution practices betray little such complexity, more closely resembling resourceful bids to simply build profits.[19] If Metzger was drawn to European titles, this, he confessed, was primarily because he could get them to play more lucrative markets. Along similar lines, Metzger described how sales head Leighton opted to avoid the existing exhibition networks for exploitation titles and instead target the drive-ins—not out of some sense that Audubon's films were too good for the former, but because the latter were "where a great deal of revenue was generated."[20] He also recalled how Leighton preferred to make her deals directly with theaters, rather than work with subdistributors, as a way to maximize Audubon's profit share. (Subdistributors were regional operations unaffiliated with the major studios, typically with strong local relationships and contacts within their territories.) "Ordinarily a producer sees possibly 10% of what his pictures bring in, because the income has to be cut into so many small pieces. In my case, I didn't have to realize so much—because I saw 100% of what was coming in."[21]

A quick case study can illustrate Metzger's opportunistic attitude to his acquisitions during Audubon's swaddling years. In the fall of 1961, following the success of *The Nude Set* and *The Twilight Girls*, Metzger left the United States on his first buying trip to Europe, during which he claimed to have viewed some two hundred titles, purchasing just four: two Max Pécas–directed films that began a fruitful relation with the director and served to introduce Elke Sommer to American audiences, namely, *De quoi tu te mêles, Daniela!* (1961) and *Douce violence* (1962) (retitled respectively as *Daniella by Night* and *Sweet Ecstasy*); a 1959 adaptation of Boris Vian's pulp crime novel *J'irai cracher sur vos tombes* (released as *I Spit on Your Grave*); and, finally, another Thevenet-Laurent film, this time the 1959 Spanish-French coproduction *Tentations*, retitled as *Soft Skin on Black Silk* for its U.S. release in late 1964.[22] Despite Audubon's track record with Laurent, Metzger harbored few illusions about the artistic merits of this last film. "It was a terrible picture about a young man who wants to be a priest," he later recalled, describing the film's plot. "His father side-tracks him into a wild life so that he will take over the father's factory. At the end of the film he winds up killing his cousin, showing his father the great error he had made in not letting him become a priest." Nor did the film contain much in the way of sex either, beyond a brief shot of Laurent's bare back and the outline of her breasts as she undresses. The limitations in the source material did, however, provide opportunities for Metzger's own filmmaking interventions: "I had a friend write a script about a boy who meets a girl on a lonely beach. They go home and make love and she tells him the story of her cousin. The cousin story was the original film. I shot 40 minutes of new film out at Montauk, because you can't tell one beach from another—beaches have no nationality. In late 1962 I cut the film, we integrated the material, and called the film *Soft Skin on Black Silk*."[23] Metzger exaggerates here, but only slightly. The original material from *Tentations* was cut to just fifty minutes in the Audubon release, to which Metzger contributed some thirty-five minutes of additional footage. Fifteen minutes of the new material comprise the framing narrative of the couple who meet at the beach; the other twenty minutes consist of three lengthy striptease sequences inserted into nightclub scenes from the original film. The framing narrative supplies the nudity the original film lacked, in the form of two women who appear topless, while the suggestive striptease sequences provide further titillation, albeit only to the point of pasties and G-strings.

This strategy of inserting explicit footage into foreign acquisitions was par for the course in the exploitation sector, where the promise of illicit spectacle was always more important than narrative coherence.[24] But these are tactics that one would expect of bottom-feeder sexploiteers like Michael Findlay or Doris Wishman, and certainly qualify any claim that Metzger was much interested in the potential "art" value of Audubon's releases at this point.[25] Metzger would later frame his work on *Soft Skin on Black Silk* as primarily an occasion to flex his filmmaking muscles and an object lesson in suggestive marketing (figure 1.2). "I had a sub line [i.e., a tagline] on the title, "A Sexual Romance." The film taught me that words mean absolutely nothing in their denotation. It is only what they connote that has meaning. . . . I [also] had 40 minutes of the Montauk film and production stills which I had taken out there showing me directing real actors. I looked just like a real director. I was even wearing dark glasses."[26] "A Sexual Romance" would indeed prove to be the first of many Metzger-authored taglines that, over the next few years, traded in vague promises of titillating profligacy: "Almost Too Hot For Comfort," for *Sweet Ecstasy*; "Too Much, Too Often" and "A Study of Physical Excess" in the case of producer José Bénazéraf's *La nuit la plus longue* (1964), retitled *Sexus* after the Henry Miller novel (figure 1.3); and "The Film That Goes Too Far!" for Metzger's first self-directed film at Audubon, *The Dirty Girls* (1964) (figure 1.4).

During Audubon's early years, in fact, Metzger seems to have been open to almost any title that invited some kind of exploitation angle. Alongside the European films that were the company's stock in trade, Metzger occasionally picked up homegrown sexploitation titles like director Joe Sarno's *Warm Nights and Hot Pleasures* (1964) and Albert Zugsmith's *Incredible Sex Revolution* (1965). Alongside the sex titles, there were also films distinguished more by their brutality than by any suggestive appeal: the 1949 Czech Holocaust film *Distant Journey*, released by Metzger in 1961 as *Hitler's Inferno*; the 1953 Brazilian western, *O Cangaceiro*, released as *The Ninth Bullet* in 1962; and a Japanese film of delinquent youth, *The Warped Ones* (1960), released in 1963 as *The Weird Lovemakers* (figure 1.5). Notably, the biggest grossing film of Audubon's early years was not a sexploitation title at all—at least, not in the conventional sense—but a nudity-free thriller about an

1.2 Poster for *Soft Skin on Black Silk*.

Source: Author's collection.

1.3 Lobby card for *Sexus*.
Source: Author's collection.

interracial sexual affair involving a light-skinned black man in the American South: the aforementioned *I Spit on Your Grave*. Promoted with the tagline "He Passed for White and They Loved It," the film was a bona fide drive-in sensation, breaking records when it debuted in the Boston area in 1962 and ultimately drumming up around half a million dollars in rentals by mid-decade.[27] It would in fact be the windfall from this film that enabled Metzger to finance the first two films that he personally directed for Audubon, *The Dirty Girls* and its sequel *The Alley Cats* (1965) (both discussed later in this chapter).

Perhaps it is better to think of Metzger's practice at Audubon's inception as more *editorial* than *curatorial*. Editing, in the more literary sense intended here, is a *text-based* process that implies the reshaping of a given text in keeping with certain standards (stylistic, typographical, or, in Audubon's case, exploitational), whereas curating is more oriented toward the creation of a *collection* via a process of selecting, organizing, and keeping. Metzger's creativity was first directed less

1.4 Publicity material for *The Dirty Girls*.

Source: Author's collection.

1.5 One of the more uncharacteristic releases from Audubon Films' early years was *The Weird Lovemakers*, an entry into the Japanese *taiyozoku* ("Sun Tribe") cycle of youth-oriented films highlighting sex and violence.
Source: Author's collection.

toward the overall creation of a cohesive and distinct brand, and more toward active interventions into his haphazard acquisitions (by the insertion of explicit footage, as well as the trimming to which Metzger subjected nearly every Audubon title). Arguably the more foundational steps were being taken by Leighton, who labored behind the scenes "with a hammer and chisel," Metzger recalled, to forge a theatrical network for Audubon's product.[28] Leighton's status as a woman booker of adult film was not entirely unprecedented: the aforementioned Doris Wishman had started her career in film as a booker for Max Rosenberg, distributor of the nudist film *Garden of Eden* (1954).[29] But Leighton quickly eclipsed any predecessors in stature and prominence. Her bid for more mainstream venues like drive-ins was a harbinger of the innovative distribution practices that would become Audubon's hallmark, garnering her an early reputation as a "crackerjack saleswoman."[30]

Leighton's marketing strategies also ensured that a large part of Audubon's story, during its first years, was made up of legal face-offs against forces of state and municipal censorship that sought to limit the circulation of adult film. The first such skirmish began in September 1961 when prints of *The Fast Set* and *The Twilight Girls* were confiscated from the Far Hills Theatre in Dayton, Ohio, setting a pattern that would recur with ever-increasing frequency over the course of Audubon's first decade.[31] The Ohio case was resolved in the theater owner's favor in just a matter of months, after Audubon filed a thousand-dollar suit for damages against Montgomery County Prosecutor Paul Young.[32] Also quickly addressed was the state of Virginia's rejection of *I Spit on Your Grave* the following year on the grounds of "low moral content," which Audubon successfully reversed simply by resubmitting the print.[33] Other cases, however, took much longer, as when the New York State Censor Board refused to issue a license for *The Twilight Girls* in the fall of 1961 unless offensive material was eliminated (basically, most of the scenes that Metzger had added to the film, together with a split-second side view of some pubic hair in the original). Audubon challenged the board's constitutional authority to exert prior restraint, and the case eventually made its way up to the New York Court of Appeals, which reversed the Board's decision on July 3, 1964—two and a half years after the film's original submission.[34]

Audubon's struggles with state censors and police confiscations during this period were part and parcel of its "hammer and chisel" approach to forging a distribution network. The legal decision that set the stage for these struggles was the 1957 Supreme Court case *Roth v. United States*, which had addressed obscenity charges brought against bookseller Samuel Roth for distributing adult literature via the postal service. Although *Roth* was the first ruling to codify obscenity as *not* a protected form of speech, it also significantly narrowed the definition of obscenity to material that is "utterly without redeeming social importance." The test for obscenity, in the opinion written by Justice William Brennan, was whether the "dominant theme [of the material] taken as a whole appeals to the prurient interest" when judged by "the average person, applying contemporary community standards," which were to be assessed on a case-by-case basis rather than as objective criteria.[35] This admittedly complicated the terrain for film companies that traded in explicit material, since they would now need to fight their battles on multiple fronts; but it also put municipal and state regulators at a disadvantage by establishing a high benchmark for unprotected expression ("utterly without social importance"). What ensued was a decade-long series of battles in which independent distributors and theater owners effectively forged the sexploitation market in the courtroom and, in the process, decimated the authority of state censor boards. (Only one, Maryland's, would survive the 1960s.)

Even in this broader context, though, Audubon stood out for the determination with which the company's lawyers took to the courts, often to a fault. Metzger seems to have taken these matters quite personally: he once described his troubles with the censors as "one profound ego assault after another," as though the censors were passing judgment on his own worthiness rather than that of his films.[36] In this regard, the drawn-out battle over *The Twilight Girls* became for Metzger a lesson in tenaciousness, paying immediate dividends when New York State cited the case in granting a license for *Daniella by Night* just two months later.[37] When the state disbanded its censorship board altogether the following year, Metzger forthrightly claimed the victory for himself: "We fought it and won. Right after [the Court's *Twilight Girls* decision], they disbanded."[38] In similar spirit, Audubon would unleash what *Variety* dubbed a "legalistic furor" a few years later when Pittsburgh Supreme Court Justice Michael Musmanno acted to pull Metzger's own *Thérèse and Isabelle* (1968) from exhibition based solely on his reading of a review in the *Pittsburgh Post-Gazette*.[39] By the time that messy and hot-tempered dispute was put to rest seventeen months later in Metzger's favor, Audubon's attorney, Edmund C. Grainger, had twice pleaded his case before the Pennsylvania Supreme Court and once before the Federal Court in Pittsburgh; Justice Musmanno was dead from a stroke days after a "bitter word exchange" that occurred during the case; and District Attorney Robert Duggan had to be admonished by the Court of Appeals for "harassment of exhibitors showing sexplicit attractions."[40]

Not that Audubon was always this uncompromising: the practice of cutting "hot" vs. "cold" versions of release prints—that is, more or less explicit versions—to navigate local regulations had long been established practice among sexploiteers, and Audubon often did the same.[41] The point rather is that the quest for legitimacy with which Audubon has often been associated needs to be understood primarily as a legal matter before it was ever an artistic one, at least in the company's early years. Yet, by mid-decade, there were signs that the issue of art was beginning to register more pressingly. Metzger's decision to retitle *La nuit la plus longue* after Henry Miller's taboo-breaking novel *Sexus* (1949) may have been bluntly cynical ("A lot of people went to the movie thinking it was the film version of that book," Metzger confessed), but it at least indicates an attempt to appropriate, however undeservedly, a more literary type of value for his films.[42] This was Metzger's first attempt to tread onto the kind of cultural territory then occupied by Miller's U.S. publisher, Barney Rosset's Grove Press, which, by the mid-1960s, was well-known for publishing the sexually explicit modernism of authors like Miller, Jean Genet, and William S. Burroughs.[43] It would not be his last.

Another sign of change came in Metzger's unusual approach to editorial inserts in another Pécas acquisition from the same time, *La baie du désir* (1964), retitled as *The Erotic Touch of Hot Skin* for its 1965 U.S. release. Pécas's original had been an erotic crime drama whose narrative begins in the aftermath of murder and then follows the slow unraveling of the murderers' cover-up scheme. In Metzger's reworking, however, two changes refocalize the intrigue away from the action proper and toward the internal disorientation of the criminal protagonists. The first of these involves a portentous and booming "voice of God" narration, which periodically intrudes over freeze-frames of the characters to describe their inner turmoil, declaring, for example, that "the pangs of guilt are strong and torturous, and the bonds that hold the guilty are in many forms." The second concerns Metzger's habitual striptease inserts, which are presented here as interior fantasies or dream sequences—interpretive-dance metaphors, as it were, for the protagonists' psychic states. For instance, the voiceover reference to "the bonds that hold the guilty" initiates a dissolve from a shot of a man's disturbed sleep to a bondage-themed sequence with a dancer tied to a cross. A subsequent example interrupts an otherwise innocuous shot of one woman comforting another to introduce a Sapphic strip number with two dancers in skimpy Greek tunics (figure 1.6).

Metzger's attempt to turn striptease into character psychology is strained to say the least, if not, in fact, fairly risible. But we do not need to take it seriously to register the shift in strategies. In Audubon's previous releases, Metzger would insert striptease acts into nightclub or cabaret scenes from the original film. More often than not, this was simply a matter of removing shots of a non-explicit female dance performance and replacing them with a newly filmed, more explicit strip number, all the while making use of existing eyelines to suture the insertion into its new home (figure 1.7). Such an approach respects the prevailing objectivity of classical film language by motivating the striptease

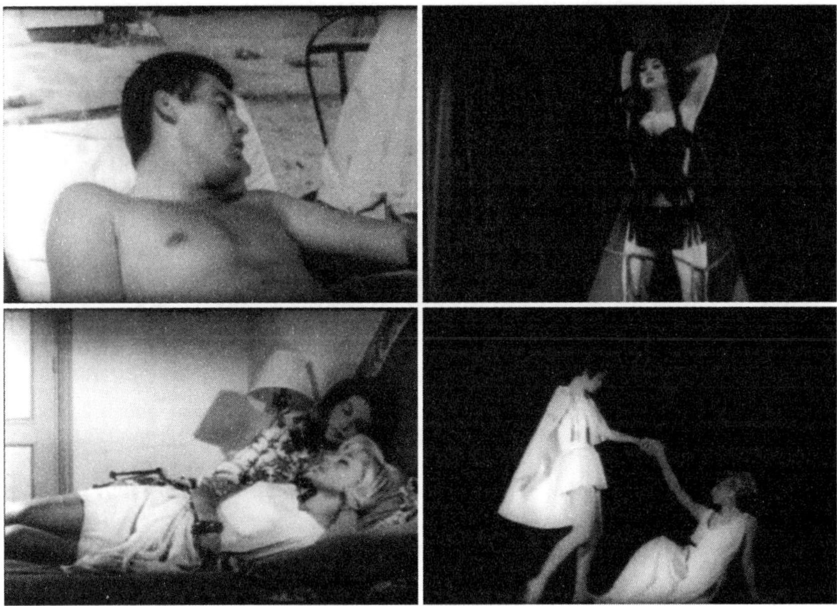

1.6 Striptease sequences representing characters' mental states. Screenshots from *The Erotic Touch of Hot Skin*.

footage in terms of the film's external narrative world: the film's action is taking place in a cabaret, so the striptease routine becomes part of that. But this is not the case for *Erotic Touch*, where Metzger's editorial tactics seemingly ask to be recognized as an approximation of postwar art cinema, a clumsy attempt to motivate the striptease numbers in terms of the interiority and subjective style that characterized the era's art-cinema narration.[44] Again, it is not necessary to debate whether these editorial intrusions have any value *as* art cinema; what matters is Metzger's attempt to model his inserts after the psychologically motivated violation of classical norms that art cinema had helped popularize in the abundant dream and fantasy sequences of a *Wild Strawberries* (1957) or an *8½* (1963). There is a difference between presenting a filmed striptease just as a cabaret act and presenting it as a psychological metaphor, just as there is a difference between retitling one film *The Nude Set* and retitling another *Sexus*. But Metzger was about to acquire a film that would require no such interventions to these ends.

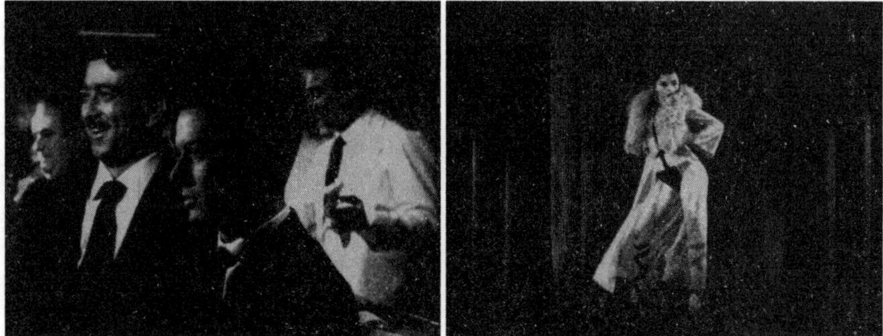

1.7 The principle of eyeline match bridges a shot from (*left*) the Spanish-French film *Tentations* to (*right*) the start of one of Metzger's striptease inserts. Screenshots from *Soft Skin on Black Silk*.

"PORNOGRAPHY HAS DISCOVERED INTELLECTUAL PRETENSION": BUILDING A BRAND, PART 2

In a 1981 overview of pornography's origins, "The Roots of Reel Raunch," critic Dan Shocket recalled Audubon's 1966 release of director Mac Ahlberg's Danish-Swedish coproduction *I, a Woman* as a turning point in the "history of sinema." Shocket's recollections are evocative enough to merit quotation at length:

> For those who reached puberty during the Sixties, *I, a Woman* was a rite of manhood equal to stroking a naked breast. The black-and-white film told of a young woman's maturation into sluthood. Most importantly, it unspooled in reputable suburban theaters. Instead of sneaking into the city, middle class adolescents could walk to a dirty movie.
>
> Theoretically, *I, A Woman* was not a dirty movie. During the mid-Sixties, any sexually mature foreign film was an art film. Bergman, Godard and Fellini are three of the many directors to gain respect and notoriety during this period. To qualify as an art film, subtitles were culturally mandatory. The distributor of *I, a Woman*, Radley Metzger, put subtitles on his Swedish purchase and found markets where no other sex films had dared to appear.
>
> Never had learning to read seemed more important to young boys. They watched the movie in awed silence. . . . Though the movies were supposedly restricted to audiences over 18, that never stopped anyone with a Red Cross

senior lifesaving card. We will never know how many youngsters saw dirty movies because of the Red Cross.[45]

The film, Shocket concluded, was the first "breakthrough" in the passage toward the hardcore boom of the 1970s, as well as a benchmark in the conflation of art and adult cinema. Yet it is a breakthrough that has remained a footnote in most histories. To the extent to which *I, a Woman* has received attention at all, this has chiefly been in relation to what Eric Schaefer calls the "shifting discourse of the 'sexy nation' ": whereas for previous generations it had been France, and particularly Paris, that defined what Americans thought of as "sexy," the period of the sexual revolution saw Americans looking to Denmark and Sweden as new, more modern frontiers of sexual liberation.[46] From this perspective, *I, a Woman* was the thin end of a cinematic wedge that, in the coming years, would see the U.S. release of increasingly explicit Scandinavian titles like the Swedish art-house film *I Am Curious (Yellow)* (1967; U.S. release, 1969), as well as documentaries like *Pornography in Denmark: A New Approach* (1970), which tracked the results of Denmark's landmark legalization of pornography in 1969.

What gets overlooked is *I, a Woman*'s role in a major reconfiguration of the theatrical market for explicit film. Two points from Shocket's recollections can be underscored in this connection: first, *I, a Woman* was "theoretically" not a dirty movie because it was released with subtitles rather than dubbed (which had been Audubon's usual practice); second, it "unspooled" in reputable theaters within easy reach of middle-class homes. And both were testament to the savvy of Ava Leighton. By his own admission, Metzger hadn't thought much of the film, which he once described as one of "the most boring pictures I have ever seen in my life."[47] But Leighton saw in it something for which her years handling art films at Janus had prepared her. She knew, for instance, that art houses of the time generally preferred subtitled foreign-language films over dubbed versions, since subtitling could convey the aura of cosmopolitan distinction to which art theaters aspired.[48] Accordingly, Metzger recalled, "It was Ava Leighton's idea to release the picture subtitled" so as to give *I, a Woman* the "patina of artistry" that would allow for first-run and art-house bookings.[49]

Once again, this was a strategy beset with risks. Audubon's bold steps into the suburbs created more legal trouble for exhibitors than any of the company's previous releases, with the result that prints were confiscated and exhibitors' permits revoked in at least seven states: Connecticut, Illinois, Indiana, Kentucky,

Massachusetts, Ohio, and Rhode Island.[50] But the strategy also brought great rewards: *I, a Woman* did the richest business that Audubon had ever seen, making it a game-changer for how explicit films were marketed and screened. The film cost Metzger a hefty $20,000 for distribution rights, but within a year and a half had brought in over three million in rentals.[51] In 1967, its first full calendar year of release, *I, a Woman* in fact accounted for around eighty-four percent of *all* of Audubon's gross profits ($2,311,946 of the company's $2,742,120 for that year), and ranked as the third highest-grossing foreign-language film in the nation (after *A Fistful of Dollars* [1964] and *A Man and a Woman* [1966]).[52] At decade's end, *Playboy* magazine would recall *I, a Woman* as "the first [sex] film to make a breakthrough into the art-house market," and credited the picture with having legitimized adult content "even in neighborhood theaters."[53] The film even made it into the 1970 report of former President Johnson's Commission on Obscenity and Pornography as the earliest example of what the commission dubbed "hybrid films"—exploitation films that "resemble art films in that many are low-budget foreign films exhibited in the original language with subtitles" and "are exhibited widely in respectable theaters for extended periods of time."[54] Whatever aspirations to the art-cinema market Metzger may have harbored for Audubon at this stage, it would seem to have been Leighton who knew how to make that a reality: she used her experience with Janus as a way of innovating within the world of explicit film and, in the process, helped create what even the U.S. government recognized as something of a new genre (figure 1.8).

Audubon's distribution of *I, a Woman* accordingly represents a test case for what scholar David Andrews has proposed as a "distribution theory" of art cinema, according to which distribution is understood as the fulcrum on which any given film's classification as "art" turns. The category of art cinema, Andrews contends, needs to be defined not at a formal level (that is, in terms of shared patterns of style, narrative, or theme), but as something that takes shape in the varying context of practices, institutions, and discourses that distribution ties together.[55] How else could *I, a Woman*—a film that, a *Variety* writer opined, had "far closer affinity" to sexploitation than to art—nonetheless go on to achieve so successful an art playoff?[56] The answer lay in the film's unique exhibition pattern, which the same *Variety* writer described as "one of the mysteries of the trade." In a handful of major cities in the United States the film had played in houses that showed both art and sexploitation fare interchangeably—theaters like the Rialto in New York or the Presidio in San Francisco. But, as Metzger

1.8 Poster for *I, a Woman.*

Source: Author's collection.

explained at the time, "everywhere else—that is, in the 95% of the country where there remains total distinction between art and exploitation houses, I have never, never permitted 'I, a Woman' to open at an exploitation theatre. In fact, the usual history is for us to follow [Michelangelo Antonioni's] 'Blow-Up' at the best art houses in town. The film eventually plays exploitation houses in some places, but it plays them last." In other words, for the film's nationwide rollout, *I, a Woman* was booked on something like the traditional Hollywood "run-zone-clearance" model, whereby it was only permitted to exploitation houses *after* it had finished its run at any given city's art house.[57] For its New York debut, moreover, the film was given a hybrid release, opening simultaneously at the Times Square Rialto (where it played in a dubbed version) and at the upscale Trans-Lux Eighty-Fifth Street art house (where it played with subtitles). The booking was not entirely out of character for the Trans-Lux: the previous year the theater had screened the Danish film *A Stranger Knocks* (1959) following a protracted legal battle with the New York Board of Regents, which had initially refused the film a license because of an implied sex scene.[58] But *I, a Woman*'s playdate still managed to raise eyebrows for those who considered the Trans-Lux one of New York City's jewels of moviegoing refinement. The theater had originally opened in 1937 as part of a chain of New York–based newsreel theaters for discriminating adults, and had won praise for an "ultra-modern" design (in the words of the *New York Times*) boasting both an Art Deco storefront and a lobby modeled after a Parisian sidewalk.[59] The critic at the *Daily News* claimed simply that "no one knows how to react" to *I, a Woman*'s screening there, while Vincent Canby, writing for the *New York Times*, noted that the film's playdates at the Trans-Lux "gave the picture a certain respectability, and opened the doors to conventional neighborhood houses that seldom play Audubon releases."[60] Archer Winsten, writing for the *Post*, reflected thoughtfully on how the film's dual opening reflected the film's contradictory appeal:

> The opening of the Swedish-Danish sexploiter, "I, a Woman," at the Trans-Lux 85th Street and Rialto theaters, accurately mirrors its double nature. It is sufficiently sensational with its body views, passionate writhings, and burlesque routines to qualify as an exploitational film worthy of a Rialto opening. It is also made with enough quality of performance and varied character to permit a serious audience to ponder its ultimate question, "Are all women like that, or is it only me?"[61]

The film's two-tier release was in this way confirmation of Audubon's approach to distribution as a form of value creation in its own right, and it cemented a dual East Side/West Side release strategy that the company would use for all subsequent New York premieres. As Metzger described the policy: "We always showed our films East Side/West Side: the West Side was popular theater and the East Side was the more sophisticated audience."[62]

But this was hardly the only change wrought in the wake of *I, a Woman*'s success. For one thing, the film seems to have initiated a change in Metzger's conception of his role vis-à-vis his acquisitions, namely a switch from an editorial approach to the creation of value toward a more overtly curatorial one. Notably, Metzger's habit of adding striptease sequences to his acquisitions dried up around this point: the last Audubon acquisition to have received this treatment seems to have been Serge Combret's 1965 *La traite des blanches*, released in the late summer of 1967 as *Hot Frustrations*, after which Metzger settled for more modest editorial interventions, such as making trims for pacing or reinserting explicit shots cut from a given film's domestic release.[63] At the same time, Metzger developed a more fine-tuned sense of Audubon as a particular brand. In the aftermath of *I, a Woman*, Audubon invested in a new logo for the company, the boxed "A" that first accompanied *Hot Frustrations*' release (figure 1.9). This was accompanied by a newfound consistency in the *type* of films that Metzger picked up for distribution—as well as those he directed himself—which began more assertively to fuse erotic appeal with modernist aspiration. *I, a Woman* defined the pattern in this respect by assuming an art-cinema model for its display of erotic effects. As the *Variety* report on the film's "mysteries" suggested, *I, a Woman*'s narrative was par for the course for sexploitation: like Russ Meyer's 1964 *Lorna*, the reporter wrote, *I, a Woman* tells the story of a woman in a "Bible-belt environment" who " 'burst[s] forth' in a lifelong orgy of sexual excess," culminating in a "mandatory last scene" in which she "receives [her] comeuppance."[64] But the film's *narration*—which is to say, the way it *tells* that story—ran closer to an art-cinema model by channeling its depiction of erotic experience through the subjectivity of its protagonist. This aesthetic torque is evident in the extended close-ups of star Essy Persson's face during the film's sex scenes, a device that coalesces an exploitation-style focus on sexual excitation with an art-cinema representation of interiority, as conveyed via subjective sound and superimposed memories (figure 1.10).[65] The film's director, Mac Ahlberg, even includes a notably Bergmanesque flourish at one point as,

1.9 Audubon's new logo in the bottom-right corner of the poster for *Hot Frustrations*. Compare the cursive logo in figure 1.8.

Source: Author's collection.

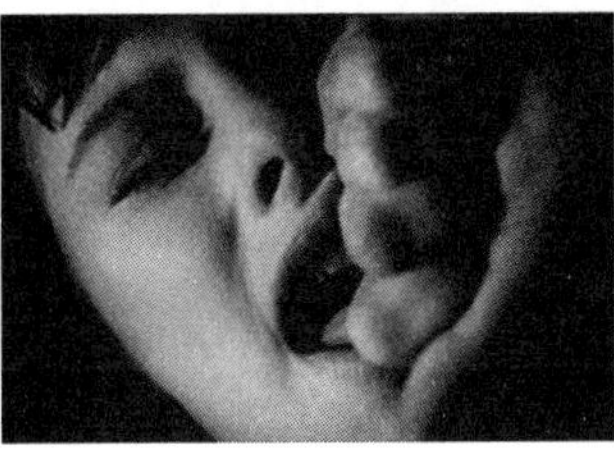

1.10 Memories of religious upbringing accompany the protagonist's orgasm. Screenshots from *I, a Woman*.

post-orgasm, Persson returns the gaze, in seeming echo of the final shot of *Summer with Monika* (1953).

I, a Woman would be the first in a series of late 1960s/early 1970s Audubon releases to dovetail sexploitation explicitness with art-house experiment. Metzger's subsequent acquisitions tended toward titles such as Max Pécas's *The Night of the Three Lovers* (1968, original title *La nuit la plus chaude*), which features a nonlinear narrative whose flashback scenes appear variously in monochrome blue, orange, and yellow; the Swedish *Vibration* (1968, original title *Lejonsommar*), another vehicle for Essy Persson, whose character reminisces over a summer of mod parties, hippie encounters, and philosophical debate; the Italian film *The Libertine* (1969, original title *La Matriarca*), which cribbed from Luis Buñuel's surrealist take on sexuality in *Belle du jour* (1967); Tinto Brass's *Black on White* (1969, original title *Nerosubianco*), a feature-length montage of S/M sex scenes, antiwar skits, psychedelic rock numbers, and even a Jean-Luc Godard parody; Seiichi Fukuda's *Madame O* (1970), a rape-revenge film that switches from black-and-white to color for scenes of sexual or violent trauma; and another Italian production, *The Laughing Woman* (1970, original title *Femina Ridens*), which combined a protofeminist sadomasochistic narrative with explicit references to pop artists Giuseppe Capogrossi and Niki de Saint Phalle. In the immediate wake of *I, a Woman*'s success, Ava Leighton had declared that Audubon would now be "aiming for a wider market for art house and regular situations"; the company's follow-up releases clearly sought to make good on that promise.[66]

In effect, what Metzger and Leighton were working to create was a public identity for explicit film aligned with what historian Loren Glass has described as the "vulgar modernism" of the era's avant-garde.[67] This is not the "vulgar modernism" perhaps best known within film studies—the version coined by *Village Voice* critic J. Hoberman to describe the ironic self-reflexivity of postwar pop culture like the films of Frank Tashlin or Tex Avery cartoons—but rather a particular inflection of late modernism whose formal experimentation was wedded to an unprecedented sexual explicitness.[68] Barney Rosset's Grove Press had been the pioneer on the literary home front. Although Grove had first established its reputation as the channel through which European authors like Alain Robbe-Grillet and Samuel Beckett found a U.S. readership, the company's brand identity mutated in the 1960s to emphasize homegrown counterculture writers like William S. Burroughs, Henry Miller, and Hubert Selby (author of *Last Exit to Brooklyn*), whose work explicitly dealt with sexual taboo. The parallel emergence of what was often called "underground film" testified to a similar conflation of formal and sexual iconoclasm, whether in the unprecedented visibility of queer content in the work of filmmakers like Kenneth Anger (*Scorpio Rising*, 1963) and Jack Smith (*Flaming Creatures*, 1963) or in Andy Warhol's filmed records of unsimulated sex, both offscreen (*Blow Job*, 1964) and on (*Blue Movie*, 1968). With obscenity law on the ropes, the act of disrobing became a common provocation in live performance, too, in works ranging from the "kinetic theater" of Carolee Schneemann's *Meat Joy* (1964) to the Broadway musical *Hair* (1967). Vulgar modernism was, in this way, a transmedia phenomenon that emerged, in Glass's words, "in the brief interregnum between high modernism and postmodernism, between the end of obscenity and the rise of pornography, as a transitional phenomenon specific to the 1960s."[69] And it was this terrain that Audubon began to encroach upon in the wake of *I, a Woman*. By the end of the 1960s Metzger would graduate from merely pilfering the title of a Miller novel to describing Grove Press as his "competitor," in a 1969 interview in which he placed Audubon's product within a broader field of explicit experimentalism that also included theatrical works like Kenneth Tynan's *Oh! Calcutta!* (which debuted off-Broadway that year).[70]

Critics, for their part, responded in kind, offering a kind of grudging acknowledgment of the vanguard aspirations that now characterized Audubon's releases. *The Laughing Woman*, for instance, "upp[ed] the intellectual percentage by volume at least to 19 per cent, which is quite a step up for the exploitation group."[71] *The Libertine* meanwhile prompted one critic to declare that "pornography has discovered intellectual pretension" before adding tellingly, "In books, this has been going on for some time, the best known recent examples being *The Story of O* and *The Image*"—both Grove Press releases (and both discussed in detail in chapter 3).[72] The change of direction was also evident in the way Audubon's titles were marketed. The vaguely connotative style of Metzger's early taglines now sharpened into a rhetoric that framed outré content as a matter of taste distinction. "Enter the private domain of the developed connoisseur," began the trailer for *The Laughing Woman*. "This is a picture for the mature, for people with strong tastes, not afraid to see truth," announced publicity material for *The Night of the Three Lovers*, adding: "If you dig the bizarre, this is it." Whereas Metzger had preferred broadly general promises of sexual explicitness for his early promotional campaigns, he now favored an address that defined sophistication in terms of a taste for sexual unorthodoxy. The French film *Michelle* (1968, original title *Sexy Gang*) introduced viewers to "a world of young people whose tastes are bizarre," while the tagline for Max Pécas's queer-themed *Her and She and Him* (1970, original title *Claude et Greta*) promised simply "a motion-picture deviation."[73] What Audubon achieved, in the process, was a redefinition of erotic capital in the image of late modernism, which implied a fusion of avant-garde representational form (derived from the codes of the art cinema) with avant-garde sexual tastes (a "connoisseur's" preference for *outré*, fetishistic forms of sexual practice).

In an essay on pornography and taste, film scholar Mark Jancovich writes that "the study of pornography . . . requires us to acknowledge that sexual tastes are not just gendered but also classed and that, as [Pierre] Bourdieu argues in relation to the aesthetic disposition more generally, sexual tastes are not only amongst the most 'classifying' of social differences, but also have 'the privilege of appearing the most natural.'"[74] In the existing literature, this insight has generally been realized in a broad-strokes dichotomy separating a variously feminized and/or middle-class erotica from a variously chauvinistic and/or lower-class porn: a kind of *Playboy* vs. *Penthouse* binary for the field of explicit sexual representation. But this is not a sufficiently nuanced framework to explain the specific field of vulgar modernism with which Metzger sought to affiliate the Audubon brand. Even if we accept that sexual tastes are "classed" (as indeed we should), the phenomenon of vulgar modernism is not well explained simply as a class phenomenon (even though, as will become clear, it was).

Rather, we need to begin with the role that publishers and distributors played in the dissemination of the era's counterculture to a broader public. If, as Barbara Ehrenreich contends, the "story of the sixties' counterculture was its co-optation," then the vulgar modernism brokered by figures like Rosset and Metzger was one of several avenues through which middle-class Americans could experience the counterculture by proxy.[75] This, after all, was an era in which Grove Press could launch a "Join the Underground" campaign on posters throughout the New York City subway system, even as a 1966 survey in *Advertising Age* revealed that the typical Grove reader was in fact "a 39-year-old male, married, two children, a college graduate who holds a managerial position in business or industry" (which would accurately describe Metzger, too, if one changed thirty-nine for thirty-seven and dropped the "married, two children").[76] It was a world in which Yale law professor Charles Reich proselytized for the values of the counterculture, first in the pages of the *New Yorker*, then in his 1970 bestseller *The Greening of America*, which presented the hippies as heralding a change of consciousness that could salve the alienation of white-collar Americans.[77] What these developments speak to was the presence of a middle class eager to participate in a curated or proxy version of the sexual ideologies from which they were a generational step apart. Perhaps not coincidentally comments in the trade press on the audience for Audubon's releases painted a similar sociological picture. Thus, Audubon's "filmgoing following," per *Variety* in 1969, consisted of the "fairly affluent middle-class public—young and middle-aged—who are inveterate movie fans."[78]

But "middle class" was a divided identity during this period, riven by a tension between a "traditional" middle class defined by a politics of civic respectability and the new cohort of what sociologist Vance Packard famously called the "status seekers," characterized by a more "modernist" or "younger" lifestyle, to which Metzger himself clearly belonged.[79] Literary historian Jordan Carroll has spoken, in this connection, of the emergence of a "type of professional-managerial masculinity that established its bona fides by showing that it could adopt a sophisticated attitude toward obscene literature"—as though the era's changing cultural winds served middle-class, midcentury white men primarily as an opportunity to burnish their sexual urbanity.[80] It is hard not to think here of Hugh Hefner's *Playboy*, which, from its origins in 1953, had sought to marry the liberationist aspect of Beat culture with a leisure lifestyle of Ivy League fashion, foreign films, jazz records, and top-of-the-line hi-fi equipment.[81] Hefner's achievement was to have pioneered a path for the mass-market popularization of the era's countercultural sensibility—of its artistic, intellectual, and, most importantly, sexual avant-gardes—to the professional-managerial classes, which was the target audience for Metzger's project as well. If, to quote Ehrenreich again, "for most grown men, the hippies' fairyland looked best as a soft-porn spectacle," then magazines like *Playboy*, Broadway musicals like *Hair*, and film distribution companies like Audubon were on hand to answer that perception.[82] This was the context in which Metzger now sought to forge his identity as a film director in his own right.

"TURNING CLASSICS INTO SEX FILMS": DEFINING AN AUTEUR, PART 1

On October 8, 1966, three days before *I, a Woman*'s New York premiere, Radley Metzger flew out to Yugoslavia's Adriatic coast to begin production on a film with the working title *Carmen 13*, scheduled for a five-week shoot at a budget of $150,000.[83] The odd title, press reports explained, was chosen because the film represented "the 13th time somebody has made a film from Prosper Mérimée's story [1845] about the cigarette girl and the soldier"—the source, most famously, of Georges Bizet's eponymous 1875 opera.[84] This was not the first film that Metzger had directed for Audubon, but it nonetheless marked a notable shift in ambition tied to the brand-image change that *I, a Woman* helped bring about (figure 1.11). Eventually retitled *Carmen, Baby* (1967), the film represented a break in precedent for Metzger on at least three counts, all of which would continue to inform his subsequent filmmaking.[85] First, the film was a significant step up in the usual production scale of Audubon releases: it was Metzger's first foray into color and anamorphic widescreen (the German-based Ultrascope process), as well as his first film requiring the building of sets (shot at the Arriflex Studios in Munich), all of which helped send the final budget beyond $200,000 and pushed the shoot seven weeks behind schedule.[86] Second, Metzger adapted the film's basic plot from the canons of "classic" literature, a conceit that he would adopt numerous times in his career. Third and finally, the film's culminating sex scene—in which a supine couple is filmed through a long row of colored glass snifters—represents the dawning of what would become a signature style in his films: "Most of [my] sex scenes contain some kind of distortion," the director later explained, "and glass is a very good method."[87]

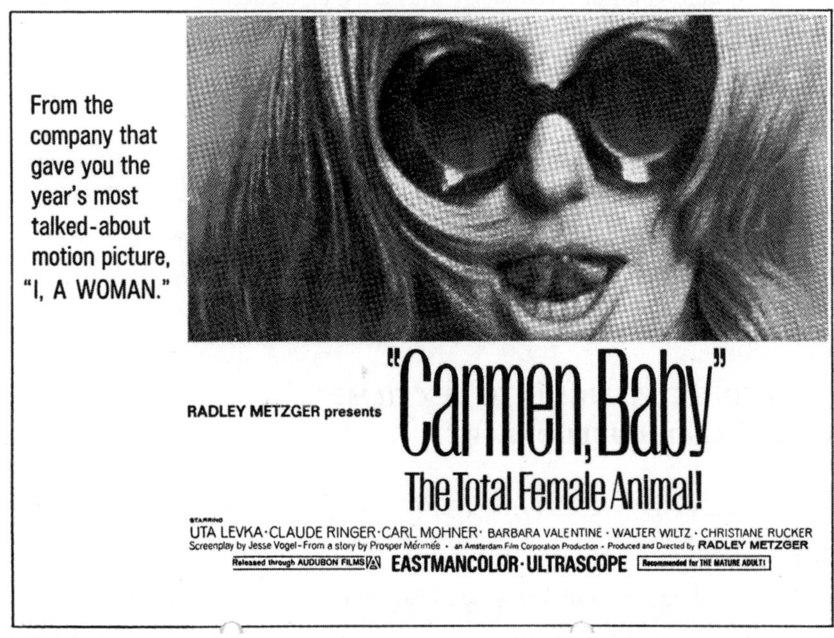

1.11 Publicity for *Carmen, Baby* played on Audubon's previous success with *I, a Woman*. *Source*: Author's collection.

The particular nature of these shifts emerges clearly through a comparison with the two Metzger-directed Audubon films that preceded *Carmen, Baby*. To the extent to which Metzger's pre-*Carmen* filmmaking has received any critical attention, this has largely been a matter of unearthing and identifying the authorial tropes that predict his mature, post-*Carmen* style, as though a kind of untrammeled teleology ran through Metzger's work in the 1960s. Bart Testa, for example, identifies *The Alley Cats* as the first example of Metzger's tendency to build "his narrative carriage around a female protagonist"—in this case, a woman, Leslie, experiencing awakening queer desire.[88] Elena Gorfinkel meanwhile notes how the trope of "sex performed by a woman's face"—which Metzger supposedly inherited from *I, a Woman*—is in fact already evident in in the scene from *The Dirty Girls* in which a female character masturbates while kissing her own reflection in a mirror (figure 1.12).[89] But such a teleology downplays the shift of gears that divided Audubon's mid-1960s rebranding from its earlier releases. Far from anticipating anything resembling the vulgar modernism to which Metzger came to aspire, both *The Dirty Girls* and *The Alley Cats* sought rather to emulate the

1.12 Production still for *The Dirty Girls*.
Source: Author's collection.

"ooh-la-la" sensibility of the late 1950s–early 1960s European imports in which Audubon initially traded. Both films were shot in Europe—*The Dirty Girls* in Paris and Munich, *The Alley Cats* just Munich—and both were released as though they were simply two more risqué European acquisitions, with no in-house publicity given to Metzger's direction nor any critical attention paid to it. *The Dirty Girls*, for example, was described in *Modern Man Deluxe Quarterly*'s special 1968 "Nude Movie Issue" simply as a Franco-German coproduction, *The Alley Cats* as a "German import" and "European-made film" in the handful of references it garnered in *Variety*.[90]

The two films were also of a piece with what Eric Schaefer describes as the "touristic" iconography of European nightlife—its parties and nightclubs, showgirls and streetwalkers—so characteristic of the imports of the time.[91] For *The Dirty Girls*, for instance, Metzger planned to make, in his words, a "three-part picture on prostitution. The story of a low, (that is, economically low) street walker in Paris, a middle girl in Germany, and a very high-level call girl in New York."[92]

The Parisian section was shot in six days, but budgetary shortages forced Metzger to abandon the New York shoot and condense the remaining two parts into a single narrative in Munich. The result is a film that incorporates the self-same appeal to Europe's permissive reputation on which Audubon's corporate reputation had been built. (The film's opening voiceover sets the tone, proclaiming, "In the streets of Paris, desire fills the night.") For Metzger, meanwhile, the film was primarily important as a much-needed confidence builder as he tested the waters of feature filmmaking for the first time since *Dark Odyssey*: "I [only] had a crew of four people," he recalled, "and I really didn't understand what it was to put together something theatrical. I had an awful lot of inhibitions . . . [but] I somehow broke through this shell and had some fun" (figure 1.13). "It's probably the single most terrifying thing I've ever done," he confessed in his 1973 *Film Comment* interview. "I had people around me who'd made maybe thirty or forty French films, and they all look at you and say, 'Well, what do we do next?' "[93] For all these reasons, *The Dirty Girls* and *The Alley Cats* are best approached less as the assertion of a nascent authorial presence than as learning experiences in which Metzger played within the limits of the Audubon brand: Metzger's authorship was, at this point, subsumed within and in service of Audubon's corporate identity, rather than the brand hallmark that it would soon become. Nor did the promotion and publicity for these films make obvious assertion of any value other than that of sex: titles like *The Alley Cats* and *The Dirty Girls* (or just *The "D" Girls* for conservative locales) hardly reflect the transvaluation of the sex film with which Metzger came to be associated.

Compare this, however, with *Carmen, Baby*, which was released on October 10, 1967, at both the Upper East Side 72nd Street Playhouse and the Times Square Rialto, and reviewed in the pages of *Box Office* as a move "into the prestige arena of color, scope [the Ultrascope process], and classic theme."[94] "Prestige" here was a matter of both literary source ("classic theme") and production values ("color, scope"), in a way that encompassed both content and form, each coalescing as part of a broader strategy of respectability that would come to define what Metzger thought of as "erotic" cinema. Metzger's appeal to the literary canon was the most obvious component of his strategy, a short-cut bid for cultural capital that deferred to the authority of the source text as a pretext for and justification of the film's explicitness. Metzger explained his approach in a 1971 profile in *Show* magazine, discussing both *Carmen, Baby* and his subsequent *Camille 2000* (1969), whose plot Metzger similarly derived from nineteenth-century literature (the

1.13 Radley Metzger in a rare cameo in *The Dirty Girls*.
Source: Author's collection.

younger Alexandre Dumas's 1848 *La dame aux camelias*): "In each case I took a highly erotic story and made a more erotic film out of it than had previously been allowed in the movies. But in each case it is less erotic than the original story on which it was based."[95] Metzger's appeal was to a kind of "good for the gander" reasoning, whereby what had been canonized in literature should also be allowed to cinema. Yet if Metzger hoped thereby to legitimize sex in film, he found little support from critics, who accused him of cultural desecration with respect to the source novella—a "vulgariz[ation of] the tragic story of Carmen," one critic complained, "turning her into a modern day tart hotly pursued by a flatheaded policeman."[96] Metzger's appeal to the literary canon in fact made *Carmen, Baby* vulnerable in a way that most other vulgar modernism was not, since it implied an underlying commitment to a traditionalist conception of "art" that the film could be accused of betraying. Few aspects of the picture were as roundly condemned as its relation to its literary source: "There have been any number of versions of both Prosper Merimee's original 'Carmen' and the Georges Bizet opera of the same name, but by far the most ludicrous . . . is the one that turned up yesterday at the 72nd Street Playhouse," New York's *Morning Telegraph* declared.[97]

There is a name for the particular landmine that Metzger had landed on here: middlebrow. Originally coined to describe commercial efforts to mass-market "the classics" (like the Book of the Month Club, launched in 1926), the idea of middlebrow was by the postwar years one of the preferred whipping boys of the critical intelligentsia. For a generation of art critics and observers, the term served as a catch-all label for what could go wrong whenever "true" or "high" art was submitted to the dictates of the marketplace. *Harper's Magazine* writer Russell Lynes provided one flashpoint in these debates in a 1949 essay that accused the middlebrow of "blur[ring] the lines between the serious and the frivolous."[98] Dwight Macdonald's famous *Partisan Review* essay "Masscult and Midcult" (1960) framed the critique in language that anticipated critical responses to Metzger's film: middlebrow culture, he contended, "pretends to respect the standards of High Culture while in fact it waters them down and vulgarizes them," citing examples that ranged from *Reader's Digest* to the film productions of Samuel Goldwyn.[99] What Metzger was guilty of, from this perspective, was a frivolous use of the cultural canon—Mérimée, Bizet—as a means to market sex films. Art critic Clement Greenberg would no doubt have derided Metzger's efforts as what he famously dubbed *kitsch*, which is what results whenever "the debased and academicized simulacra of genuine culture" are appropriated for a kind of spurious respectability.[100] Unlike other exploitation filmmakers whose work pursued a kind of pulpy experimentation—the work of the Amero brothers, say, in the United States, or of Jess Franco and Jean Rollin in Europe—Metzger's aspirations to fuse art and sex remained bound to the safety of the classics. Worse, he had committed what Lynes's essay had described as the middlebrow's most pernicious move: he had mixed up the "lowbrow arts . . . with middlebrow ideas of culture," from which "the highbrow turns away in disgust."[101]

The elitism of the critics' responses to Metzger's film is obvious. Less so is what *Carmen, Baby*'s critical drubbing shared with the director's own filmmaking ambitions. Metzger's drive to gentrify the sex film, as we have seen, was part and parcel of a new postwar culture in which matters of cultural taste and sensibility became royal roads to social status.[102] But the denigration that *Carmen, Baby* received was simply the flip side of the same coin. In a context in which taste served as a significant source of distinction, the critical elites strove to erect a *cordon sanitaire* protecting the sphere of "true" art against its upwardly mobile, middle-class pillagers. To tar a work with the middlebrow brush was the strategy of choice for critics seeking to condemn those who were suspected of selling the Muses short. "It must be obvious to anyone that the volume and social weight of middlebrow culture," Greenberg had complained, presents "a more serious threat to the genuine article than the old-time pulp dime novel [or] Tin Pan Alley . . . ever has or will."[103] Metzger's fault, from this perspective, was to have assumed that the process of "turning classics into sex films," as the *Show* interview put it, was sufficient alchemy to turn sex films into art cinema.[104] The same quest for status that motivated Metzger to "upgrade" the aesthetic standards of explicit filmmaking also ensured his rejection by a critical establishment that used the middlebrow label to ward off pretenders.

But there is another label for describing *Carmen, Baby*, one that was complexly entangled with middlebrow—namely, erotica, the very term with which Metzger would associate his work. As explored in the introduction, the concept of erotic art has often been used to describe works that combine sexual content with artistic intent or value. Where this becomes difficult, though, is that this very mix of elements almost by definition invites the middlebrow critique. Given the popular prejudice that would separate art and pornography as mutually exclusive terms, any aestheticization of explicit sexual content—such as Metzger intended—risks being seen as a similarly "pretend" aesthetics aiming for a similarly "pretend" respectability.[105] The point here is not that Metzger's erotica *is* or *was* middlebrow—which is an evaluative label more than a descriptive one—but that it could not have escaped the stigma.[106] What more egregious instance of art's adulteration could there be than the apparent charlatanism of a sex filmmaker turning to the classics?

It is ironic, then, that the one area where *Carmen, Baby* elicited some praise was for its direction, such that mockery of Metzger's narrative pretension often existed side-by-side with grudging acknowledgment of his visual style. Vincent Canby at the *New York Times* captured the dichotomy well, describing how the film "has a rather classy look" despite its "heated sexual shenanigans."[107] The anonymous critic for *Box Office* struck a similar note, commenting that "There's at least one improvement in the sexploitation film, the photography. Now, if they'd do something about the writing!"[108] Metzger's innovations in this regard bespeak a rather different orientation from his approach to the film's narrative:

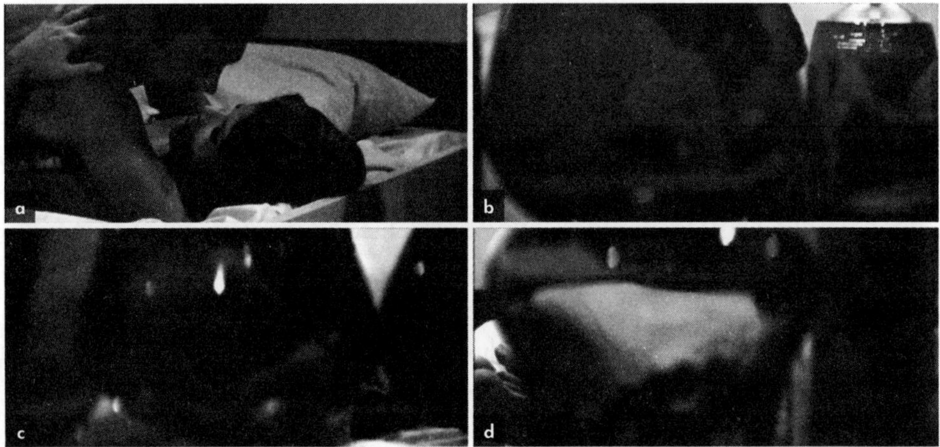

1.14 Sex refracted through colored glasses in a single tracking shot. Screenshots from *Carmen, Baby*.

if the latter looked back to the perceived authority of a literary classic, then the former appealed to the contemporary cachet of an art and avant-garde cinema that had begun to disentangle visual style from classical standards of narrative clarity and causality. The standout sequence in this respect—the film's stylistic climax, if not yet its narrative one—is the aforementioned scene with colored glass, in which Carmen (played by Uta Levka) makes love to pop singer Baby Lucas (the film's version of the picador Lucas from the Mérimée novella).[109] Two lengthy moving shots—the first lasting some ninety seconds, the second nearly four minutes—depict the action refracted and distorted through a row of barely translucent colored glasses (figure 1.14). Concealing the action even as they hint at its possible visibility, these dolly shots provide the first instance of what Gorfinkel has insightfully described as a "trajectory toward abstraction" in Metzger's work in which "it is *style itself* that is being eroticized."[110] That is to say, the formal conceit of these shots invests the glass surfaces with a weight of their own that counterbalances the sensuous action behind the glasses: optics itself here becomes the object of vision, in tension with the sexual display.[111]

Did *Carmen, Baby* qualify as art cinema, then? The critic who decried Metzger's "desecration" of Mérimée didn't think so: on the issue of the film's style, she mocked Metzger's presumed assumption that "art" was just a matter of photographing the love scenes "through rose-tinted glasses."[112] Evidently what was "vulgarization" in relation to the classics was "pretension" in relation to adult film: in neither case, the argument went, was Metzger able to operate at the level at which art was to be found. Yet this objection only underscored the contradictory conception of art that Metzger's strategies of respectability sought to straddle, at once canon in its narrative content and vanguard in its style. In attempting to reclassify the sex film, Metzger was appealing to schizoid registers of artistic value that yoked a genteel deferral to the classics to a modernist insistence on the autonomy of visual style.

It is tempting to psychologize Metzger in this respect, as though his scattershot approach to artistry was the result of an overcompensation. Despite the learning experiences of *The Dirty Girls* and *The Alley Cats*, Metzger remained besieged by a kind of imposter syndrome, fearing that he was "perhaps a film fan misplaced" and that "maybe the love of motion pictures is not enough to carry you into making motion pictures."[113] He further described his anxieties in making *Carmen* in a way that implied an analogy with his own ethnic background: "You know I felt sort of like the first Jew in the Country Club. . . . His standards will be twice as high as anyone else, in order to prove himself."[114] Even as he took his first step toward a transvaluation of explicit filmmaking, Metzger evidently remained every inch the City College graduate with a catch-as-catch-can cinephilia and a desire to prove himself. But he had also exposed a conflict in his conception of artistic value that his subsequent films, so far from resolving, would develop into one of the very hallmarks of his authorship.

"AN AMALGAM OF '60S SEXUAL EXPOSURE AND '30S GENTILITY": DEFINING AN AUTEUR, PART 2

Whatever the critics' opinions, *Carmen, Baby*'s box-office performance served as proof of concept for the new direction in Metzger's filmmaking: it would become the biggest grossing film that Metzger ever directed under his own name, ultimately pulling in close to two million dollars ($1,758,885 by April 30, 1969, according to *Variety*).[115] The one-two punch of *I, a Woman* and *Carmen, Baby* helped make 1967 the most financially successful year in Audubon's history at that point (with the company recording an overall income of $1,725,744, more than five times greater than the previous high of $314,630, reported for 1966).[116] It was even rumored that the film's success spurred Metzger to sign the picture's star, Uta Levka, to a multiple-picture deal, although nothing ultimately happened to that end.[117] What Metzger did do next was to direct a picture with Essy Persson, the star of *I, a Woman*: an adaptation of Violette Leduc's lesbian novella *Thérèse et Isabelle* (1966). For the sake of my argument, though, I want to leave that film to the next chapter, in order to look at the picture he made *after*, for which he returned to the winning formula of *Carmen, Baby* with another explicit updating of nineteenth-century literature, this one starring French actress Daniele Gaubert, fresh from a headline-making divorce from the son of Dominican Republic dictator Rafael Trujillo.[118]

The film in question, *Camille 2000*, involved the most ambitious shoot of any of Metzger's self-directed Audubon titles. Filmed largely on location in Rome, *Camille 2000* was scheduled for eight weeks of principal photography, starting October 28, 1968, with an estimated budget of $750,000; by the time the film wrapped, however, its costs had run over a million, with production having spilled over to mid-January. Metzger's gentrifying aspirations were again apparent, this time in the lavish baroque and neoclassical buildings he chose for his locations—the Palazzo Brancaccio (constructed in 1880, also used in William Wyler's *Roman Holiday* [1953]), the Teatro Valle (1726), and the Villa Miani (1837)—with only a few days' filming on soundstages in late December at the Dear Studios in Rome.[119] Like *Carmen, Baby*, moreover, the film placed one foot each in cinema's prestige past and its vanguard present: a remake of sorts of MGM's 1936 Greta Garbo vehicle, *Camille*, Metzger's film boasted some of Italy's foremost young filmmaking talent, both in front of and behind the camera, including actor Nino Castelnuovo (the male lead in Jacques Demy's *The Umbrellas of Cherbourg* [1964]), composer Piero Piccioni (director Francesco Rosi's composer of choice), and cinematographer Ennio Guarnieri (a frequent collaborator of Lina Wertmüller's).

Among these new collaborators, however, few had greater impact on the look of the film than set and costume designer Enrico Sabbatini, who had previously worked on the sci-fi fashions in Elio Petri's *The Tenth Victim* (1965), and would go on to an extraordinarily distinguished career, including costumes for *The Laughing Woman*. *Camille 2000* was, in fact, Sabbatini's first turn at set design in film, and his creations for the project were standout examples of the Pop-Art futurism of 1960s Italian cinema that had clearly caught Metzger's eye. (Piero Poletto's set designs for *The Laughing Woman* and Flavio Mogherini's for *The Libertine* are other notable instances.) Part of Sabbatini's mandate for the film was to link *Camille*'s protagonist—the tubercular courtesan Marguerite in Dumas's text, here a heroin addict—to a sense of doom and the nonliving. "We tried to give Camille a very dead milieu," Metzger recalled. "Nothing around her lived. She was always dressed in either white or black, and the décor of her room was filled with unreal things—plastic, phosphorescent stuff."[120] In terms of costuming, Metzger's intent was realized not just in an absence of color, but also in Sabbatini's use of inorganic materials, such as a dress with collar and sleeves of transparent plastic bars in the opera scene where Armand (Castelnuovo) first meets her and a metallic halter in a later S/M party. In terms of sets, meanwhile, Sabbatini came through with a show-stopping all-white design for Marguerite's bedroom, replete with a transparent inflatable bed, plastic furnishings, multi-paneled mirrored walls, and other "sci-fi accoutrements," as the *Playboy* critic described them.[121] Most reviewers felt compelled to make wry jabs at Sabbatini's outré furnishings—A. H. Weiler at the *New York Times* jokingly commented on *Camille 2000*'s likely appeal to "every red-blooded voyeur and admirer of plastic décor"—and the plastic bed in fact became the source of one of Metzger's favorite stories of the film's production.[122] "We were working with very long lenses," Metzger recalled, "which meant that the focus was very, very critical. The actors would be in bathrobes and whatever. We'd rehearse the scene, work out the camera movements, which were very delicate. They'd take off their clothes. They would lie on the plastic furniture, the beds, and the body heat would change the inflation of the furniture, so the focus was not right."[123] There were even reports in the trade press that Metzger was planning to put the bed on a nationwide tour in conjunction with the film's opening, as though in an effort to transform theater lobbies into real-life extensions of the erotic fantasy worlds depicted on screen (figure 1.15).[124]

Whatever else it may have been, then, Metzger's eroticism had by this point clearly crystalized as an attention to the specifics of mise-en-scène. In this, he would echo or anticipate many of the leading theories of the erotic imagination in the late twentieth century. In a celebrated 1967 definition, for example, psychoanalytic theorists Jean Laplanche and Jean-Bertrand Pontalis argued that fantasy is a *staging* of desire, a psychosexual mise-en-scène ("*la mise-en-scène du désir*," in their formulation), an insight shared by U.S. sexologist Robert J. Stoller, who described eroticism as a matter of *theater*, in which each detail of staging counts.[125] Extrapolating from this point, fashion historian Alistair O'Neill has more recently suggested that eroticism in film should, then, be seen as "more about sofas and sheets than sequences and shots"—although in the case of *Camille*

1.15 Poster for *Camille 2000*.

Source: Author's collection.

2000, the point might be reframed as "sofas and sheets and the sequences and shots they inspire."[126] For what becomes clear in the sex scenes of *Camille* is the way in which Sabbatini's innovative set design served as a catalyst for Metzger's stylistic experiments. Set design and film technique fused in an approach to sex scenes that built upon the play with refractive surfaces begun in *Carmen, Baby*. For the scene in which Armand and Marguerite first make love, for instance, Metzger uses the circular panel of mirrors around the bed, as well as the mirrored ceiling and floor, to transform the image into a repetition of frames within the frame. The lovers' naked bodies are multiplied even as their reflections are inescapably partial: the image paradoxically withholds where it seems most fulsome (figure 1.16).[127] A similar displacement from bodies onto optics structures a subsequent sex scene: in a standout, minute-long take, Metzger's camera racks focus repeatedly between Marguerite's face in the background and a vase of camelias in the foreground, keeping time with her panting breaths as she is brought to orgasm (figure 1.17). Vision here becomes a kind of embodied ancillary to Marguerite's sexual pleasure, which is less the object of a visual representation than the very thing that governs the shifting relations of visibility within the shot.

There are two emergent devices of Metzger's cinema wedded together here. One, making its first appearance in his films, is the trope of the *modern room*, which would recur, for instance, in the library within the medieval castle of *The Lickerish Quartet* (1970)—also designed by Sabbatini, and discussed in the next chapter—as well as the abstract set design for Dr. Seymour Love's apartment in the hardcore *The Opening of Misty Beethoven* (1976). The other is what might be called the *glassy image*—a reliance on reflecting or refracting surfaces which would serve as Metzger's strategy of choice for, in Gorfinkel's words, "presenting sex as aesthetically mediated or dematerializing."[128] Although the tropes do not always go hand in hand in Metzger, their combination in *Camille 2000* has the unique effect of giving *spatial* expression to the tensions first articulated in

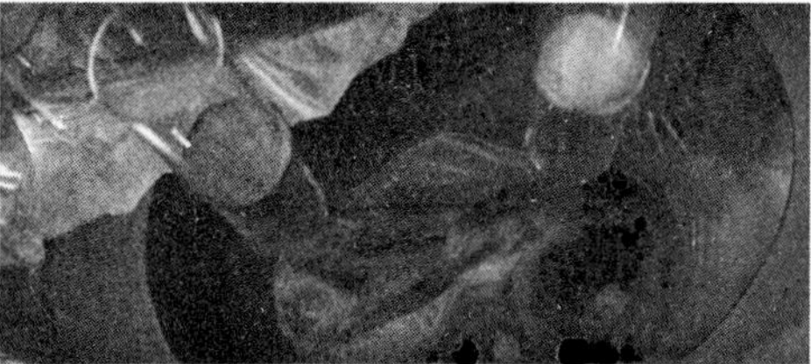

1.16 Mirrored reflections around a plastic bed. Screenshots from *Camille 2000*.

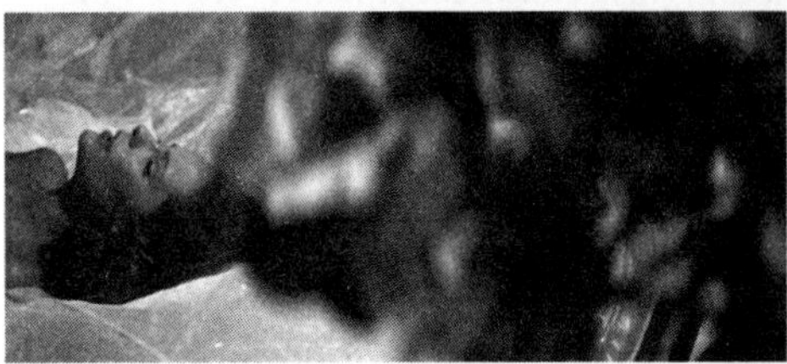
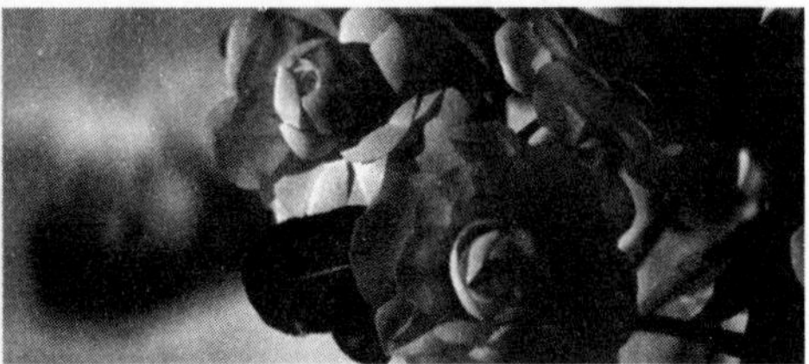

1.17 Racking focus between Camille in the background and a vase of camellias in the foreground. Screenshots from *Camille 2000*.

Carmen, Baby's conception of *aesthetic* value. Metzger's approach to interior space has often been understood as a two-sided one. In a 1999 essay, critic Bart Testa described two different approaches to the staging of sex in Metzger's films: the "*Playboy*-mansion styled orgy" and the "twosome sex scene."[129] But note how the distinction, in *Camille 2000*, opens out onto competing registers of cinematic art: on the one hand, the lavish interiors of the film's historic villas in which said orgies occur, which corresponds to a gentrifying, middlebrow appeal; on the other, the experimental design of the modern room for the "twosome" sex scenes, for which Metzger deploys the stylistic autonomy of art-cinema technique. Put another way, Metzger's divided idea of art manifests itself in *Camille 2000* and elsewhere as a very particular sort of architectural incoherence, the secret chamber of a Pop-Art eroticism hidden within the sumptuous palazzos of a genteel past.

What is furthermore evident is that Metzger had, by this point, thrown out just enough red meat for auteur-minded critics to sink their teeth into. The meaning of "auteur" had to travel a certain distance first, though. Originally imported from postwar French cineaste circles to the United States in Andrew Sarris's "Notes on the Auteur Theory in 1962," the notion of the director as auteur defined the terrain on which debates over film art would be waged in American film criticism of the era.[130] Certain filmmakers, whose work displayed a "distinguishable personality" and "personal style," were now sacrosanct as the medium's foremost artists, their films celebrated as the expressions of their directors' sensibilities. Others could meanwhile be damned, whether as mere studio functionaries or as overrated technicians whose work lacked personal spark, the dreaded category of "metteur-en-scène." But soon there was a third class that Sarris and his acolytes had never expected or intended: the gray zone occupied by the "cult auteur" who seeks or achieves auteurist recognition despite working within cinema's less legitimate subcultures—in exploitation, "B" movies, and beyond, far removed from the fields where "art" might be expected to thrive.[131] Metzger was one of the early beneficiaries of this slippage, and the then-twenty-five-year-old film reviewer Richard Corliss—future lead critic at *Time* magazine—was his first benefactor, albeit a two-minded one. In a full-page review in the *Village Voice*, another first for Metzger, Corliss declared *Camille 2000* the director's "most poignant and polished testament to his aching desire for cinematic respectability," offering as proof the sheer density of the film's intertextuality with the current art cinema:

> You want a sumptuous production? Metzger created most of it, and what he couldn't create he bought—talented technicians like director of photography Ennio Guarnieri (cameraman on "L'Avventura" and "La Dolce Vita," cinematographer for "Ape Regina"), composer Piero Piccioni ("Bell' Antonio," "Il Diavolo"); and designer Enrico Savvatini [*sic*], whose flaccidly futuristic sets and costumes from "La Decima Vittima" he revised for "Camille 2000." . . . You demand cinematic allusions? "Camille" includes an off-hand reference to the scene in "Vivre sa vie" where Karina and her lover exchange cigarette smoke by kissing. . . . And at a prison-garb costume party that wavers in audacity between a Hugh Hefner nightmare and a Jean Genet wet dream, a circular table has as its center-piece a nude girl in chains: on her right thigh is written in lipstick the word FANGELSE, which is Swedish for "Prison" and the title of Ingmar Bergman's early allegory.[132]

He also wrote admiringly of Metzger's command of film technique, even as he criticized the filmmaker's inability to match technique with dramatic value.

> A completely realized Metzger film will have to await the ebbing of his early exclusive interest in filmic and sexual technique. We can imagine him plotting the mechanics of a tracking shot or analyzing the balletics of ecstasy, but not working on a deficient script or extracting a bit of life from his attractive but atrophied actors. . . . It may turn out that Metzger's competence simply does not extend to the direction of actors. If this is so, our disappointment would be for the loss of a potential genre. Metzger's hung-over romanticism keeps hinting that it might produce a successful amalgam of 60s sexual exposure and 30s gentility. . . . Metzger's intentions to become an Ophüls of the

orgasm, a concupiscent Cukor, are the most appealing aspect of the man and his gaudily proficient films.[133]

This was the most detailed critical attention that Metzger had yet received as a filmmaker, and it describes the contradictions that Metzger's "aching desire for respectability" had already produced in his films. 1960s "sexual exposure" and 1930s "gentility" is a formulation that neatly captures a style of vulgar modernism paradoxically beholden to a studio-era model of quality filmmaking, as though Metzger's divided cinephile ambitions would best be realized in the authorial signature of a would-be Ophüls versed in Bergman and Godard.

Yet Corliss was clearly interested to see where this "amalgam" might lead. He was one of a small handful of reviewers in mainstream publications to give sexploitation cinema any critical attention—others included *Life*'s Richard Schickel, the *New Yorker*'s Brendan Gill, *Variety*'s Addison Verrill, and the *Los Angeles Times*' Kevin Thomas—and the only one who consistently gave that attention to Metzger.[134] In the process, Corliss helped establish a critical perspective on Metzger that has had lasting influence on the way his films have subsequently been discussed. At the heart of that perspective lay a comparison with the other preeminent director of sex films of the era, with whom Metzger shared initials: Russ Meyer. Both R. M.s accrued significant name recognition in the late 1960s and early 1970s. While Metzger was establishing his authorship with what one critic dubbed "class sex" films like *Carmen, Baby* and *Camille 2000*, Meyer was courted by producer Richard Zanuck and made two films for Twentieth Century-Fox, *Beyond the Valley of the Dolls* (1970) and *The Seven Minutes* (1971).[135] Both, moreover, represented in Corliss's eyes the divided trajectories of sex cinema in the 1960s as these related to issues of class and taste hierarchy. "If Radley Metzger is an orgasmic Ophüls," Corliss wrote in a review of Meyer's *Cherry, Harry & Raquel!* (1969), "Russ Meyer is the Swingin' Sam Fuller of the nudies. Whereas Metzger inhabits a European climate of elegance, decadence, and sexual metaphor, Meyer is genuine, impure, adulterated, no bullshit, working-class American. . . . Metzger's characters drown their satyriasis in Dom Perignon. The Meyer Guys quench their thirst with a case of Bud, and no symbolism about it."[136] Meyer's approach to explicit film corresponded with the more-bang-for-your-buck principle of what Bourdieu described as the proletariat's "taste of necessity": his was a cinema of "gargantuan girls . . . Silicone freaks with breasts large enough to halt . . . traffic on Wall Street." Metzger's, meanwhile, was more in line with the patient remove of bourgeois sensibilities, slowly luring his viewers "into an exclusive, personal relationship with the material on the screen."[137]

The implied class dialectic separating these two filmmakers has subsequently recurred in almost every scholarly study of Metzger.[138] But such a reading once again reduces the field of erotic representation to a broad-strokes class divide ("working-class" vs. "sophisticated," "lowbrow" vs. "middlebrow," etc.) and, in the process, flattens out the tensions to which Metzger's own films gave testimony. Metzger's arriviste relation to culture, this chapter has suggested, shaped an aspirational style that conflated heterogeneous registers of cinematic "sophistication"—a deference to the classics, both literary and filmic, that simultaneously enveloped a bric-a-brac style of postwar art cinema—bringing into combination the most contradictory intuitions of distinction in a way that the majority of critics continued to disparage as a grotesque homage, "pretentious and pornographic" and "bad and dishonest," to quote two reviews of *Camille*.[139] As Metzger would come to learn, his attempt to transvaluate explicit film would, for many, only ever be legible as a form of misplaced erudition.

Not that he had much to complain about at the time. As the 1960s drew to a close, Metzger and Leighton were sitting pretty. Boosted by a high-profile photospread in the May issue of *Playboy*, *Camille 2000* opened in the summer of 1969 as the debut film for two new Manhattan theaters, the Cine Lido (on West Forty-Eighth Street) and the Cine Malibu (on East Fifty-Ninth Street).[140] This variant on the company's East Side/West Side strategy was a deliberate snub on Audubon's part of the Times Square houses that, Leighton told the trades, were now no longer "commensurate with [Audubon's] new image."[141] The film grossed close to a million before the year was out (specifically $865,996), helping to make 1969 the company's third successive year with net profits in the vicinity of two million dollars.[142] Metzger, meanwhile, took the opportunity of the film's success to burnish his own image, too. His 1969 fashion-plate profile in *GQ*—discussed in the opening of this book—was only one in a series of press reports that associated Metzger with the jet-setting lifestyle that *Camille 2000* had only depicted. Readers of film magazines now learned of the filmmaker's "plush" Manhattan apartment and newly acquired real estate in Paris and Rome, while Audubon press releases described Metzger as a filmmaker who "journeyed all over the world" to film in the "internationally famous playgrounds" of the elite. His name was by this point a regular entry in *Variety*'s weekly list of airline travelers to Europe and back, whether because of buying trips for Audubon acquisitions or because of his own filmmaking. (He made transatlantic flights every *month* in 1968, except for the end of the year when he was shooting *Camille*.) If, as one observer of the era's "jet-age society" quipped, "it is now an accepted dogma that in order to be better known one must be in orbit much of the time," then Metzger was definitely in orbit at the decade's twilight.[143]

But success was measured not in lifestyle change alone. Metzger and Leighton used their string of recent box-office hits to diversify the Audubon brand into related media. Just prior to *Camille*'s release, Audubon announced the formation of a new music division, Ethel Music, to release LP versions of Georges Auric's score for *Thérèse and Isabelle* and Piero Piccioni's for *Camille 2000*.[144] Next, in September, came the announcement of Audubon Books, a publishing division under the editorship (and in many cases pseudonymous authorship) of *Camille 2000* screenwriter Michael DeForrest, with plans to publish both novelizations of Audubon's films and outside manuscripts.[145] A handful of previous Audubon releases had received book tie-ins—the release of *I, a Woman*, for instance, had been accompanied by a Dell paperback translation of Siv Holm's source novel; *Carmen, Baby* was novelized by Award Books; and Leduc's *Thérèse and Isabelle* was reissued as a paperback tie-in with Metzger's 1968 adaptation—but Audubon's decision to go in-house gave the company a new outlet for burnishing its brand identity.[146] On the one hand, books could be explicit in a way that wide-release films at this point simply could not.[147] On the other, Audubon used its publishing division to move beyond the market for erotic fiction, in a seeming effort to become something more like a lifestyle brand. Outside manuscripts published during Audubon Books' brief, two-year existence included a 1970 reprint of the first volume of John Galsworthy's *Forsyte Saga* novels (1906–21), released as a tie-in to the 1969–70 broadcast of the BBC's *Forsyte Saga* series on the Ford Foundation's National Educational Television network, and, strangest of all, *Collected Speeches of Spiro Agnew* (1971), as though catering to an imagined public that balanced a taste for well-heeled erotica with an investment in proto–*Masterpiece Theater* television and Nixon-era culture-war politics (figure 1.18).

Pulp adaptations of sexploitation films were hardly uncommon in the 1960s, but Metzger's sights were set considerably higher than those of the fly-by-night publishers that usually churned such material out.[148] Once again Grove Press

1.18 Cover of Audubon Books' *Collected Speeches of Spiro Agnew* (1971). *Source*: Author's collection.

seems to have been on his mind. At the start of the decade Grove had innovated the genre of the "film book" by launching a series of lavishly illustrated paperback screenplays of landmark art films, beginning with Alain Resnais's *Last Year at Marienbad* (1958) and *Hiroshima mon amour* (1961). Rosset's company had subsequently made notable moves into film distribution, first, in 1966, by purchasing Amos Vogel's legendary Cinema 16 library, then with the acquisition and release of *I Am Curious (Yellow)*, which Grove gave lavishly illustrated film-book treatment to while the film was held up on obscenity charges.[149] It is not hard to imagine that Metzger, who had begun to think of Grove as his "competitor," decided to encroach upon Rosset's bailiwick in response to Grove's encroachment upon his.

Topping all of these developments, however, was Metzger and Leighton's decision to go public in 1969 to finance Audubon's further expansion, with a planned issue of 250,000 common shares at ten dollars apiece. According to the proposal, Metzger would own 43.4 percent of the company and Leighton 28.8, with the public holding a 24.4 percent stake (the remaining 3.4 percent accounted for by other "officers and directors").[150] The company's filing with the Securities and Exchange Commission revealed just how rich the last few years had been for the company, provoking a flurry of interest in the trade press.[151] As *Variety*'s then owner Syd Silverman punned, Audubon had clearly found the "formula for sexcess": the company had never made a loss on any of its pictures and, since 1964, had operated as an entirely self-sustaining enterprise, without borrowing from any source.[152] Also included in the SEC filing, moreover, were plans to secure the company's footing on the Upper East Side market by acquiring a theater there, as well as to establish a 16mm department to distribute its films to colleges, service organizations, and social clubs. Audubon had flirted with exhibition before—in early 1963, Metzger briefly took out a lease on the celebrated Charles Theatre repertory house on Twelfth Street and Avenue B, with an announced policy of showing "select foreign and American films"—but the new plan was for something else entirely: a permanent showcase for Audubon's output among New York's toniest residences, a scant three years after *I, a Woman* had first breached the neighborhood.[153]

Yet, short of Audubon Books, none of these aspirations would come to pass, as a sudden drop-off in box office the following year prompted Metzger to shelve the public offering. The company's biggest business in 1970 came from *The Laughing Woman*, with a gross of just $334,500, while Metzger's own *The Lickerish Quartet* proved a major box-office disappointment ($186,019 in the same year).[154] In all, the company's market share dropped by a staggering 50 percent in 1970 alone, which seemed to create something of an identity crisis for the Audubon brand.[155] Metzger's next project, *Little Mother* (1972), was a deliberate attempt to move away from erotica to make a political drama, and his acquisitions similarly broached new genres: pickups in 1971 included director Yves Boisset's *A Cop* (1971, original title *Un Condé*), which had drawn controversy in France for its depiction of police violence, and the low-budget oddity *The Zodiac Killer* (1971), made by the founder of a West Coast pizza chain in hope of spurring the public to catch the Bay Area serial killer.[156] Metzger also tried that year to engineer a five-picture deal with British horror director Pete Walker for exclusive rights to his films in the United States and Canada, although this too came to naught.[157] Audubon would never again release a film with the head-turning impact of *I, a Woman*, nor would it regain the prominence it had briefly achieved at the end of the 1960s.

In the end, the conditions under which a project like Audubon's could thrive were perhaps too fragile to be sustained for long, made possible only in the lag between the weakening of obscenity law, on the one hand, and the rise of hardcore pornography, on the other. Audubon's lawyers had done their part in chiseling away at obscenity restrictions, yet the success that this brought the company was soon eclipsed by the advent of hardcore feature films, first on the West Coast with Sherpix-distributed 16mm titles like *Mona* (1970), *Adultery for Fun and Profit* (1971), and *School Girl* (1971), then with the luminous success of director Gerard Damiano's epochal *Deep Throat* in 1972. Metzger would eventually adapt to these changes too, albeit taking care to keep his and Audubon's names out of things. But before we follow Metzger on that path, there remains the question of what, if anything, Metzger's films contributed to the art-cinema modernism—vulgar or otherwise—to which he so dearly aspired: pictures like *Carmen, Baby* and *Camille 2000* may have been too obviously compromised by their middlebrow ambitions, but the same cannot so easily be said of his two other films from this period.

CHAPTER 2

"THE NEXT STEP WILL BE TO SHOW 'IT'"

A Media Ontology of Eroticism

If there is fantasy in pornography, it is not of sex, but of the real.

—Jean Baudrillard

The noted postwar critic Parker Tyler was drawn to moments in film that tapped into the sexual undercurrents roiling beneath Hollywood's smooth surfaces. He called them "crevices," those details or loose ends that pop out at the expense of the whole and allow the spectator's fantasies to "creep through and flower."[1] One of Tyler's favorite crevices, in this respect, was whether characters in a film have sex or not: "Do They or Don't They?" he asked in the title of a 1970 essay in Barney Rosset's *Evergreen Review*.[2] Of course, thanks to strict censorship under the Production Code, American studio films of previous decades couldn't explicitly show sex; at best they could allude to its possibility—an embrace between lovers, a swell of music, fade out to a brief ellipsis, then fade back in.[3] *Something* has happened, but exactly what is left to the spectator. By the end of the 1960s, however, the crumbling of censorship opened up a new avenue for speculation where sex was concerned. Referring to the "new brand of skin flick in which screwing *au naturel* is ostensibly performed in full view of the camera," Tyler proposed that the operative question was no longer "Do they or don't they?" but instead "Are they or aren't they?"[4] Whereas the old question was about the characters in the fiction (do the fictive characters have sex?), the new one was about the performers in front of the camera (are the actors actually having sex?). Is it all just let's pretend, or is there "actual entry of organ into involved aperture"?[4] And what difference does it make anyway?

Rather a lot, it turns out. Art, Tyler opined, "is a formal representation of life," and "not life itself." Actual sex performed on camera, from this perspective, would compromise "fact-fiction methods," a problem he attributed to a "new literalism" in film inspired by an unholy alliance between cinema verité methods and pornographic prurience. Hardly a prude himself—he first came to prominence in Greenwich Village's queer literary scene when his first book, *The Young and Evil* (1933), coauthored with Charles Henri Ford, was banned in the United States—Tyler nonetheless expressed disdain for the "paltry, token affair" of actual filmed sex in favor of the more evocative pleasures of "sheer aesthetic illusion." His preference, accordingly, was that sex should remain "a fiction, and a fiction that doesn't have to be fortified by visible entry." The "search for fact," he declared, should respect some limits. The fictive act of sex between two characters does not require verification from the actual enactment of sex by the performers, any more than the genuineness of a man's ardor should be gauged "by measuring the vibration of his orgasm by an electrical attachment."[5]

In retrospect, Tyler's questioning is apt to seem naïve, the legacy of a moment when the practice of simulated sex—even "*au naturel*"—could not confidently be presumed by filmgoers. Naïve or not, this worrying about the implications of actually filmed sex was remarkably persistent among observers of explicit films throughout this period. Alongside those reactionary voices that considered explicit material a *moral* problem to be censored, there evidently also existed a competing recognition of filmed sex as a specifically *aesthetic* or *film-theoretical* conundrum. For example, Andrew Sarris, doyen of American film critics in the 1960s, made the same argument as Tyler in response to Vilgot Sjöman's notorious *I Am Curious (Yellow)* (1969). Sarris had no personal objection to the film's explicit content, which includes a moment in which the protagonist actually kisses a flaccid penis, but feared that the closer films came to showing actual sex, the less they would succeed as dramatic art: filmed sex, he wrote, "destroy[s] the fictional façade of cinema."[6] And, to return to the subject of this book, in a review of Radley Metzger's *The Lickerish Quartet* (1970), *Village Voice* critic Richard Corliss argued that the same dilemma lay at the heart of Metzger's recent filmmaking:

> Metzger has realized that the next step in fictional sex films will be to show "it" namely, fucking. But how can a director reconcile the fictional reality of his characters with the documentary reality of his performers? When a couple starts going at it in a stag film, the audience is aware, not of "characters" resolving a plot development with this or that sexual technique, but of

> two rather pitiful people performing the love act for a camera. The fiction film with a "real" sex scene will have taken the trouble to create an illusion, only to surrender it once Warren Beatty and Julie Christie (or whoever) hop into bed. . . . [Metzger is] interested in th[is] question and its ramifications for this kind of film.[7]

Like Tyler's, the tone here is one of waggish amusement, as though the matter at hand was best treated as theoretical scuttlebutt and innuendo. Yet Corliss's analysis captures with precision the medium reflexivity or self-consciousness that was arguably Metzger's distinctive contribution to the "vulgar modernist" ferment of the late 1960s, when his work turned repeatedly on these issues. How, to paraphrase Corliss, do fictional and documentary realities relate to one another in the cinematic representation of sex? What does cinema's basis in live-action photography imply for the rendering of sexually explicit material on film? And where does eroticism fit into the picture? These questions refer to the fundamental properties or inner workings of film—what film scholars call the medium's *ontology*—which this chapter explores through the two movies in which Metzger best realized his aspirations for an art-cinema model for erotic film: *Thérèse and Isabelle* (1968) and *The Lickerish Quartet* (1970).

Before we turn to those films, though, it will be helpful to locate the matter at hand within what were, at the time, already long-standing issues of film theoretical debate. The "problem" of actual filmed sex is one that speaks to the ambiguous status of the photographic image in narrative film: as a photograph, the image is a visual document of something that has *actually happened* in front of the camera; in terms of the film's narrative, however, that same image also belongs to the *fiction* that the film is weaving. Cinema, one might say, is a medium of direct *presentation* (of the reality filmed by the camera) that is coopted to a mode of *representation* (of the fiction that that reality is supposed to depict). The scene of the fictional Rick bidding the fictional Ilsa adieu that ends *Casablanca* (1942) is also, first and foremost, a record of the real Humphrey Bogart and the real Ingrid Bergman play-acting in front of a camera. More than that, however, the photographic image's presentational aspect always threatens to ruin its representational ambitions: the fiction of a period drama, say, will be betrayed by the actor who has forgotten to remove his Apple watch, or by the boom mike visible at the top of the frame.

In the early decades of writing about film, this ambiguity was usually raised in relation to the question of whether cinema was—or could be—a new art form.

Cinema's photographic function as a means of recording reality was felt by many to be incompatible with the representational orbit of art proper. Accordingly, if cinema was to fulfill its promise as what early theorist Béla Balázs described as "an independent, basically new art," it would need somehow to transcend the brute realism of the photographic record.[8] What mattered, in other words, was the *difference* that cinema could introduce into the events that it photographs, since, as Soviet filmmaker Vsevolod Pudovkin opined, "It is *exactly this difference that makes the film an art*."[9]

But sex was early on recognized as a threat to that balancing act. In his overlooked late essay "Marginal Notes on Eroticism in the Cinema" (1957), the film theorist André Bazin argued that a tendency toward pornographic display was endemic to cinema—a "basic ingredient" of cinematic fascination—even though, in his opinion, the filmed record of "actual sexual emotion" was "contrary to the exigencies of art."[10] With the popularization of explicit film in the 1960s, critics finally had to confront head on the dilemmas that earlier theorists had warned of: whereas a murder in a crime film does not require the actual slaying of the actor, a hardcore scene is inevitably a record of actors having sex, and, in this way, anathema to the suspension of disbelief on which cinematic illusion depends. One cannot simply "act" visibly penetrative sex, nor can a visible erection be just pretend.[11]

But if all this is the case, then it is also clear that cinematic eroticism will require a careful negotiation with the properties of film itself. If eroticism, as I have been discussing it, is constituted in the "gap" that intervenes before the direct encounter with taboo, then eroticism *in film* requires that the filmmaker push against the grain of the medium's own affordances: what cinema's presentational aspect allows for—a photographic record of taboo—is exactly what eroticism must avoid. In which case, Metzger's erotic cinema will need to be approached not simply in terms of a sociology of taste, the backdrop for the previous chapter, but as a matter of medium ontology as well, which is the subject of this one.

"TO SAY SOMETHING IS TO MURDER IT": WORD AND IMAGE IN *THÉRÈSE AND ISABELLE*

Even before the release of his *Carmen, Baby* in the fall of 1967, the extraordinary and ongoing success of *I, A Woman* (1966) convinced Metzger of his next project: an obvious attempt to cash in on *I, A Woman*'s notoriety by casting its lead, Swedish actress Essy Persson, this time in an adaptation of Violette Leduc's semiautobiographical queer novella *Thérèse et Isabelle* (1966). First announced by *Variety* in

April 1967 in the unfortunately titled "Leduc Lesbo Love Film for Audubon," the project was touted as "another rung up for [the] indie company and [a] departure from exploitation," with a half-million-dollar budget more than three times that of *Carmen, Baby*. Whereas Audubon's rivals "usually slap together some libido-pitched nonsense," the article explained, Metzger's firm was seeking a "bigger market" by making a prestige picture with " 'literary' trappings." Production on the film was, moreover, timed to "coincide with publication of novel by Farrar, Straus and Giroux in the U.S."[12]

Nor was it only through an appeal to literature that Metzger sought to "upgrade" Audubon's cultural capital. Shot entirely on location in France between August and October 1967, *Thérèse and Isabelle* was effectively Metzger's attempt to make a French art film (figure 2.1).[13] For the score, Metzger secured the services of noted French film composer Georges Auric, who had previously provided scores for filmmakers like Jean Cocteau, René Clair, and Marc Allegret. For the film's setting, he chose the picturesque, thirteenth-century Royaumont Abbey, located in Val-d'Oise, some twenty miles north of Paris.[14] Once the rough cut was assembled, Metzger flew the heads of the Brandt, Walter Reade, and Art Theatre Guild theater chains to Paris for a private preview screening. The film was promoted in trade ads as a "sizzler from France," and was even reviewed in the pages of *Variety* in the "Foreign Film Review" section (figure 2.2).[15] Like *I, a Woman*, it was released in both subtitled French and unsubtitled English versions, with Metzger explaining that the French version was to add a "touch of class" for art-house bookings while the English dub was "for the grinds."[16] Metzger also replicated *I, a Woman*'s release strategy for the film's New York debut, on May 14, 1968, in a "dual world premiere" at the Trans-Lux 85th on the Upper East Side and the Rialto Theater in Times Square, at both of which the film set opening week records ($19,960 and $32,844, respectively).[17] The film would go on to play continuously at the Trans-Lux for four months, and at the Rialto for half a year, eventually grossing some $2.4 million (just shy of 40 percent of Audubon's entire gross between 1968 and 1970).[18]

Metzger's opportunistic attempt to make a film that could be marketed as French art cinema has drawn ridicule among later commentators. (Bart Testa's withering 1999 assessment of the filmmaker identifies *Thérèse and Isabelle* as Metzger's closest emulation of 1960s European art film, but one whose "very proximity reveals its measure as erotic kitsch.")[19] But it is arguably less the film's *cinematic* masquerade, than its relation to its *literary* source that is most relevant

2.1 Location shooting for *Thérèse and Isabelle* at the luxurious Pré Catalan restaurant in Paris.
Source: Author's collection.

to an understanding of Metzger's formal strategies. In choosing Leduc's work, Metzger was not only upping the scandalous ante of *I, a Woman*—this time with Persson in a lesbian drama set in an all-girls boarding school—but was adopting a very different strategy of adaptation, one that appealed not to the conservatism of a preexisting middlebrow canon (as per *Carmen, Baby*'s free updating of Prosper Mérimée) but instead directly to the vanguard of sexually explicit, French-sourced literary modernism that had heretofore been the bailiwick of publishing houses like Grove Press and its Evergreen Review.[20] With *Thérèse and Isabelle*, Metzger was in fact embarking on his most serious-minded attempt yet to poach upon the cultural capital of the era's vulgar modernism, by signing his name to the adaptation of what tie-in promotion described overtly as an "underground masterpiece" by "one of the great and controversial writers of her day."[21]

A figure at the margins of the existentialist movement, Leduc was indeed emblematic of the convergence of avant-garde experiment and obscenity that

2.2 "A Sizzler from France." Advertisement for *Thérèse and Isabelle. Independent Film Journal*, July 9, 1968.

centrally shaped the field of underground film and literature discussed in the last chapter. She initially wrote *Thérèse et Isabelle* as the opening section of her semi-autobiographical 1955 novel, *Ravages*, only for her publisher, Éditions Gallimard, first to reject the novel on grounds of its explicit homosexual content, and then eventually to accept it only after Leduc agreed to excise its first section, which became *Thérèse et Isabelle* when it was released as a stand-alone work in the wake of her scandalous 1964 memoir *La bâtarde*. In one of the last interviews before his death, Metzger claimed to have communicated with Leduc, who apparently gave him a single instruction before he started his adaptation: "Don't make a dirty picture."[22] Whether or not the resulting film was in fact a "dirty picture" would be loudly contested in the film's reviews, as we will see. Less up for dispute, though, was Metzger's close allegiance to Leduc's text, which he used as the verbatim source of Thérèse's voiceover as she revisits the school as an adult, recalling her past trysts with Isabelle in a series of flashbacks. Unlike his previous literary adaptation, *Carmen, Baby*, which had simply borrowed the *plot* of Mérimée's novel, Metzger's approach to *Thérèse and Isabelle* showcased the taboo-breaking *prose* for which Leduc was infamous. Yet this has an important effect on the film. Whereas Metzger's style has commonly been associated with the peekaboo play of visibility afforded by reflective and translucent surfaces (his "glassy images," as discussed in the previous chapter), *Thérèse and Isabelle* sources *its* erotic effects rather differently, in the figurative capacity of Leduc's prose to hint at things that Metzger's camera is unable to show. A number of reviews in fact commented on Metzger's unusual strategy in this respect, noting how the voiceover shouldered the burden of the film's sexual representations: the film is "explicit in a slightly unexpected way," noted the reviewer for *Independent Film Journal*, since "it's the sound track (and sub-titles) as well as the visuals that drive the message home."[23]

A sequence midway through the film demonstrates the approach, depicting the consummation of the two girls' relationship behind the altar of the school chapel. The first half of the scene is composed around three principal shots: a medium shot of the young Thérèse (Persson), which tracks backward before her as she enters the chapel and walks toward the altar (figure 2.3a–b); a static distant framing of Isabelle (Anna Gaël) waiting at the altar, into which shot Thérèse enters from the foreground and approaches her lover, the two eventually sinking down in an embrace (figure 2.3c–d); and a lengthy tracking shot that reverses the movement of the first, beginning on the altar, with only the girls' intertwined feet visible, and then slowly retreating away, back up the aisle (figure 2.3e–f). The voiceover of the grown Thérèse, taken directly from the novel, accompanies this near two-minute reverse track:

> I tore at her uniform and crushed the hairs beneath. The blood rose into my cheeks, into my throat. Her hand was making it difficult for me to breathe. I was sobbing without a sound, without tears. Isabelle was sobbing too as she pressed her hand against my uniform. I dug her neck into my teeth. Her lips were trying to find mine in my hair, in my neck, in the folds of my uniform. I pushed her against the floor, I nailed her hands against it with the palms of mine. I hugged her with all the strength of my repentance, I breathed her in, I pulled her tight against my belly and made a loincloth for myself. She was melting my ankles and knees into delicious decay. I burst with warmth

> like a fruit, I was running with the same liquid sweetness. There were pincers softly tearing at me, oh so softly. I was following everything inside her, I could see with my inner eyes the light in her flesh. In my head I had a Thérèse with opened legs, straining up to the sky, who was receiving all that I was giving. We hugged to our hearts all the Thérèses and Isabelles who would make love to one another later with other names. We rolled, intertwined, down a slope of shadows. We held our breath so that life and death should come to a halt. I stormed her mouth as one storms a beleaguered city: I was hoping to plunder and destroy both her entrails and my own. Isabelle cried in panic. I persevered. Isabelle called for help.[24]

As the camera continues tracking back over the monologue's end, the older Thérèse (also played by Persson) steps into the foreground (figure 2.3g). (The distant feet of her younger self, now in the shot's background, are presumably provided by a body double.) In a recurrent trope of the film, Thérèse's present and past selves thus come to occupy the same physical and visual space, into which the older Thérèse has folded herself as a spectator of her own sexual memories. The film cuts to a medium close-up of the young Isabelle, writhing on the floor in orgasm: "It's coming upwards," she cries. "In my legs, in my knees. It's coming higher and higher" (figure 2.3h). The film's two timeframes further intertwine over a series of shot-reverse shot cuts in which the adult Thérèse now communicates with her memory of the supine Isabelle (figure 2.3i–j). "Tell me," the present Thérèse commands, to which the past Isabelle seems to respond, "I love you." "Again!" "I love you." "Again!" "I love you." Sexual representation has here become the province of words alone, while what we are asked to look at is something more like the act of memory itself.

Not that Metzger's approach in *Thérèse and Isabelle* is always this coy; still, in all of the sexual scenes between the two girls there is an effect of disjunction between voiceover and visuals. The protagonists' second sexual encounter, for example, switches between visual and literary registers of explicitness, moving from the former to the latter as the action builds: although the scene begins with the visual display of sexuality (topless nudity as the girls strip before each other), it soon defers to a medium close-up of Thérèse's ecstasy—Metzger's preferred trope of "sex performed by a woman's face" (Testa)—while the voiceover takes over to explain what is happening off camera.[25] "Her face was traveling all over me, her face was exploring me. There were lips seeing and touching what I

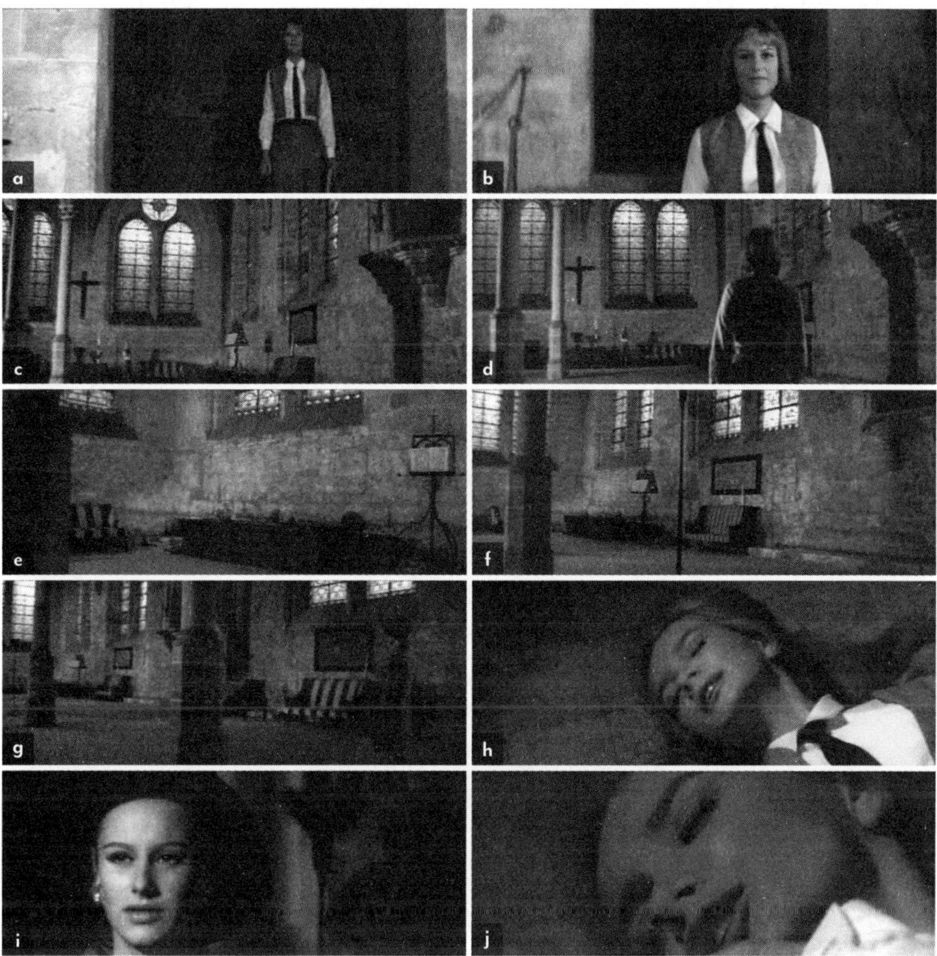

2.3 Past and present intertwine in the consummation of Thérèse (Essy Persson) and Isabelle's (Anna Gael) mutual desire. Screen captures from *Thérèse and Isabelle*.

would never see. I was humiliated for her. Indispensable and ignored, that was what I was with my face so far away from Isabelle's. A saint was licking away my soils."[26] The third and final sex scene—rendered in a single three-minute long shot of the protagonists embracing next to a pond, their bodies reflected in the waters—meanwhile features a curious mismatch between sound and image throughout: although Thérèse and Isabelle's naked bodies are shown, their visible actions do not correspond with the remarkably explicit descriptions in the voiceover. "Isabelle straddled across me. The sea monster inside me was coiling its tentacles once more. I felt her secret lips against my buttock. I felt for her hand, I put it against my back, I guided it down beyond the edge of my spine, I left it pressed against the edge of my anus"—none of which is given in what we actually see, which remains limited to supine caressing and kissing.[27]

It would be tempting to ascribe Metzger's strategy here to the restrictions placed on the film image; that is, the literary word is called upon to *say* what the film image cannot *show* (or at least could not show under the conditions of film industry regulation within which Metzger was working). But such a reading overstates the ability of the word to directly "say" in the first place. For what is striking about Leduc's prose is not its explicitness per se but the way in which that explicitness coexists with a kind of metaphorical obscurantism, so that her literary articulations of sexuality seem riven between a disarming frankness, on the one hand, and a tendency to spin out into metaphor and symbol, on the other. In an insightful essay on Leduc's work, literary scholar Alberta Gallus interprets Leduc as a writer "haunted" by a tension between her effort to evoke the embodied experience of sex and an awareness of the impossibility of finding literary means adequate to the task.[28] Yet instead of paralyzing her writing, Gallus suggests, that awareness produced a distinctive style that self-consciously reenacts the impossibility it confronts. In her 1970 autobiography, *La folie en tête*, Leduc herself recalled her difficulties in narrating the youthful sexual experiences of *Ravages*: "Everything we write will be absent. Would I describe a stone for a hundred years, my text will not have the hardness, the disdain, the hermeticism of the stone."[29] This proto-Derridean notion that words can only enact a kind of deferral of what they seek to describe is repeatedly manifest in Leduc's *Thérèse et Isabelle* in Thérèse's refusal to accommodate Isabelle's need for a word to describe the intensity of what they experience. "Say something, Thérèse." " 'Talk,' she said. 'Tell me about it.' " " 'Talk,' Isabelle begged. 'I'm all alone' "—in the face of which Thérèse stands firm in her resistance: "To say something is to murder it."[30] The metaphorical excess with which Leduc's prose is often charged is fueled by an awareness of language's inadequacy in capturing the embodied experiences that her writing ceaselessly puts into play. Put another way, Leduc's highly figurative style is not a response to some form of internal censorship or prohibition but rather an articulation of the limits of language itself, in relation to which female desire and sexuality gets constituted as an absence or a gap.

It is not enough, then, to say that Metzger uses Leduc's novella to say what cannot be shown, for Leduc's text—like Thérèse—refuses straightforwardly to "say" in the first place. Rather, the film's use of Leduc generates a kind of ouroboros effect at the level of erotic representation: where Leduc often draws on metaphors to hint at what cannot be said, Metzger uses Leduc's words to hint at what cannot be shown.[31] One is perhaps reminded of the paradox identified by André Bazin in another of his 1950s essays, this one on director Robert Bresson's 1951 adaptation of George Bernanos's novel *Le journal d'un curé de campagne* (*Diary of a Country Priest*, 1936). There Bazin noted that Bresson, forced to cut from the original book, had removed not its most "literary" material—the writing of the journal—but in fact the most visual and sensory. "Of the two," Bazin noted, "it is the film that is literary and the novel that is teeming with images"—a claim that could equally apply to the relation between Metzger's *Thérèse and Isabelle* and Leduc's source text. But with one important difference. The relation between the literary word and cinematic image in Bresson's film, at least in Bazin's analysis, serves to demonstrate the divergent properties of each medium—"side by side, using the means at its disposal, in its own setting and after its own style"—which is to say, what each medium *can* do.[32] But the relation between word and image in Metzger's adaptation instead clarifies what each medium *can't*: the word cannot say what it means nor can the image show what is to be seen, at least if both are to remain erotic art. What we call eroticism in any given medium might then be said to have a certain medium specificity, in the sense in which it emerges from a fundamental friction with the affordances of the medium in question.

Not that Metzger's critics were particularly interested in engaging things on this level. In a familiar pattern, Audubon's continued success in building an art market for its films fueled backlash on the part of those who disputed the presumption of art in the first place. This time, however, the vitriol came with a slightly different flavor. Whereas Metzger's deference to the literary canon in films like *Carmen, Baby* and *Camille 2000* (1969) opened him up to charges of middlebrow desecration, *Thérèse and Isabelle*'s affiliation with the literary underground baited critics into engaging its taboo content. For some the explicit depiction of queer sex provoked outrage: Wanda Hale, critic at New York's *Daily News*, opined that the film "should be shown in an outhouse, not an arthouse."[33] For others the spectacle of what *Variety* described as "things which have never been seen on screen before" required novel adjectives to express their objections, as when the National Catholic Office for Motion Pictures objected to a "cunnilingual" scene.[34] Others, still, sought to remain aloof and above it all, like Andrew Sarris who shrugged off the supposed controversy by dismissing *Thérèse and Isabelle* as a "bore." "It is hard to see what all the talk of a 'breakthrough' is about," he concluded.[35] Metzger himself would partly have agreed with Sarris, at least in retrospect, acknowledging in later years that he should have gone further. "A hundred percent gay story was a very frightening concept in 1968," he explained, admitting that his own uncertainties led him to film two different endings. The ending used for the film's initial release recuperates Thérèse to straightness by suggesting that her lesbianism was just a "phase": in a distant framing, the adult Thérèse leaves the school grounds and approaches a car parked outside, at which point a cut to a closer view reveals a man who has been waiting in the passenger seat all this time. "We don't want to be late to our own wedding," he reminds her as she gets in, and they drive off. The other ending, restored for the 1999 DVD release by First Run Features, simply omits the closer view: Thérèse enters the vehicle and drives away from the school, with nothing to suggest anyone else in the car but her. In the years that followed, Metzger claimed to have tracked down every print with the straight ending and buried them "in an unmarked grave."[36] As well he should have: the film's original ending not only betrays the spirit of Leduc's original but also contradicts the aesthetic strategies that keep sex and sexuality in this film on the side of the *un*represented. The gaps and deferrals that structure the film's presentation of queer sexuality are brought up short by Thérèse's ultimate submission to heterosexual union, which is clearly and unambiguously visualized in a medium close-up of her impatient husband. If *Thérèse and Isabelle* has anything to contribute to the vulgar modernist ferment to which Metzger aspired, it is, contrariwise, in its insistence that eroticism inheres not in what an image can show or a word mean, but in the negative or inverse of each medium's function—that is, in the way in which the image can be made *not* to show, nor the word to mean. This, at any rate, will serve as a working hypothesis from which to turn next to *The Lickerish Quartet*, Metzger's most sustained and self-reflexive engagement with the relation between film art and filmed sex.

"IT'S ONLY A FILM": ART AND SEX IN *THE LICKERISH QUARTET*

The Lickerish Quartet announces its ambitions from its opening frames with a quote from Luigi Pirandello's absurdist 1921 play *Six Characters in Search of an Author*: "all this present reality of yours—is fated to seem a mere illusion to you tomorrow." The idea gets an immediate workout: the film dissolves into grainy, black-and-white images of a naked man and woman engaged in foreplay, only for the camera

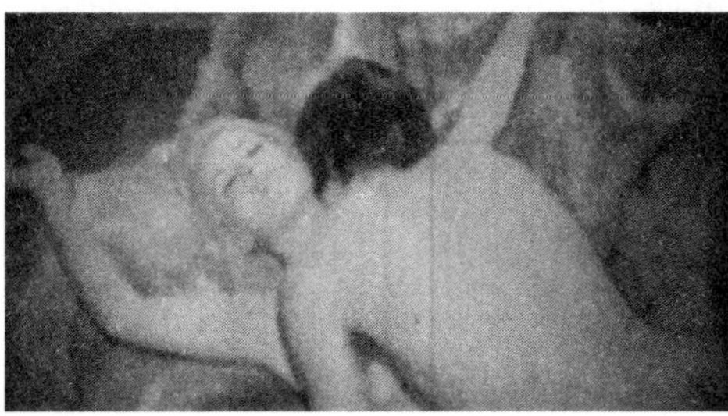

2.4 The opening shot reveals a film within the film. Screen captures from *The Lickerish Quartet*.

to pull back to reveal that what we are seeing is, in fact, cinematic illusion—footage of a stag film projected onto a portable screen (figure 2.4). What we might have assumed to be the "reality" of the film, the black and white footage, is less "real" than "reel," a film within the film—a "mere illusion," perhaps, and certainly a new level of reflexivity in Metzger's filmography to that point.

Even before it went into production, in fact, *The Lickerish Quartet* bore a particular freight. It was the first time since *The Alley Cats* that Metzger had worked from an original script, cowritten with *Camille 2000*'s scribe Michael DeForrest, whom Metzger had recently promoted to editorial director of Audubon's new publishing division.[37] The announcement of the project in August 1969 (under the working title "Hide and Seek") was clearly timed to coincide with Audubon's move to a public offering, and the film's production built upon the ambitious template of *Camille 2000*: a six-week Italian shoot on a $500,000 budget, with principal filming done largely on location throughout November and early December at the lavish thirteenth-century Castello di Balsorano in Abruzzo, plus a single day on the soundstages of the legendary Cinecittà studios in Rome.[38] The film built upon *Camille* in another way, too, since it was planned from the outset as a starring vehicle for Silvana Venturelli, who had turned heads in the earlier film in the minor role of Olympe.[39] For its orchestral soundtrack, meanwhile, Metzger hired Stelvio Cipriani, who had impressed Metzger for the "nice job" (Metzger's words) he had done with the soundtrack for *The Laughing Woman*.[40] But most important of all, *The Lickerish Quartet* was the film in which Metzger most openly placed his auteurist cards on the table, forgoing his usual dependence on literary sources to instead ground his script in his own reflections on cinema—specifically on what he called, in later interviews, the "impermanence" of film. As he recalled the project's germination:

> Michael DeForrest and I got together, and I said "Let's do a movie about the impermanence of film." That was the initial thrust. When I did my first movie, *Dark Odyssey*, we had a lot of screenings for investors, for exhibitors, screenings for distributors. Screening, screening. And it occurred to me, attending every screening, that the nature of the audience actually affected the presentation. Now, I went into film, as opposed to theater, because I like the permanence of it. Celluloid is permanent. And what occurred to me was the impermanence of celluloid. Sometimes you actually thought you were in the presence of different actors. The timing was different. The dialogue was communicated in very, very different ways. And I said "Let's do something that visualizes that same variation in seeing movies."[41]

The film would become the only one of Metzger's own films to receive tie-in publication through Audubon's book division—not as a novelization, but, uniquely, in the form of a published film script, equivalent to Grove Press's "film book" screenplays of contemporary art films, as though *The Lickerish Quartet* were a legitimate object of close reading equivalent to the scholarly analysis of literary texts (figure 2.5).[42] It is the film of which he would remain, for the rest of his life, the proudest.[43]

What, then, might a close analysis of *The Lickerish Quartet* reveal? Metzger's own reflections on film's impermanence indicate a preoccupation with how a film image's photographic realism—what is often misleadingly thought of as its objectivity—can nonetheless get activated in different ways for different viewers, as realized in *The Lickerish Quartet* via a plot that follows the fantasies and traumas unearthed among three family members who view a stag film. Where this achieves an interest beyond mere relativism, however, is in the way the film ties the three individuals' responses to the stag film to different "modes" of the photographic image's relation to reality. That relation, in *The Lickerish Quartet*, is a threefold one. There is in the first instance the image's status as a document (that is, as a material *record* of the reality it represents); there is also the image's status as a copy (that which *resembles* or *looks like* the reality it represents); and there is, finally, its status as *art* (i.e., an expressive vehicle that *transforms* the reality it represents).[44] For *The Lickerish Quartet*, as we will see, it is only in becoming

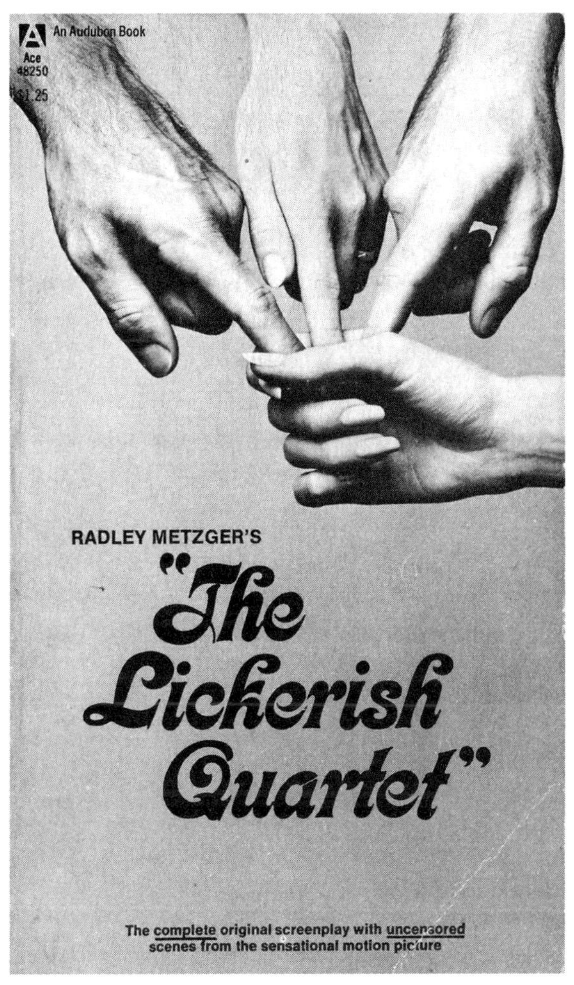

2.5 The front cover of Audubon Books' publication of *Radley Metzger's Lickerish Quartet* (1970).
Source: Author's collection.

erotic art that the photographic image is able to answer to the traumas and fantasies that it awakens in its raw state. The passage between these modes, accordingly, becomes the film's major structuring principle.

To begin with the first of these modes, and to return to the film's opening shot. Offscreen voices are heard over the whirring of a film projector. "Well, don't take it so seriously," a woman complains. "It's only a film. Why don't you fix it?" "It's too dark to see anything," a man replies. "You want to let me try?" offers another man with a younger voice. The film cuts to show the projector, beaming directly into the camera. "I honestly think these pictures are more trouble than they're worth," the first man responds, before a series of shots reveals the sources of the voices: a middle-aged man (Frank Wolff) operating the projector, a similarly aged woman (Erika Remberg) lounging on a divan, and a young man (Paolo Turco) who appears to be their son, all watching the film within a cavernous and lavishly appointed ballroom. Much of what they have to say, in the ensuing conversation, concerns the conditions of the stag film's making—the "reality" behind the "illusion"—even as they begin to layer other, complementary distinctions upon this Pirandellian binary. The father, for instance, is concerned with the performers' acting abilities: "I wonder if they're really enjoying it or if they're just faking? . . . I'd like to know how many times they had to do it before they got a good take." The woman, meanwhile, introduces the issue of class difference and sex work, as she muses disparagingly—and hypocritically, we will see—about the performers' social identities: "This one looks like she's been around. I wonder where they find the girls to act in these things. . . . They're probably just prostitutes." The "lowness" of the performers' class status in turn gets associated with the material qualities of the stag film itself, whose degraded, beat-up quality draws complaints from the boy: "It's not a very good one," he observes of the film, elsewhere declaring it "a bit crude." Stag films have, of course, long been associated with a kind of technological regression and shoddiness, a kind of materialization at the celluloid level of the low cultural status they occupy. And this quality is central to the distinction that *The Lickerish Quartet* draws between its own aspirational status as erotic art, as rendered by Hans Jura's sumptuous color cinematography, and the brute, black-and-white realism of sex on film.[45] "We had to dupe it [the footage] about six times before it looked crude and ugly enough for a stag film," Metzger explained. "And this is a fundamental principle of hard-core. . . . When you say hard-core looks lousy, what you really mean is it looks illegal."[46] Distinctions of legality and class appeal, even the broader division between softcore and hardcore—all here get tied to the material substrate of celluloid film itself.

Where materiality matters most, however, is in the stag film's status as tangible evidence of something that the performers did in front of a camera. In viewing the film, the family members see *through* the staged action to ask about the people underneath, raising questions about who the actors are, what it must have been like on set, and so forth. The footage is, in other words, experienced less as a fictive representation than as a documentary record of actions preserved on celluloid. This is what film scholars, following turn-of-the-century philosopher Charles Sanders Peirce, habitually describe as the *indexicality* of the film image—the fact that the image is directly *caused* by what it represents (by the interaction of reflected light rays on the chemical emulsion of the celluloid film strip) of which it therefore serves as a material trace.[47] And film theorists have frequently had recourse to bodily metaphors in describing this existential bond. The most famous example is provided by André Bazin, who contended that the photographic image was subject to a "mummy complex," spawned from the same impulse to embalm the dead and preserve the past into the present.[48] The celluloid image is both the emanation or imprint of a body and, in its materiality, a body in its own right. What the stag footage of *The Lickerish Quartet* thereby accomplishes is the very incarnation that *Thérèse and Isabelle* evades.

But this has two specifiable consequences for the film's unfolding action, each pertaining to one of the two sides of the Pirandellian binary. First, the footage provokes memory and fantasy on the part of the family members, affording us glimpses into the sexual anxieties that each will have to confront in what is to come. A casual reference to the stag film "look[ing] like something they made during World War Two" provokes black-and-white flashbacks to the father's memories of first meeting his wife in wartime, when she was a prostitute and he a GI. Meanwhile, the son's view of the film is repeatedly interrupted by quick cuts to images of demonic torture, bestiality, and rape from a painted mural in the ballroom. And the woman protests too much when her husband snidely asks if she could "do the things" she is watching in the stag film ("Never!" she curtly responds). Second, and more mysteriously, the stag film will itself "becomes flesh" as a result of the actions that the family now takes. They decide to get out of the house and visit a fairground, where they watch a motorcycle stunt show. One of the stunt artists appears to be the blond woman from the film they have just been watching at home (Venturelli), seemingly spawned from the family's private screen and directly into their reality. Struck by the coincidence—and imagining that the woman must have been tricked into performing in the stag film—they invite her home to watch the movie with them.

This is the point at which the film directly activates Metzger's interest in the impermanence of his medium. Hoping to use the evidence of the stag reel as an opportunity to proposition the woman, they play the film for her only to find that the stag film has *changed*—that, while the depicted action remains the same, the blond woman in the stag film no longer resembles their guest. (The footage was reshot by Metzger with a different actress.) What comes to the foreground in this second screening is, then, a second mode of the photographic image: not its status as an index—as a tangible trace of what it represents—but its status as, in Peircean terminology again, an *icon*, which refers to the image's relation of *likeness* or *similarity* to its object. The questions that the family members now ask of the footage accordingly shift to the axis of resemblance: Why does the woman in the stag film no longer resemble the woman from the carnival? Why is their viewing of the stag footage no longer like their previous viewing? Of course, in the typical photographic image, iconicity and indexicality are wed in mutual confirmation: the image *looks like* what it represents because it has been *caused by* the same, hence the platitude that "the camera never lies." But *The Lickerish Quartet* wants to trouble this positivist epistemology by treating iconicity as something fluid: what the image documents cannot be known if what it looks like cannot be determined.

Critics at the time were quick to pounce on what they perceived as the banality of Metzger's art cinema posturing on these themes. For Judith Crist, writing in *New York* magazine, Metzger seemed to "have in mind a sort of 'Last Year in Shmutsville,' " while *Variety* similarly opined that "in today's post-Resnais cinema such material is old hat."[49] Obscured by such derision, however, was the way the film explicitly ties its ontology of the photographic image to the operations of erotic fantasy: the more indeterminate the images of the stag film become, the more they intertwine with the character's fantasy lives. The father's confusion about the film begins to bleed into a confusion about his own memories: from this point on, the images of the black-and-white stag film will become increasingly indistinguishable from his wartime flashbacks, in which the blond woman now enacts the role of his wife. His wife's curiosity about the identities of the film's performers meanwhile intensifies, as the woman from the fairground parrots her earlier question about where they get "the girls to make these films." And the son recounts a childhood vision of St. Margaret the Virgin and her apocryphal torture by a dragon—the source, it becomes clear, of the mural images to which the film continues to cut, as well as of his thinly veiled sexual fright. (He describes the saint's wound as an "ugly gaping hole" and refers to the "shiny length" of a snake "swelling out inch by inch.") The very indeterminacy of the indexical image has accelerated the troubling fantasies that the stag film first set in motion, and whose resolution will now require the intervention of a third modality for the photographic image.

Metzger always denied having seen Pier Paolo Pasolini's 1968 *Teorema* before making *The Lickerish Quartet*, but the action that now follows resembles the Italian film enough that critics, then and since, have drawn the connection: like Terence Stamp in the Pasolini film, the woman from the fairground seduces each member of the family in turn and, in so doing, saves them from what ails them.[50] Each scene of seduction, moreover, explores a distinct stylistic register that works in counterpoint with the stag film's raw documenting of the sex act. If the stag film can be considered a kind of degree zero of filmed sex, then the three seduction scenes serve as displays of directorial virtuosity, each of which capitalizes on a different expressive use of the medium. In the process, moreover, Metzger's film shifts the status of the image once again, this time to assert its presence as art. What is at stake in the seduction scenes is not simply the image's capacity to document sex, or to show something that looks like sex; rather, it is the capacity of the medium to uncouple the photographic image from its basic recording function and offer, instead, an *aesthetic* transformation of its object—that "alteration of resemblance" that, according to philosopher Jacques Rancière, "produces what we call art."[51]

The first two seduction scenes—of the man and the boy, respectively—are conceived according to two aesthetic registers that have long been thought of as opposed poles in cinematic expressivity: a fast-paced editing-based approach on the one hand and a long-take, moving-camera style on the other. The first of these scenes was the only sequence for which a set had to be constructed—a sparsely furnished, all-white library, designed by Metzger in collaboration with his art director from *Camille 2000*, Enrico Sabbatini, and constructed at Cinecittà. The idea behind the scene, Metzger later recalled, was inspired by a television performance of Diahann Carroll covering the Little Anthony & the Imperials' song "Goin' Out of My Head" (1964), in which Rorschach blots revolved behind her; somewhere along the line, this morphed into the idea of a sex scene in which a couple writhe around a library floor that has been printed with dictionary definitions of sexual terms.[52] During scripting, Metzger conceived the scene in terms of swirling camera movements, perhaps in keeping with the Diahann Carroll inspiration; but he opted during postproduction for a fast-paced montage approach that would give greater vitality to middle-aged actor Frank Wolff's sexual exertions: "It was an older man with a young girl," Metzger explained, "and the cutting helped suggest the effort and the spirit in the spine of the scene."[53]

But montage also serves as a means of linking sexual insecurities to their resolution. Two different approaches to editing shape the scene's structure in this respect. In the scene's first half—before the sex proper begins—editing moves us back and forth in time, as a series of cuts take us once more to the man's wartime experiences. As his recollections intrude, the man is prompted to confess his potential sexual inadequacies. "[My wife] says I'm impotent," he explains to the fairground woman. "I'm not. But when she says it, I start to believe it must be true." "I didn't think you're impotent," the woman replies, by this point lying supine and naked on a central table. The film cuts to a final flashback memory of a gun firing and an unidentified man tumbling down a flight of stairs, suggesting that the man's present sexual hesitancy has its source in an act of murderous violence. Once the sex begins, though, Metzger's editing shifts from a temporal orientation—between present and past—to a spatial one—cutting from the couple rolling around to the words printed on the floor, most of which serve to literalize the man's restored potency: "phallus," "prick," "priapism," "testicle," "fuck," and the like (figure 2.6a–f). Whether in terms of the man's psychosexual insecurities or in terms of actor Frank Wolff's apparently feeble gyrations, montage here becomes a kind of aesthetic Viagra, the expressive form for virility's restoration.

This is not the case, however, in the son's sex scene, which Metzger instead built around three long takes: a handheld shot as the son and the woman dance with one another in the castle; a lateral tracking shot, interspersed with some cuts to close-ups, as they dance their way outside through an olive garden; and a static extreme long shot as the two make love on a grassy hillside. Metzger's original intent had in fact been to film the leadup to the sex scene in a single unbroken shot, from inside the castle to outside, but abandoned the challenge because "the place was [too] difficult to meander around.'[54] He also explained his long-take, long-shot approach as an attempt to "get a pristine, Garden-of-Eden atmosphere, [in which] a cut would have been jarring."[55] What matters here, then, is not the accelerating dynamic of male potency, but instead an aesthetic framework in which the son can experience penetration as natural and prelapsarian pleasure rather than demonic defilement (figure 2.7).

It is with the third and final sex scene, however, between the woman and the wife, that the protagonists' memories begin to achieve some clarity, as the wife is finally made to acknowledge her repressed former life as a sex worker. Her reconciliation with her past begins gradually, in a conversation with her husband

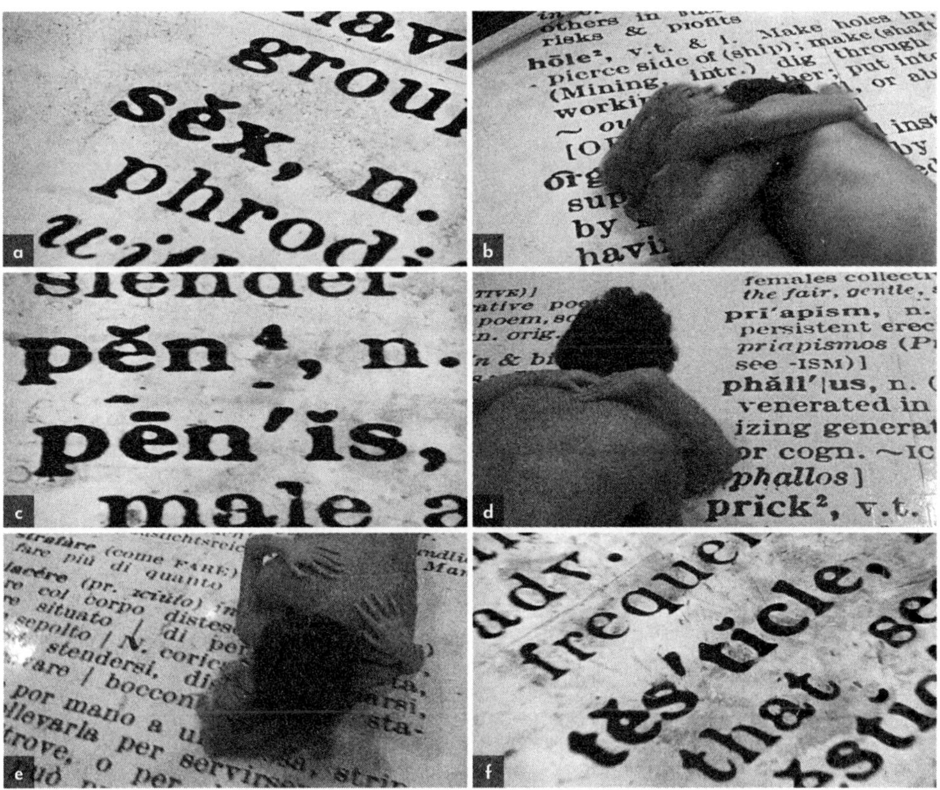

2.6 A montage sequence from the library sex scene. Screen captures from *The Lickerish Quartet*.

where she, once again, disparages the woman from the fairground: "She's just a carnival tramp." This time, however, the husband leaves nothing to implication: "It takes one to know one," he replies. He holds her feet to the fire once more when she claims that the two of them first met at an elegant party in St. Tropez: "I found you in a whore house," he corrects her. But words can only do so much in a film in which, as Linda Williams aptly observes, "sexploitation style . . . substitutes for the talking cure" as a means for repairing trauma.[56] The wife flees to the ballroom, where she starts up the stag film alone: a girl-on-girl scene in which the woman from the carnival is being tied to a bed. That same woman now enters the ballroom, standing next to the screen on which she is also being projected, and the wife once more tries to draw distinctions: "I'm not like that," she says of the performers in the stag film.

2.7 The long-take/long-shot style of the olive-grove sex scene. Screen captures from *The Lickerish Quartet*.

But the lesson she has to learn is that she is precisely "like that." Another of cinema's aesthetic affordances reveals this: namely, the capacity of editing to introduce discontinuities and substitutions within an unfolding action. The wife looks back at the screen to discover that she is now in the stag film itself. Puzzled, she stands up, suddenly naked, in front of the projector, images of herself projected onto her flesh (figure 2.8a). "Who are you anyway?" she asks. "I'm the girl from the carnival," the woman replies. But the wife recalls that she herself is also a girl from the carnival, as she now remembers leaving home to join the circus at the age of thirteen. A cut back to the screen, where the wife and the blond woman are seen making love in the stag film (figure 2.8b). Seated in front of the screen, the blond woman begins to caress and then masturbate the wife, who looks back to the screen to see that the blond woman's place in the film has now been taken by her husband (figure 2.8c–d). The wife climaxes in time with her own screen self's orgasm, and, with that, the mysterious woman is gone: the camera pulls back from a closeup of the wife to reveal the husband sitting where the woman was a moment earlier. The stag reel continues to unspool, however, and what it next shows finally lays bare the shared trauma by which the three family members have been scarred. Within the stag film, the husband and wife are lying on the bed in postcoital embrace: a little boy enters the room, his mouth falling agape in terror as he beholds his primal scene; then a man bursts in threateningly and is shot by the husband, cueing the earlier image of a man falling down a flight of stairs. The wife, the film would have us surmise, was already married when she prostituted herself to the husband; the son is in fact the product of that previous marriage; and the husband an interloper who murdered his predecessor in front of his family.

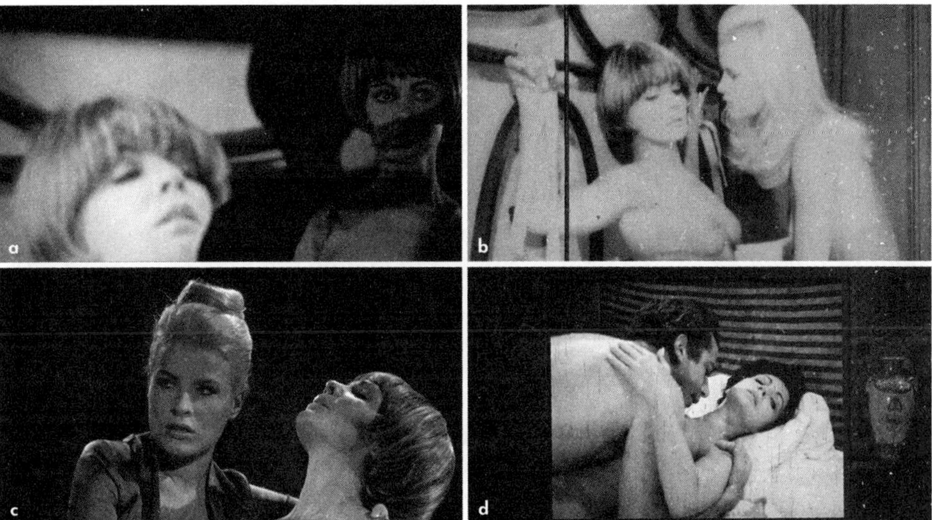

2.8 Discontinuity editing in the wife's seduction scene. Screen captures from *The Lickerish Quartet*.

The wife's repressed memory, the son's sexual disgust, the husband's impotence—all have their origins in this event, and all get repaired in a tripartite experience of sex that asserts itself in three distinct aesthetic terms. The psychic drama of the patriarchal nuclear family in this way gets correlated with the film's reflexive interrogation of the photographic image: just as trauma must be acknowledged if the husband is to take his place next to his wife, so must the raw document of filmed sex be sublated into erotic style. Once again, as with *Thérèse and Isabelle*, Metzger's erotic art aligns itself with a repudiation of cinema's most basic affordance: artistry is a matter of stylistic operations that move beyond the imperative of documentation, a matter of "faith in the image" rather than "faith in reality," to refer to the famous distinction drawn by Bazin.[57]

Perhaps *The Lickerish Quartet* is, in this respect, only the confession of a problem to which his earlier films had already presented the solution. Ever since *Carmen, Baby*, Metzger's proclivity for displacing the direct visibility of sex through reflective and translucent surfaces had been an established component of his endeavor to align filmed sex with a discourse of taste. Erotic artistry had long implied for Metzger a renunciation of "mere" visibility in order to explore alternative strategies that *dis*semble, rather than *re*semble, the object of representation. Only in the case of *The Lickerish Quartet*, there is one last riddle to pose, one last substitution, in the film's final moments: the husband and wife are still "in" the stag film, making love on screen, but are now being watched by a different group of characters in the ballroom, the performers from the original stag reel that began the movie. In a replay of the film's opening scene, the performers comment snidely on the husband and wife, the same way the husband and wife once commented on them, and then head out to the fairground. The process has in other words begun all over again in what is ultimately exposed as a kind of infinite regress. It is in this ever-renewed effort to reclaim filmed sex for erotic art that Metzger's authorship finds its form.

Even if for many the jury was still out on the question of his artistic seriousness, the release of *The Lickerish Quartet* in October 1970 made Metzger a filmmaker at least worthy of serious discussion. Arch-Pop-modernist Andy Warhol gave the film his imprimatur in a four-word blurb widely used in publicity: "Outrageously kinky masterpiece. Go!" (figure 2.9). The months following the film's release saw Metzger basking in the spotlight of a critical attention he had long hungered for. In December he was featured on WABC's radio morning show *AM New York*; the same month, he was a guest on *The Merv Griffin Show*, one of the most popular late night talk shows of the time; the following March, he gave lectures at the "Filmmakers Seminar" of New York University as well as to film students at Columbia University, the latter with a screening of *The Lickerish Quartet*; he was a talking head in a couple of public radio and television shows, on WNET's *The Great American Dream Machine* in March and on Dick Pyatt's *Seminars in Theatre* in April; and, in May, he was awarded "Best Producer" at the Colgate University Film Festival (in attendance with Robert Altman, who received the "Best Director" prize), again with a screening of *The Lickerish Quartet*.[58] Perhaps most remarkably of all, New York's Museum of Modern Art approached Metzger to request prints of all his films for their archive and, in January, hosted "An Evening with Radley Metzger," featuring a screening, yet again, of *The Lickerish Quartet* (figure 2.10).[59] Surviving audio of the postscreening Q&A reveals a Metzger basking in the audience's attention, thanking one viewer who compared the film to Alain Resnais's *Last Year at Marienbad* (1958) and announcing his acquisition of film rights to a new work by absurdist playwright Fernando Arrabal (the

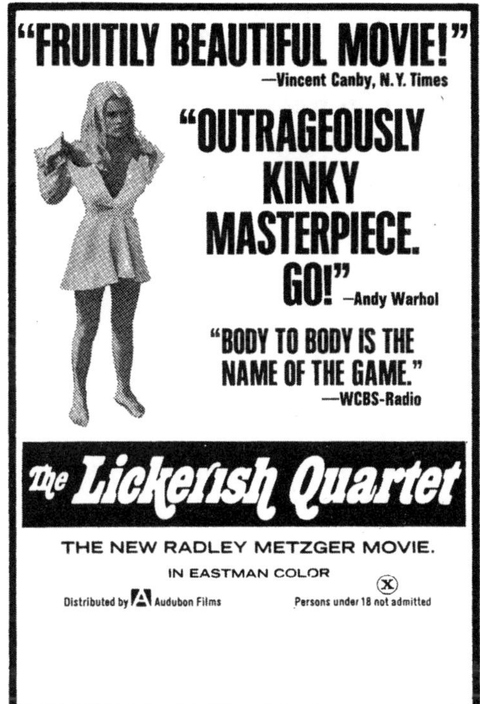

2.9 Publicity material for *The Lickerish Quartet*.
Source: Author's collection.

progenitor, with Alejandro Jodorowsky, of the "Panic Theater" movement).[60] In that brief moment, Metzger's aspirations to the cachet of the erotic avant-garde had seemingly been fulfilled.

At the same time, the very obviousness of his aspirations inevitably tarnished his work as kitsch in the eyes of establishment film critics. In his study of taste in American society, historian Lawrence Levine explains how popular art gets "transformed into esoteric or high art precisely at that time when it in fact *becomes* esoteric, that is, when it becomes or is rendered inaccessible to the types of people who appreciated it earlier."[61] The wrinkle for Metzger, however, was that the critics who served the temple of film "art" refused to honor his esoteric appeals. For every art-cinema move Metzger could make there was a critic ready to smack him down with a "Last Year in Shmutsville" jibe. Ironically, for a filmmaker who had sought to introduce distinction to sex films, Metzger came to be treated by some as a director unable to understand the distinctions that purportedly separated filmed sex from film art in the first place. Things boiled over in

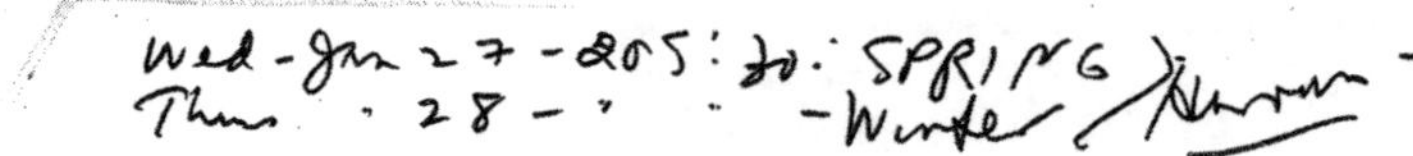

The Museum of Modern Art Department of Film

11 West 53 Street, New York, N.Y. 10019 Tel. 956-6100 Cable: Modernart

CINEPROBE

Tuesday, January 26th at 5:30 p.m.

AN EVENING WITH RADLEY METZGER.

Screening of THE LICKERISH QUARTET. 1970. Produced and directed by Radley Metzger. Photographed (Eastmancolor) by Hans Jura. Sets and costumes by Enrico Sabbatini. Edited by Amedeo Salfa. Screenplay by Michael DeForrest from the original story, 'Hide and Seek', by Metzger and DeForrest. Music by Stephen Cipriani. Photographed at the Castle of Balsorano (Italy) and Cinecitta Studios (Rome). A co-production of Cinemar Productions (Rome) and Peter Carsten Productions (Munich). With Silvana Venturelli (The Girl), Frank Wolff (The Man), Erike Remberg (The Woman), Paolo Turco (The Boy). 90 minutes. Courtesy Audubon Films.

Mr. Metzger will be present for a discussion with the audience after the screening.

"lick-er-ish (lĭk'ə r ĭsh) adj. Archaic. 1. eager for choice food. 2. greedy. 3. lustful. Also, liquorish [earlier lickerous (influenced by lick and liquor with substitution of -ish for -ous), ME likerous, repr. an AF var. of OF lecherous, der. lecheor gourmand, sensualist. See lecher.] " American College Dictionary.

" An erotic duet for four players. "

" ... all this present reality of yours -- is fated to seem a mere illusion to you tomorrow..." - Pirandello, Six Characters in Search of an Author.

Radley Metzger is not only a filmmaker. He has been an exhibitor (he bought the Charles on Manhattan's Lower East Side) and a distributor (I, A WOMAN: his company is Audubon Films). Metzger grew up in Washington Heights, and the Audubon Theatre (now the San Juan Ballroom) was the name of the first theatre he visited. Ushering at the Strand Theatre on Broadway he earned money to attend City College of New York where he graduated with a B.A. in Dramatic Arts. He had hoped to be an actor. During the Korean War Metzger edited training films, and after his service worked for a small distributor of foreign films. He helped compile the trailers and assisted in the dubbing of these films. With the capital raised he produced his first film (in both English and Greek), a fast moving drama of Greek immigrants in New York - DARK ODYSSEY (retitled to PASSIONATE SUNDAY). The film did poorly, and Metzger turned to that genre of the 60's for which he has become known. FILMOGRAPHY: DARK ODYSSEY (1961), DIRTY GIRLS (1964), ALLEY CATS (1966), CARMEN BABY (1967), THERESE AND ISABELLE (1968), CAMILLE 2000 (1969), THE LICKERISH QUARTET (1970). Mr. Metzger has acquired the motion picture rights to Arrabal's 'The Garden of Earthly Delights'.

Future Cineprobes: (All filmmakers will be present.)

Feb. 2 - ERNIE GEHR (WAIT, REVERBERATION, HISTORY, SERENE VELOCITY, STILL).
Feb. 16 - STORM DE HIRSCH (AN EXPERIMENT IN MEDITATION - A New Work-in Progress, THE TATTOOED MAN, and others.)
Feb. 23 - BARBARA LODEN (WANDA.)

2.10 Handbill for Metzger's appearance at the Museum of Modern Art in New York City, January 26, 1971.

Source: Courtesy of the Museum of Modern Art, New York.

a heated 1971 interview on *Newsday* film critic Joseph Gelmis's radio show, *The Movies*, in which Metzger was repeatedly asked to differentiate his work from what Gelmis referred to as the "male stud films on Eighth Avenue":

GELMIS: What word would you use to distinguish *that* from the kind of film you made, your latest film, *The Lickerish Quartet*. *I'm* not drawing the analogy. I'm asking *you* to draw some sort of word definition or distinction which is satisfactory to you.

METZGER: Well, I don't know. I think that, outside of the fact that they're probably both photographed on Eastman Kodak stock, I can't think of any relation. It's very similar to if I said "Please tell me the difference between you and Al Capone."

GELMIS: I could.

METZGER: Sure you could, but posing the question itself implies a relationship. . . .

GELMIS: What I'm having a problem with is pinning you down on any level where you will say "I do make value distinctions or judgments." Do you yourself make value judgments or distinctions? Or when you walk down Seventh Avenue and you see all the peep shows and the places where they have all these little booths where the guy puts the quarter in—

METZGER: Well now, Mr. Gelmis. I don't know if you saw *Thérèse and Isabelle*, but nobody is going to wait three months on a production, to get Georges Auric to write his score. . . . You saw the color in *The Lickerish Quartet*. Nobody is going to spend the hours and the days and the weeks waiting for the right sunlight to photograph that, if they didn't have some seriousness of purpose.[62]

By this point in his career, Metzger had evidently begun to bristle at critics' derogatory responses to his work: Gelmis's categorization of his pictures as "sex films," he was surely aware, was not just a judgment on the films themselves but, more personally, implied a dismissal of Metzger's authorial self-image. (Metzger liked to compare genre categories with wine labels, which allow people to exercise a kind of *faux* discernment without necessarily knowing anything about wine.) Perhaps this is why, for his next picture, he would try to answer his critics by proving his art-cinema credentials outside of the sphere of sex. If so, however, he had been baited into a bad mistake.

"NOT WORTH THE EFFORT": *LITTLE MOTHER* AND THE LIMITS OF METZGER'S MODERNISM

The film in question, *Little Mother* (1972), provides an interesting limit case for the argument of this chapter and, as such, a suitable conclusion for its themes. Metzger's modernism, I have been suggesting, precipitated around the conundrum that cinema's indexicality was felt to pose for the question of erotic art. How, then, would he approach filmmaking in, as he put it, a "non-erotic climate?"[63] What direction would his interrogations of visuality take outside the province of vulgar modernism? In his own words, Metzger's answer was to film a "psychological, political drama" loosely based on the life of Eva Perón, with a complex flashback structure that would dramatize the "disparity between what people do and what people say they do."[64] (The film's narrative form prompted one critic to waggishly dub the film "*All About Eva* (Perón).")[65] Yet the film's dreary reviews—"perfunctory," "out of fresh ideas," "obsolete"—showed Metzger squandering the precarious capital that *Lickerish* had briefly brought him.[66] Whatever ambitions Metzger had for the film were quickly disavowed: when he rereleased the film two years later, he renamed it *Blood Queen* and promoted it as straightforward sex-and-violence exploitation (figure 2.11).

Shot in four weeks in Yugoslavia in early 1972 on a reported budget of over $500,000, *Little Mother* was never quite the departure from previous form that Metzger had suggested.[67] Few critics were able to resist mentioning the "generous views" Metzger afforded of star Christiane Kruger, in the Perón-like role of Marina; and, indeed, the film contains one of the director's most memorable "glassy images," in a shower scene in which Kruger's body is pressed up against the shower stall's frosted glass (figure 2.12).[68] The scene prompted some half-ironic auteurist musings on the part of the *Independent Film Journal*'s critic, who noted how the image of a "nude body pressed *against* glass" called to mind the scene from *Carmen, Baby* in which Metzger had "filmed lovemaking *behind* colored glassware."[69] A more thoroughgoing auteurist take might, however, have detected thematic continuities, too, in the way *Little Mother* extends Metzger's preoccupation with the relation between the screen and what it shows, only in this case transferred from the realm of sex to that of politics.

Along similar lines, Metzger's object of interrogation in *Little Mother* is not the sex film, as in *The Lickerish Quartet*, but rather the television newscast. The film's

2.11 Poster for *Little Mother*'s 1975 re-release as *Blood Queen*, on a double-bill with the similarly retitled *The Cop*.

Source: Author's collection.

2.12 A signature "glassy image." Screen capture from *Little Mother.*

overall narrative form is bookended by two corresponding scenes in which the "Little Mother," as she is known, appears to her people in a television broadcast. In the first, the film's programmatic opening scene, Marina launches her campaign for election to vice president of her unnamed country by celebrating a local soccer team's victory before the news cameras. The scene ends with Marina throwing a ball to the team and then cuts to show the same images playing on a black-and-white television screen; another cut shows Marina and her aide, watching those images on the television (figure 2.13). The Little Mother expresses disappointment at the newscaster's commentary and orders that it be changed in subsequent broadcasts. In the film's final scene, Marina, now president, appears on the balcony of a government palace while a prerecorded film of her Christmas message is projected onto a screen to the cheering crowds below. A political assassin shoots her in the back of the head as she watches herself onscreen (figure 2.14a–b). During the resulting chaos, the film repeatedly cuts away to a group of people watching the broadcast of her Christmas message on television in a shop window, unaware that the message is not live and that the woman who is addressing them has just been killed. The unwitting newscaster announces that the station will now return to the "celebrations in progress" at the palace, and the television screen turns to static, the last image of the film (figure 2.14c–d).

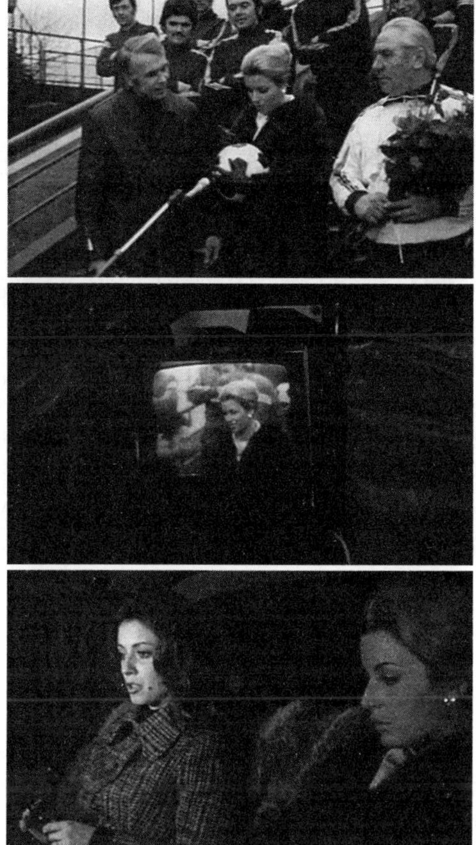

2.13 *Little Mother* begins by demonstrating how political manipulation intercedes in the "liveness" of a television broadcast. Screen captures from *Little Mother.*

No less than in *The Lickerish Quartet*, Metzger's concern is with the reliability of the moving image, only here in a context not of memory and sexual fantasy, but of political powerplays and media control. Just as the film itself begins and ends on that point, so also is the beginning and ending of Marina's political career similarly framed. As shown in a flashback, she first comes to public attention as a television weather girl who, during a live broadcast of a cholera outbreak, spontaneously braves the quarantined area to help the afflicted, seizing the interest of the news cameras. The Little Mother's political rise is in this way charted in terms both of her control over her mediated image and of her ability to control the attention of others *through* that image, even after her death. Nor is it only the thematic switch from sex to politics that reshapes Metzger's reflexivity here, but a corresponding change in the nature of the media involved, from film to television. Whereas celluloid cinema's "mummy complex," as we have seen, associates

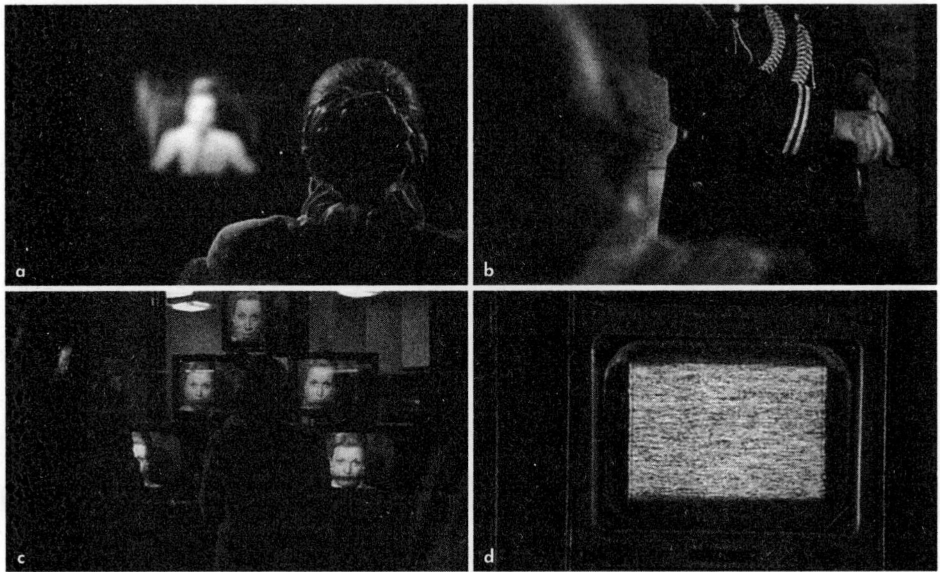

2.14 In the film's climax, Marina (Christiane Kruger) is killed while people watch her supposedly "live" Christmas television address. Screen captures from *Little Mother.*

the medium with a past that it preserves (thus making it an appropriate springboard for *The Lickerish Quartet*'s themes of memory, repression, and trauma), television's ontology has historically been understood in relation to the present-tense simultaneity of event, transmission, and reception. During the 1950s, for example, Bazin himself published a series of pieces on the "provisional essence" of television, which he understood as rooted in *liveness*—and thus in opposition to the cinematic capacity to mummify time that was central to his theory of film.[70] Of course, one might object, television need be no more "live" than cinema, as is manifestly clear from prerecorded shows, reruns, and the like.[71] But as Jane Feuer argued in a seminal 1983 essay, "The Concept of Live Television: Ontology as Ideology," the *idea* of television's liveness has nevertheless persisted: even if television is not in fact live at any given moment, liveness remains as part of the medium's ideology, as a key to its hold on our attention.[72] Television is—or rather, *was*, before the internet—the medium for breaking news, sports broadcasts, presidential addresses, and other events that require updating in real time. But the Little Mother intuits the strategic utility of liveness, too: her decision to enter the quarantined area is, for example, a calculated one, designed to exploit the presence of a near-at-hand camera crew to turn herself into a news story. It is, furthermore, the presumption of liveness that, at the film's end, allows Marina to continue to exert her sway from beyond the grave over the people watching her Christmas broadcast on television.

Yet, unlike *The Lickerish Quartet*, these media themes get engaged only in isolated moments toward the film's beginning and end, without being harnessed to the film's showier narrative flourishes. A number of critics took Metzger to task, for example, for the film's complex flashback structure—repeatedly cutting back to uncover the various maneuvers and betrayals that lie behind Marina's ascent to power—which many dismissed as a pointless exercise in empty formalism. The usually sympathetic Archer Winsten, critic for the *New York Post*, wrote that the film's "backward and forward method of narration . . . manages a degree of suspense, but . . . doesn't seem worth all the effort," concluding "this is a picture that tries to fool the eye and mind, pretending to offer a great deal more than is ever really there."[73] (Amusingly, the clippings collection of New York's Museum of Modern Art include an unidentified critic's handwritten notes from *Little Mother*'s press screening: "Nonsensically edited," "What's going on?" and "Flashbacks—too many," are some of the reviewer's thoughts.)[74] The film was also subject to the most savage review of Metzger's career—already quoted in part in the introduction to this book—in which the New York *Daily News*' Rex Reed castigated Metzger's film as a "downright comical" effort that played like an "old Joan Crawford tearjerker . . . complete with soft-core Playboy-Penthouse erotica thrown in to keep the audience awake."[75] Metzger's aspirations to prove himself as more than just a "skin-flick maker" had resulted in embarrassing exposure: the film was at once his first major commercial failure, barely surviving on screens into 1973 after a nationwide rollout the previous October, and the object of a critical drubbing for which he no longer had any cover.

The sense in which Metzger was trading in a kind of art-cinema kitsch had long been a charge of the filmmaker's detractors and would remain so throughout his life. Critics at the time who derided the Brechtianism of Metzger's clapperboard opening to *Camille 2000* ("as if he were Ingmar Bergman") or who mocked *The Lickerish Quartet* as "post-*Marienbad*" hackwork were only laying the groundwork for Bart Testa's eloquent 1999 critique of Metzger's style as a "deracinated aesthetic . . . lifted from hard-won forms and modes of expression—here art cinema—and replanted as isolated effects."[76] Metzger's media-reflexive trope of the "screen within the screen" would become a case in point: first deployed in *The Lickerish Quartet* in relation to cinema, and then in *Little Mother* in relation to television, the device would harden into something of a stylistic tic in Metzger's subsequent cinema, as later chapters will show. At the MoMA screening of *The Lickerish Quartet*, Metzger linked the technique to the influence of Orson Welles's 1946 stage production *Around the World* (an adaptation of the 1873 Jules Verne novel) as well as the Czech multimedia group Laterna Magika, both of which involved interactions between film projection and live-action performance. But he also explained his fondness for this trope simply as an "occupational hazard" for any cinephile who has been "exposed to pictures so much," which is indeed how it sometimes registers.[77] Such, for instance, is the opinion of Linda Williams, who, noting the trope's appearance in Metzger's 1978 remake of *The Cat and the Canary*—the second and last time that the director sought to break free of the category of "sex film"—complains that it serves merely as a "clever" gag, lacking the "more resonant avant-garde sensibilities" of his earlier work.[78] (The instance in question is discussed in this book's conclusion.)

Still, one should beware of throwing the baby out with the bathwater. Whereas Testa wants to dismiss Metzger out of hand as a "charlatan" for whom "no critical recuperation should be sought," Williams strikes a more partial, and to my mind more satisfactory position: Metzger's modernist aspirations failed primarily when he strayed outside the province of the sex film.[79] This chapter has shown why that might be, on at least two counts. Foremost is the vulgar modernism within which Metzger had established his authorial credentials: the broader context of sexually explicit modernism during this period gave Metzger's work a traction (or, less charitably, an alibi) that he simply abandoned in attempting a film in a "non-erotic climate." But it is also the case that Metzger's investment in the *materiality* of his medium had an applicability to the question of filmed sex that it lacked elsewhere. The cinematic image's paradoxical status as, at once, a representational fiction and a presentational fact is rarely more fraught than in the case of sex, where, as we have seen, the fiction of sex on screen ultimately requires the fact of sexual contact in front of the cameras. The problem of sex for aesthetics thus acquires a unique aspect in the case of photographic media when compared with the other arts: namely, the impossibility of containing sex to the sphere of representation alone. The point holds across the spectrum of sexual contact: just as the representation of a visible kiss on the lips in a fiction film requires the performance of an actual kiss, so too does a visible erection require real sexual arousal. To recall critic Richard Corliss's question: "How can a director reconcile the fictional reality of his characters with the documentary reality of his performers?" Metzger's answer is, arguably, a conservative one: cinema's indexicality becomes, in effect, the media-ontological trauma—metaphorically equivalent to the primal scene—that cinematic artistry is called upon either to overcome (in *The Lickerish Quartet*) or to hold in check (in *Thérèse and Isabelle*). That Metzger's answer perhaps disappoints is not, however, the same as his not answering the question, which is where Testa's dismissal oversteps.

Finally, what also emerges from these considerations is a new perspective from which to return, once more, to the erotica/porn distinction, only this time in media-technological terms. Pornography of course receives one of its most celebrated definitions as what Linda Williams called a "frenzy of the visible," a genre marked by the compulsive drive to see—and thus to know—the hidden truth of sexual pleasure.[80] Pornography, on this reading, is more than just one cinematic genre among others, but is something like the fullest realization of the medium's basic affordance as a technology of vision; cinema, in turn, is more than just a technology of recording, but part of a will to knowledge of which pornography represents an outer limit. Eroticism, however, bespeaks a very different orientation, at least if we heed Metzger's lesson. As Metzger's work suggests, eroticism inheres not in the *consummation* of a medium's affordances than in their avoidance or deferral—less a "frenzy" of the visible, perhaps, than its refraction and redirection. Eroticism, in Metzger's hands, is a matter of circumventing the indexical record of sex (in *Thérèse and Isabelle*) or of subjecting that record to an aesthetic transformation (in *The Lickerish Quartet*).

My point here is not to argue that the eroticism/porn distinction is in some instances a matter of taste distinction (as discussed in the previous chapter) while in others related to media affordances (as discussed here). Rather, it is to suggest that distinctions in taste can take material form in the relations that get established between sexual representation and the properties of the media of representation.[81] Nor is my point limited to Metzger's work or his era. Take, for example, the soft-focus visual style that characterizes erotic media as diverse as 1950s *Playboy* photoshoots and 1990s softcore thrillers, which has commonly been understood as a strategy of distinction crossbreeding lowbrow sexploitation style with the purported respectability of pictorialist photography.[82] But what really matters for eroticism, I would contend, is less pictorialism per se than how its characteristic use of soft focus introduces a kind of interference or gap into the relation between a photographic image and what it represents. Likewise, if the aesthetic diversity of the sex scenes in *The Lickerish Quartet* can tell us anything, it is surely that it is this very gap, in which aesthetics in general coheres, that catalyzes eroticism rather than the connotations of any singular aesthetic like pictorialism. Metzger had tethered his auteurist reputation to an approach that displaced or refracted the indexical record of sex in favor of its artistic transformation. What he could not have foreseen—and what the next chapter explores—is how subsequent developments in the sphere of adult film would throw that approach into crisis.

CHAPTER 3

"THAT'S NOT HIS REAL NAME"

Pseudonymity and the Porn Auteur

One of the best gags in Radley Metzger's hardcore films occurs early in *The Opening of Misty Beethoven*, shortly after noted sexologist Seymour Love (Jamie Gillis) first encounters sex worker Misty Beethoven (Constance Money) in a Parisian porn theater. "Is that your real name?" he inquires. "No, it's not. I took it to sound more important," she replies. "What was it before?" "Delores Beethoven," Misty deadpans.

In one sense, this is an elementary bait-and-switch gag: Misty's claim that she changed her name to "sound more important" should imply "Beethoven," not "Misty," as the status-seeking moniker. But the absurdist twist—that somebody named Delores Beethoven would rename herself Misty for grandiosity's sake—also offers a wink at the parodic aspirationalism found in so many porn pseudonyms of the era: the Gerald Graystones, Henri Pachards, and Candida Royalles of the industry, among many others. Few of those names, though, have been more prominent in histories of hardcore pornography's Golden Age than "Henry Paris," the *nom de porn* that Metzger created for himself for a series of five hardcore features—*The Private Afternoons of Pamela Mann* (1974), *Naked Came the Stranger* (1975), *The Opening of Misty Beethoven* (1976), *Barbara Broadcast* (1977), and *Maraschino Cherry* (1978)—shot over a breakneck twenty-three-month period beginning in the summer of 1974. As Metzger himself later recalled, "It's strange but at the time, 'Henry Paris' became much more famous and successful than I did."[1]

Metzger's motives in adopting the alias aren't hard to decipher. As with most pseudonyms, the Henry Paris name was taken for simple reasons of cover, specifically *legal* cover owing to Metzger's fears of prosecution given the dubious legality of hardcore filmmaking. The director's shift into hardcore was spectacularly ill timed in that respect: Metzger's decision to enter the growing market for XXX films came *after* the seminal 1973 obscenity case of *Miller v. California*, which reinterpreted the "community standards" benchmark for obscenity in local rather than national terms. That ruling effectively shifted regulatory power back to state and municipal bodies, resulting in a surge of injunctions against hardcore exhibitors and distributors.[2] "It was a worrying time and we were scared," the director later recalled. "I learned that [*Variety* critic] Addison Verrill intended revealing that I was the director of *Pamela Mann*, and so I spoke to him and had to beg him not to."[3] Metzger was right to be scared, too: his move into hardcore coincided with the 1974 arrests of dozens of individuals involved in the production and distribution of the pioneering *Deep Throat* (1972), and the resulting convictions of eleven—including star Harry Reems—for conspiracy to transport obscene materials over state lines. (The convictions were eventually overturned because *Deep Throat*'s production predated the *Miller* ruling, a condition that wouldn't have applied to Metzger.) Above and beyond these real legal worries, however, the Henry Paris pseudonym also served Metzger as a form of *brand* cover on the part of a director-distributor who wanted to preserve the authorial reputation and identity that he had worked so long to secure, both as a director in his own right and as head of Audubon Films. Again, Metzger: "I had done, by that time, [a number of] features and I guess there was a sameness to them: people would go to see them and expect something. And I felt that I didn't want . . . people to go and expect what I was doing. . . . The one thing I don't think is fair is misleading the public."[4]

That more complicated motives were in play, though, becomes clear from what happened once the beans were spilled. Henry Paris proved to be a fig leaf that was almost immediately torn off, both by the adult and the mainstream trades. The *Independent Film Journal*'s review of the very first Henry Paris film, *The Private Afternoons of Pamela Mann*, had already dropped a major hint by describing the film as "directed by a 'Henry Paris' which we understand is a pseudonym for a well known name in the 'soft' market," a point that *Playboy* magazine echoed two months later, describing Henry Paris as the "nom de film . . . [of] an established movie-maker whose soft-core exploitation flicks are famous for their deluxe style."[5] And then, in April 1975, *Variety* revealed the truth, as Metzger had feared it would, in an article goadingly titled "Metzger Too Soft for His Name on Hardcore 'Naked' [*Naked Came the Stranger*]."[6] Yet, despite the exposé, Metzger *continued* to use the Henry Paris name, turning it into an alter ego of sorts, the Mr. Hyde to his established auteurist persona as a purveyor of "class sex" erotica, even to the point of toggling between names, when his 1976 film *The Image* was released as a Radley Metzger film sandwiched between the release of two Henry Paris pictures (*Naked Came the Stranger* and *Misty Beethoven*). Metzger's use of a porn pseudonym was thus quite unlike that of other former sexploitation filmmakers like Joe Sarno and Doris Wishman, who sought simply to bury and conceal their work in hardcore.[7] With Metzger, what began as a "false name" adopted for reasons of legal protection and brand identity morphed into the rather different category of the *heteronym*, which refers to the use of imaginary identities to write in distinct styles and construct distinct authorial personas.[8] In the process, Henry Paris shifted from being a mask to a masquerade, a cover that confessed to its own ruse. "That's not his real name," declares star Gloria Leonard of "dynamite director Henry Paris" in the trailer for *Maraschino Cherry*, adding "but that's his *mishegoss*." In similarly playful spirit, *High Society* magazine's 1977 catalog of adult filmmakers represented Henry Paris with a picture of a man with his back turned to the camera, but then described him in the accompanying capsule as a former "master of soft-core" whose "*Therese and Isabel* [*sic*] . . . is considered a classic"—a claim that gives the game away even as it pretends to be playing it (figure 3.1).[9]

But what, if anything, was the method behind the *mishegoss*? This chapter considers how "Henry Paris," as both pseudonym and heteronym, worked to introduce a distinction into Metzger's filmography that allows us to rethink Metzger's relation to the categories of "hard" and "soft" into which adult film has ordinarily been divided. For, in adopting his "Henry Paris" alter-ego, Metzger

PARIS, HENRY
One of the very best directors and filmmakers in porn today, Paris was a master of soft-core before he tackled the harder stuff. His *"Therese and Isabel"*, the story of a love affair between two French schoolgirls, is considered a classic. Among his porno efforts are *"Naked Came the Stranger"*, and *"Maraschino Cherry"*.

3.1 Who was Henry Paris? *High Society* magazine drops some clues in its 1977 special collector's edition, *Who's Who in X-Rated Films*.

was not simply covering—or turning—his back; he was also clarifying who "Radley Metzger" was and had been in the first place.

"METZGER HAS BECOME OBSOLETE": PORNO CHIC AND THE LIMITS OF TASTE

Distinction is, of course, the operative word for any discussion of Metzger. Prior to his hardcore turn, Metzger's work in the adult-film market had been fueled by a combination of middlebrow literariness and modernist aspiration that, by the early 1970s, saw him variously crowned the "aristocrat of the erotic," "auteur of the erotic," and "master of the erotic."[10] The reception of *The Lickerish Quartet* in late 1970 represented a pinnacle in this regard, but a pinnacle for which a banana peel was already being prepared. That banana peel came in the form of the "porno chic" era, so dubbed by *New York Times* writer Ralph Blumenthal in 1973, to refer to the legal emergence of theatrically exhibited hardcore features.[11] Gerard Damiano's *Deep Throat* and Jim and Artie Mitchell's *Behind the Green Door*, both 1972, are typically cited as the era's bicoastal clarion calls—the former from New York, the latter San Francisco—although they were significantly anticipated by dozens of smaller-scale, 16mm features like the Sherpix-distributed titles *Mona* (1970) and Alex de Renzy's *Pornography in Denmark: A New Approach* (1970), as well as Wakefield Poole's experimental queer hardcore film *Boys in the Sand* (1971).[12] But firsts are less relevant here than the demoralizing effect these developments had on the existing market for adult film. Softcore cinema would continue to be made—even experiencing a brief "chic" of its own thanks to Just Jaeckin's *Emmanuelle* in 1974—but its formal evasiveness on the representation of sex began to seem simply pointless, resulting in a dwindling market share.[13] Go hard or goodbye seemed to be the unwelcome lesson for many filmmakers. Even before the porno chic era, Metzger's peer Russ Meyer admitted to rooting for U.S. Customs officials who had seized a print of the boundary-pushing Swedish film *I Am Curious (Yellow)* (1969). If the film passed the censors, Meyer explained, "every crummy producer in the in the country will be out with sex-exploitation films showing everything, and the whole business will be ruined."[14] Filmmaking brothers John and Lem Amero, meanwhile, had just finished their surrealist sexploitation film, *Bacchanale*, in 1970, when a chance viewing of *Mona* in Times

Square sent them back to the studio to add hardcore inserts. "I immediately knew that if hardcore sex was going to be the norm," John recalled, "nobody would pay for imitation."[15] Others, meanwhile, took the hardcore turn as their cue to leave, such as Barry Mahon, who transitioned out of sexploitation fare like *Fanny Hill Meets Dr. Erotico* (1967) to make independent children's movies like *Jack and the Beanstalk* and *Thumbelina* (both 1970).

What all these filmmakers were responding to were fears about the *market viability* of nonexplicit adult film. What Radley Metzger had to deal with, in addition, was an almost existential threat to his authorship—the defunding of the very kind of erotic capital on which he had built his reputation. The vulgar modernism to which Audubon and Metzger had heretofore aspired now appeared to be nothing more than a placeholder for the subsequent rise of a hardcore that neutralized its provocations. This, in fact, provides further context for the critical drubbing Metzger had received for *Little Mother* (1972), in which he had continued to mine his trademark veneer of art-cinema eroticism, despite the fact that *Deep Throat*'s release had rendered his style a seeming relic. "Maybe in this era of 'Deep Throat,' the soft-core simulated sex of Radley Metzger has become obsolete," cautioned George Anderson of the *Pittsburgh Post-Gazette*.[16] "Alas, it's 1973, and we've already seen *Deep Throat*," added Rex Reed in his scathing review for the *Post*. 'By comparison, *Little Mother* . . . seems outdated and out-raided."[17]

To clarify the problem Metzger now faced, it is useful to recall historian Steven Marcus's *bon mot* from his pioneering 1966 study of nineteenth-century literary erotica, *The Other Victorians*: "Literature possesses . . . a multitude of intentions, but pornography possesses only one."[18] For Marcus, "literature"—meant here in the evaluative sense, that is, *good* literature—is characterized by multiplicity, narrative and formal complexity, and a concern with human relations; but pornography is essentially repetitive, literal, and interested in organs rather than people. However one assesses Marcus's sentiment, there is no question that it speaks to the long-established schism that has been felt to divide the realm of pornography from that of "art." That distinction is, of course, a historical one—rather than an absolute—which, in this case, traces its origins to developments in eighteenth-century moral and aesthetic philosophy. In the hands of thinkers like Immanuel Kant and Friedrich Schlegel, aesthetic value came to be defined through a negation of bodily stimulus and excitation, in repudiation of a much older conception that saw artistic beauty and eros as intimately linked.[19] The birth of the field of aesthetics in its modern sense was premised on an ascetic ideal of *disinterestedness*, for which Schlegel provided the watchword when he warned, "Physical excitement is the end of all art."[20] Yet the obvious problem here is that physical excitement is hardcore's specific goal. The birth of modern aesthetics thus also set the conditions for the category of pornography as the negative marker for that which was excluded from the realm of art. As theorist Pasi Falk notes, pornography has long served as the "paradigmatic case of the *anti-aesthetic*": it cannot be seen as having any complexity of intentions, because the instincts to which it appeals are at loggerheads with the contemplative distance that the aesthetic attitude requires.[21]

But we have also seen that there exists, at the precise point of tension between the poles of art and pornography, the field of erotica, which Metzger in the late 1960s had made his own. A category of explicit representation that nonetheless operates *within* the contemplative aestheticism of legitimate art, erotica finds itself on the contentious frontier of distinction, poised on the knife edge between embodied stimulation and aesthetic disinterest. It must always carry the promise of sexual arousal in order to maintain its identity and not simply be absorbed into the realm of art, just as it also maintains an aestheticism that defers against the "merely" pornographic. This is what Elena Gorfinkel, in a discussion of the stylization of Metzger's films, has described as the "soft-core predicament"—a "prohibition of the explicit sexual act" that is balanced by an array of viewer compensations, including aesthetic stylization and lavish production values.[22] The paradox of hardcore imagery, for Metzger, was that it threatened to upset this delicate balance by collapsing his filmmaking into the pornographic immediacy that his aestheticism was designed to offset.

Accordingly, Metzger's first response to the porno chic wave was to try to renegotiate his established brand of "class sex" filmmaking within the context of the new license for explicitness. The result, *Score* (1973), was an adaptation of a short-lived off-Broadway play by Jerry Douglas, telling the story of a bisexual married couple, Elvira (played in the film by Claire Wilbur) and Jack (Gerald Grant), who seduce naïve newlyweds Betsy (Lynn Lowry) and Eddie (*Boys in the Sand* star Cal Culver). Shot in Yugoslavia in the late summer of 1972, just weeks after the release of *Deep Throat*, *Score* marked a new approach on Metzger's part to erotic sophistication, one indebted less to the art-cinema accents of *The Lickerish Quartet* than to modish currents in sexual lifestyles: it was a film that capitalized on the era's interest in "swinging" culture and the brief vogue of what *Newsweek* christened "bisexual chic."[23] Queer female desire had been a theme of Metzger's work ever since *The Twilight Girls* (1961), of course, but *Score* goes further by depicting all possibilities for sexual coupling, male-female (a threesome between Elvira, Betsy, and a telephone repairman), female-female (Elvira/Betsy) and—far rarer for adult film of the time—male-male (Jack/Eddie). More radically still, the film was distributed in two different versions, with a hardcore cut for the film's New York release (at the Cine Malibu and Cinema Village) in which it is surprisingly only the *male* duo's coupling that is represented with unsimulated imagery.

Perhaps this is why the film has come to be identified, albeit tentatively, with queer film history.[24] Its empathetic, nonjudgmental depiction of male-on-male sex finds few parallels outside of early queer hardcore, with the exception perhaps of Andy Milligan's 1965 short *Vapors*. Metzger's casting of Cal Culver, moreover, suggests a calculated appeal to gay male audiences: under the porn name of Casey Donovan, Culver was already something of a queer icon by this point—not just for his role in *Boys in the Sand*, but as a frequently featured model for *After Dark* magazine—and the director cast him after viewing Wakefield Poole's breakthrough film.[25] Still, Metzger thought of *Score* not as a "queer film" per se but as simply another step in his continued experimentation within the sphere of erotic film. The result, though, was a movie that even he found impossible to categorize. "I don't know what name you'd give it," he explained, "but I think it's beyond soft core" (figure 3.2).[26] The explicit footage in the New York release shows too much to fit happily within softcore's borders—specifically, unsimulated male-male masturbation and oral sex, together with possibly simulated anal penetration—yet *Score* also falls short of expectations of hardcore: the explicit images account only for a bare handful of minutes, couched in an otherwise Metzgerian mise-en-scène that obscures bodies behind reflective and translucent surfaces. Meanwhile, the film's queer nonnormativity—accentuated by the casting of Culver—raised issues for marketing that were significant enough to attract trade attention. Dubbing *Score* a "sexploitation milestone" in its 1973 review of the softcore version, *Variety* nonetheless confessed to "puzzlement" regarding the possible response of "the straight male audience to the gay sex scenes, heretofore a strict no-no on the sexploitation market." The film's box-office fate, the critic concluded, was likely in the hands of "newly liberated femme audiences [who] may well turn-on to it all, offsetting any straight male hysteria."[27] These

3.2 A different type of sex film.

Source: Author's collection.

uncertainties account for the film's unusual release pattern, whereby the film's New York premiere was delayed while Metzger and Leighton experimented with marketing strategies in other cities. "Test for 'Right Sell' to Wrong Sex" was the title of a subsequent *Variety* article enumerating the varied campaigns: "Pic has been test dated around the country with three different campaigns, at least two of them avoiding pic's real subject matter. . . . A pitch to straights worked in Weathersfield, Conn., a gay sell didn't work well in Los Angeles and a flat-out exploitation 'straight' pitch worked in a number of drive-ins and in Atlanta."[28] The inclusion of hardcore footage for the film's eventual New York release in August 1974—for which Metzger decided to appropriate *Newsweek*'s coinage and sell the film as "Bisexual Chic"—seems in this context to have been something of a Hail Mary in response to these uncertainties.[29]

Who was *Score* for in the end, then? For "newly liberated femmes" or New York's gay male subculture? Was the film ersatz hardcore for queer audiences or erotica for the swinging crowd? As Jamie Hook observes, the difficulty of categorizing the film reveals how "dominant and regulatory 'commonsense' and hegemonic conceptions of desire and sexual expression as embedded in the western sex-gender system have stymied the development of categories through which to name films that simply do not conform to governing expectations for how sex (queer or straight) is to be represented."[30] Perhaps predictably, then, the film was not a box-office success, with low grosses everywhere except, ironically, in New York, where the explicit cut was likely buoyed by gay filmgoers.[31]

In a later interview, Metzger explained how the one-two disappointments of *Little Mother* and *Score* convinced him that he would now have to throw his hat into the hardcore ring. "You never like to see your grosses go down," he put it. "We were always self-financing. So when the gross would go down it would impact on the next picture you were going to do."[32] "So I sat with Ava [Leighton]," Metzger elsewhere recalled, "and we said well, maybe we just have to do it, just to put the company financially back on keel."[33] *Score* had been an object lesson in the kind of contortions Metzger would have to perform in attempting to preserve his auteurist reputation in a changing market: it saw him shift from the vulgar modernism of *The Lickerish Quartet* and reposition himself as a tastemaker in sexual lifestyle choice; it dabbled with greater explicitness but in the process confused expectations. His next step was to meet those expectations, even at the cost of his auteurist identity.

"EVERYTHING SHE DOES IS ANONYMOUS": THEMATIZING PSEUDONYMITY IN THE EARLY HENRY PARIS FILMS

Looking back at the production of *The Private Afternoons of Pamela Mann*, Metzger claimed no intent for the film other than to make money: "We did this to produce revenue. There was no overview, no saying 'Well, now I'm in . . . this part of my career and this will be the first.' " One thing, though, is clear: he approached the project with a measure of wry humor, both for the circumstances in which he found himself and for the genre in which he was now working. The experience of making the film seems in fact to have been a relaxed and happy one. After years of increasingly ambitious runaway productions, Metzger found a "freedom that I never had before" in the reduced circumstances of a six-day shoot with a bare crew on the streets of Manhattan and in friends' apartments (including Ava Leighton's, which doubles as Pamela Mann's own). "It was suddenly Disneyland. It took a lot of pressure off. It was almost a new way of filming."[34]

Metzger's initial idea for the film winked at his own situation as a director now working undercover: a movie about a woman who leads a sexual double life. This idea gave him the character name—a friend had told him about a real woman named Pamela Mann who secretly ran a sexploitation talent agency out of her New York apartment—and it also gave him the plot: a man (played in the film by Alan Marlow) hires a private detective (Eric Edwards) to secretly film his wife Pamela (Barbara Bourbon) during her "private afternoons." Like *The Lickerish Quartet* before it, *Pamela Mann* interrogates its own status as an explicit film, only this time with a detached, ironic amusement at the protocols of the burgeoning hardcore genre. Gerard Damiano's *Deep Throat*, for instance, gets name-checked early on, in dialogue that plays on the 1972 film's second life as codename for the Watergate informant. "We went to a dinner party last night," the husband explains to the detective, "and the conversation naturally came up: the impeachment and Deep Throat. Pamela confided in me that she would like very much to do that number if she could." The film's first hardcore scene, when Pamela fellates a stranger at Sutton Place Park, continues along this line by ludicrously hyperbolizing the conventions that Damiano's film had helped make *de rigueur*: not only is the stranger whom Pamela deep throats played by the notoriously well-endowed Marc Stevens ("Mr. Ten-and-a-Half," one of the burgeoning New York porn scene's early loop performers) but the culminating money shot (industry jargon for a close-up of male ejaculation) was filmed in super slow-motion at four hundred frames per second, using a special camera apparently developed at NASA.[35] The trope of the money shot is in Metzger's hands exaggerated to the point of absurdity, all to the accompaniment of thunder and lightning effects on the soundtrack. (The director also toyed with some fourth-wall-breaking humor in the deep throat scene, instructing Barbara Bourbon to gag on Stevens's penis, turn to the camera, and say, "That was the best gag in the film." The footage survives in existing outtakes but was not used for the finished film.) Metzger's cheeky teasing of hardcore even extends to a running gag throughout the film that pokes fun at debates over obscenity law during this period. From time to time an opinion pollster (played by Doris Toumarkine, Metzger's editor on *Score* and his first two Henry Paris films) shows up to ask Pamela for her views on social issues totally unrelated to the plot. At the end of the film, the pollster walks unannounced into the Manns' bedroom. "Who *are* you?" the husband asks, to which she replies, "Oh, I'm here to give the film socially redeeming values."[36]

Whatever his intent for the film, the cumulative effect of Metzger's approach is to ironize the mechanics of hardcore.[37] In her 1989 study of the genre, film scholar Linda Williams famously described the "animating fantasy" of hardcore as the attempt to visibly represent the "truth" of female sexual pleasure.[38] The formulaic trope of the money shot is, on this interpretation, at once the fulfillment of hardcore's will to knowledge and the sign of its failure: it provides a representation of sexual climax, but only as a phallic proxy for what remains *un*representable, namely, the woman's pleasure.[39] In *Pamela Mann*, this same "animating fantasy" gets deflected into a parodic hall of mirrors. The detective's clandestine filming certainly produces visible evidence of Pamela's sexual encounters, even as the interpretation of her desire remains willfully obscure. "You've asked me to find the common denominator, the essence of Pamela Mann," the detective acknowledges, but all he can offer the husband is comically pompous psychobabble. "It couldn't be more clear: the need for degradation, for reassurance, from observing the very act in which she feels so insecure." The final twist is that, with the exception of the naïve detective, *nobody's* desire is what it seems: in the concluding scenes, it is revealed that all of the sexual encounters have been staged by the Manns as part of a game to keep their marriage exciting, and the detective is one in a long line of gumshoes hired under false pretenses to film Pamela having sex with other men. Even the one sex scene that does *not* include Pamela plays as a cameo of these themes of pretense and masquerade, when Pamela's

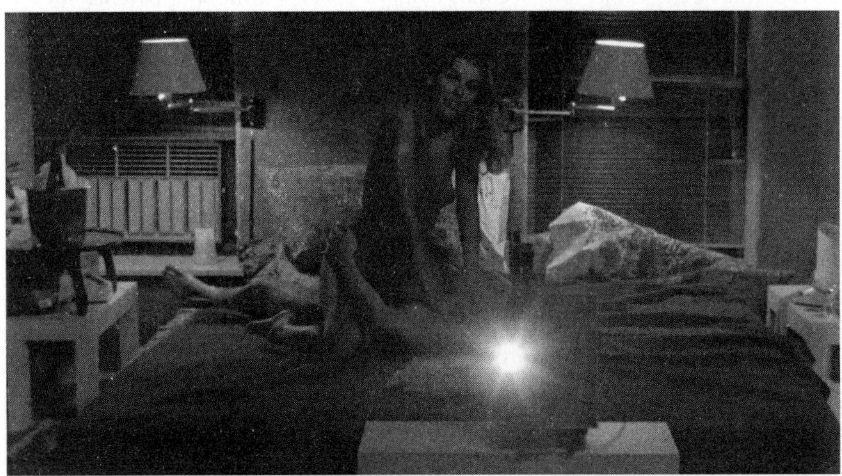

3.3 Pamela (Barbara Bourbon) and her husband (Alan Marlow) have sex while watching the filmed projection of her earlier sexual encounters. Screen capture from *The Private Afternoons of Pamela Mann*.

sex worker friend—played by Georgina Spelvin, star of Damiano's *The Devil in Miss Jones* (1973)—pretends to be convinced by a client who pretends to be a gay man who wants her to turn him straight. (Spelvin's appearance here reunited her with Metzger for the first time since Audubon's swaddling years, when he filmed her for the inserts for *The Twilight Girls* [1961].)[40] The overall effect is to retroactively deflect hardcore's will-to-knowledge into what *Variety* dubbed a "mini-Pirandelloesque" examination of desire's false fronts and decoys.[41] The *Deep Throat* quest to uncover the "truth" of female sexuality gets displaced onto a play of mediated simulations, culminating in a sex scene that reenacts the film's play of facades as cinematic self-reflexivity: the Manns' bedroom becomes an impromptu movie theater as Pamela screws her husband to the accompaniment of the detective's footage of her earlier encounters projected on the wall (figure 3.3). The detective's attempt to uncover the "essence" of Pamela Mann ultimately leads him nowhere: "Everything she does is anonymous," he concludes. "There's no identity."

Pamela Mann debuted in New York on December 24, 1974, at Times Square's World Theatre, where it was immediately recognized as a vanguard for narrative sophistication in hardcore. Rocco Bonelli at *Screw* affirmed it as "the best porno film to date . . . [having] little resemblance to what we think of as a hard-core flick," and Al Goldstein selected it as *Screw*'s film of the year, a distinction also bestowed by adult-film periodical *Adam Film World*.[42] "Most porn films have a one-idea premise that serves as an excuse for continuous 'loops'—sex scenes," wrote a reviewer for the porn magazine *Flick*, adding that "*Pamela Mann* is notable because it gives us . . . a lot of humor and clever plot twists to keep us entertained between the loops."[43] Even mainstream periodicals like the *Independent Film Journal* acknowledged *Pamela*'s distinction, describing it as "one of the more interesting porno flicks to come down the pike."[44] The film was also more profitable than any film Metzger had directed to date: shot on Super 16mm on a budget that the director recalled merely as "modest," *Pamela Mann* pulled over $350,000 during its thirteen-week run at the World alone and went on to enjoy successful runs in other cities over the course of 1975.[45] According to *BoxOffice* magazine's metrics—which measure performance as a percentage of "normal" performance per theater—*Pamela Mann* started its run at the World outperforming *every other film* then in release in New York City. The only notable bumps in the road, in fact, were abroad: it was banned outright in London and cut in Sweden to eliminate a disturbing and tonally jarring scene in which Pamela is kidnapped and raped by two radicals.[46] (Like the other sexual encounters in the film, this one has been staged by Pamela and her husband: the radicals are later revealed to have been the Manns' maid and driver in disguise, played by Darby Lloyd Rains and Jamie Gillis respectively. Yet the spectator doesn't know this during the scene itself, which, in consequence, reads as a very violent rape. Metzger himself would later seek to downplay the scene's offensive impact by claiming that he "never thought of it as a rape scene." But this was disingenuous. He didn't really care one way or the other, as is clear from his made-for-cable compilation film, *The World of Henry Paris* [1981], in which he included the sequence as a stand-alone without bothering to include the play-acting reveal.)[47] Metzger had in any case surprised himself: on a bare-bones six-day shoot he had turned out the most profitable film in his directing career so far, and he had done so with a plot that riffed off the pseudonymous conditions of the film's own making.

Something similar might be said of the director's next foray into hardcore, *Naked Came the Stranger*, only with the proviso that the motif of pretense here registers less as a plot device *within* the film, but rather *intertextually*, that is, in the relations the film flags with other texts. Unlike *Pamela Mann*, Metzger's second hardcore title was a literary adaptation, specifically of a best-selling erotic novel of the same name that had been rumored for film adaptation since its successful release in the summer of 1969. That novel was an infamous, sex-in-the-suburbs potboiler that, at its peak, reached third place on the *New York Times* best-seller list, and, by the time Metzger began filming, had been through three paperback printings at Dell Publishing (figure 3.4).[48] In later years, Metzger explained his interest in the novel in terms of its sketch-like structure, which, he argued, lent itself to the format of a hardcore film.[49] What likely added extra appeal, though, was the fact that the novel offered a playful experiment in pseudonymity that mirrored Metzger's own situation during this period. *Naked Came the Stranger*, the book, had first been released under the name of one "Penelope Ashe," described on the back cover as a "demure Long Island housewife," with an accompanying photograph of her stroking a Russian wolfhound. But the woman depicted was not Penelope Ashe, who did not exist, but one Billie Young, and the actual writing of the book was by a team of twenty-four *Newsday* journalists, each responsible for a chapter, under the direction of columnist Mike

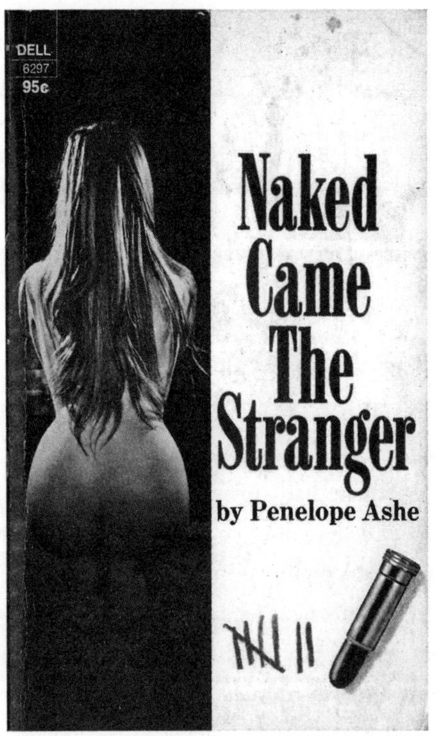

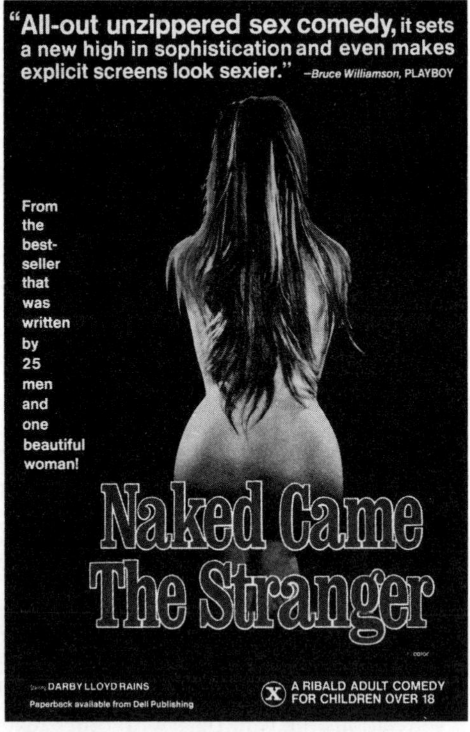

3.4 From book to film. Book cover (*left*) and poster (*right*) for *Naked Came the Stranger*.
Source: (*left*) Courtesy of Barricade Books; (*right*) Author's collection.

McGrady, Young's brother-in-law, who had asked her to be the media "face" of the project. McGrady's plan had been to spoof the American public's literary standards by trying to make a bestseller out of intentionally awful writing. (As he put it in a memo to his writers, "true excellence in writing will be quickly blue-penciled into oblivion.")[50] The book's unexpected success gave dramatic proof of McGrady's concept—and an object lesson, perhaps, for a filmmaker who was beginning to play his own pseudonymous games.

The pseudonymity of the novel was in one respect quite different from that of Metzger's Henry Paris films. For McGrady's joke to work, the novel's authorship had to be revealed, which occurred in August 1969, when nine of the novel's male writers were introduced on *The David Frost Show* as "Penelope Ashe," walking on stage to the tune of "A Pretty Girl Is Like a Melody."[51] Metzger, by contrast, was more reluctant to reveal himself at this point, for reasons discussed at the beginning of this chapter. At the same time, Metzger's pseudonymity also *resembled* that of the *Newsday* writers in the way it gave him scope for creative gameplay. Just as McGrady and his team used "Penelope Ashe" as a license for the fun of bad writing, so Metzger used "Henry Paris" to experiment with an atypically (for him) playful style of cinephile reflexivity. More akin to the freewheeling spirit of a French New Wave film like François Truffaut's *Tirez sur le pianiste* (1960) than to the self-serious art cinema that had previously been his model, Metzger's *Naked Came the Stranger* abounds in winking nods to its own processes of cinematic artifice. This is not just because of the numerous callouts to classic Hollywood film—Astaire and Rogers in particular are frequently invoked—but because of the way the film's leads, married radio hosts Billy and Gilly (Levi Richards and Darby Lloyd Rains), toy with the film's signifying conventions: Gilly, for instance, repeatedly breaks the fourth wall to address the camera and, at one point, seems to control the film's musical soundtrack, calling out "Music!" as she plots her extramarital affairs. She also manages to turn the film into a silent movie when, during a tryst with the Valentinoesque-named "Sheikh" (played by Gerald Grant, from *Score*), she declares her desire to "go back to a simpler time." The film's diegetic sound suddenly goes mute, the color photography switches to sepia, and title cards substitute for audible dialog (including one that reads "Shoot it in my wet cunt"—words that likely had never appeared on a silent-movie title card before!). Metzger even sneaks in a clue to his authorship when Billy and Gilly watch the filmmaker's own *Camille 2000* (1969) on television in a concluding bedroom scene that, like *Pamela*'s, centers on an act of spectatorship.

"Why don't they show the Garbo version?" Billy complains. No other Metzger picture is so wittily engaged in its own status as a film.

Naked was, in every respect, an attempt to step up in scale following Metzger's success with *Pamela Mann*. Its production budget was unprecedented for a hardcore film—with some reports even making the unlikely claim of $300,000 and above—which the director showcased in the film's elaborate settings and locations: a waterfront mansion in King's Point, New York, the ballroom of the Hotel St. George in Brooklyn Heights, even a rented London double-decker bus, on which the director shot a sex scene as it drove up and down New York's Fifth Avenue.[52] The tie-in with the novel also boosted the film's visibility in the mainstream press—making *Naked Came the Stranger* the unique case of a hardcore film that was also a presold property—as did the premiere on May 21, 1975 at the World Theatre, to which Metzger cheekily invited the *Newsday* writers without alerting them to the film's explicitness. ("There were quite a few of us," McGrady later recalled. "Unfortunately, we brought our wives and it was a hardcore movie.")[53] These factors made *Naked Came the Stranger* another huge moneymaker, its eventual fifteen-week run at the World even topping *Pamela Mann*'s gross to the tune of around $430,000.

Yet despite Metzger's evidently broadening ambitions in hardcore, *Naked Came the Stranger* remained thematically of a piece with the earlier film. Just as *Pamela Mann* had been a film about people putting each other on, so *Naked* was itself a kind of con, or rather a nested series of cons, extending metatextually from the original *Newsday* hoax, through the film's own peekaboo pseudonymity, and on to the gag of its premiere, in which the original tricksters were tricked in turn. A wittily pseudonymous riff on an infamously pseudonymous novel, *Naked Came the Stranger* was appropriately marketed in its trailer as a "put-on of a put-on" and reviewed as an "all-out spoof of pornography."[54] It is as though Metzger's initial Henry Paris films simply could not stop sounding the alert as to their own charade, flagging masquerade not just as the condition of their authorship but as a term in their textuality too. To what end, though?

"SOME FUN AT GUESSING GAMES": DIONYMITY AND *THE IMAGE*

One clue to an answer can be found in literary theorist Gérard Genette's essay "The Name of the Author," from his collection of essays *Paratexts*, in particular his reflections on what he calls the "pseudonym effect." This "pseudonym effect" occurs in situations when a reader—Genette discusses only literary examples—is aware of the fact of a pseudonym, aware, that is, that a pseudonym is being used, irrespective of whether the reader knows the author's real identity or not. In the case of not knowing, the pseudonym-effect functions equivalently to anonymity in that it provokes curiosity about who the author might be. In the other instance, when the reader *does* have the information, "the pseudonym is included in his [the reader's] image, or idea, of that particular author, so that inevitably (although in varying degrees from reader to reader) he considers pseudonym and patronymic [i.e., the real name] together."[55] What Genette calls "single pseudonymity" (as per "Henry Paris") splits, in this latter case, into what he calls "dionymity" (to produce "Paris/Metzger"), whose function is to imply an operation of self-differentiation within the author's body of work. What Genette is pointing to may be banal in the case of porn: we are familiar with the way in which porn pseudonyms shape on-set identities that performers keep separate from their private selves. The question, though, is what such self-differentiation accomplished in the case of the Paris/Metzger dionym?

Consider, in this respect, the aforementioned *The Image*—an adaptation of *another* famously pseudonymous text, Jean de Berg's 1956 S/M novel *L'Image*, published by Éditions de Minuit—which was the one picture released under Metzger's own name during his Henry Paris period.[56] A coproduction with French sexploitation director Max Pécas's Les Films du Griffon, the film was shot in August of 1973, nearly a full year before the director's hardcore turn.[57] (The shoot involved a week in Paris for exteriors and a party scene, and—bizarrely—five days in the New York City townhouse of notorious attorney Roy Cohn, where Metzger filmed a variety of interiors, including the dungeon where the S/M games are played.)[58] But it was released much later, hitting the screens of New York's Eastside Cinema and the Bryan West on February 4, 1976, a little more than a month before Metzger's third Henry Paris film, *The Opening of Misty Beethoven*, debuted at the World on March 18—so that in fact both *Misty* and *The Image* were in first-run release in New York at the very same time.[59] What is it, then, that gives *The Image* the Metzger stamp while *Misty* is a Henry Paris production? Three hypotheses can bring the stakes of the Paris/Metzger dionym into focus.

1. Perhaps the film bears Metzger's name because it was in keeping with the strategies of literary adaptation that established his reputation in the late 1960s. For *The Image*, Metzger opted to follow his approach to his earlier adaptation of *Thérèse and Isabelle* (1968): passages from the source text are lifted verbatim for

the film's voiceover narration, this time with the addition of chapter headings that correspond precisely to those in de Berg's novel. Metzger was also following the template of *Thérèse* by capitalizing on the countercultural cachet of underground literature. S/M themes had begun to achieve a particular prominence within the literary underground in the years leading up to Metzger's production of *The Image*. These were years in which Grove Press began publication of a three-volume set of the writings of the Marquis de Sade (in honor of the 150th anniversary of Sade's death) while the Evergreen Book Club released English translations of both *L'Image* itself and its equally pseudonymous S/M predecessor, Pauline Réage's 1954 *Story of O*.[60] Both *L'Image* and *O* were swiftly enshrined as key literary reference points in debates about the possibilities of pornographic art, whether in the affirmative (as in Susan Sontag's 1967 essay "The Pornographic Imagination," which treated the books as exemplars of "psychic disorientation" in modernist art) or in the negative (in Andrea Dworkin's 1974 *Woman Hating*, whose discussion of these books reads as a thinly veiled critique of Sontag for the "double think" of confusing woman's sexual subordination as "mystic experience").[61] Both, moreover, constituted a new front in the taste politics of erotica to which Metzger may have wanted to add his name.

The politics of naming is in fact important for understanding how Metzger's *The Image* relates to *L'Image*. The original publication of *L'Image* was not just pseudonymous but, in its initial printing by Éditions de Minuit, self-consciously evoked the "pseudonym effect" by means of a preface by Pauline Réage herself, who relished the opportunity to extend the rampant speculation to which her own book had been subject to another's: "Who is Jean de Berg?" she wrote. "This question gives me a chance to have some fun at guessing games." The novel's first-person narration—a supposed record of "Jean de Berg's" exploits with a dominatrix and her sex slave—was not, in Réage's view, to be trusted: "I doubt that a man could be responsible for this volume. It sides far too often with the women's point of view."[62] Promotional material for Metzger's adaptation further underscored the mystery in a pressbook that reprinted Réage's preface, adding: "Today, two decades after these words were written, few know for sure whether Jean de Berg is the pseudonym of a male or female. The most persistent rumor would have it that 'THE IMAGE' was the effort of a collaboration between one of France's leading novelists and his wife or mistress, while another rumor, almost as stubborn, claims authorship for Réage herself." (The "most persistent rumor" is closest to the truth: *L'Image* was written by Cathérine Rstakian, who, the year after publication, married novelist Alain Robbe-Grillet, taking his name.)[63] In the case of the *film* adaptation, by contrast, Metzger's name is appended in an unusually grandiloquent style, with the credit title "Directed by Radley Metzger" withheld until the film's very last moment, somewhat akin to Orson Welles's directorial credit at the end of *Citizen Kane* (1941). In a total reversal of his approach to *Naked Came the Stranger*, Metzger refuses to extend the original novel's pseudonym effect to his own directorial authorship, opting instead to assert his name with unavoidable finality, immediately after "The End" appears on screen.

This difference of approach begs to be interpreted in relation to distinctions of perceived literary value as they relate to gender: if, in the case of *Naked Came the Stranger*, Metzger wanted to join the *Newsday* writers' boys-club parodic masquerade of woman-authored erotica, then with *L'Image*, he appropriated a work of genuine woman-authored erotica to his own authorial signature, much as he had done with *Thérèse and Isabelle*. This dynamic was also in play in the tie-in republication of *The Image* by Grove Press, in which Metzger finally closed the circle he had been pacing around Rosset's organization for the better part

3.5 Front cover of Grove Press's 1975 version of *The Image* "with over 60 photographs by Radley Metzger."
Source: Author's collection.

of a decade: released some months ahead of Metzger's film and boasting over sixty production stills, Grove's publication actually *made no explicit reference to the movie*, but instead presented the illustrations as "an extraordinary series of photographs by Radley Metzger"—as though Metzger had been conscripted by Grove to create a *fumetti* version of de Berg's novel.[64] The reprint in this way does double duty, both as a literary work on de Berg's part and as testimony to Metzger's photographic artistry, with both artists' names prominently featured on the book's cover (figure 3.5).

Yet at this point our initial hypothesis needs emendation, for the truth is that Metzger's proclivities for literary adaptation extended into his Henry Paris work, too, not just in *Naked Came the Stranger* but also in *Misty Beethoven*, which was a "hardcore updating" of George Bernard Shaw's 1913 *Pygmalion* (and thus a return of sorts to the more middlebrow leanings that had guided Metzger's choice of literary sources in *Carmen, Baby* [1967] and *Camille 2000*).[65] The practice of adaptation, in and of itself, is not sufficient to differentiate "Radley Metzger" from "Henry Paris," such that an alternative vector of distinction will need to be found.

2. A second hypothesis shifts attention from the literary sources themselves to the sexual acts they depicted. That is to say, perhaps *The Image* got the Metzger stamp because it was a film about S/M at a time when texts like *O* and *L'Image* had established S/M as the royal road to the kind of erotic legitimacy to which Metzger aspired. Fueled in part by Grove Press's publication of Sade's writings, sadomasochism had been one of the lodestones of the vulgar modernism discussed in this book's first chapter. Sade himself became what historian Elisabeth Ladenson describes as a "sort of libertine Dalai Lama" for the counterculture; and it was Sade who Sontag evoked as a precursor in her essay defending the novels of Réage and de Berg as "serious literature."[66] Even though the advent of theatrical hardcore in the early 1970s took the shine of this vulgar modernist ferment, Sadean themes continued to carry the torch of ongoing efforts to legitimize explicit film for a "class" audience. The years surrounding *The Image*'s release represented a mini-"vogue" for S/M films across the art-sex spectrum—whether in art-house titles like Liliana Cavani's *The Night Porter* (1974) or Pier Paolo Pasolini's *Salò* (1976, itself based on Sade's unfinished novel *The 120 Days of Sodom*), in European softcore releases like Just Jaeckin's Réage adaptation *Story of O* (1975), or in homegrown hardcore films like Alex de Renzy's *Femmes de Sade* (1976), prompting pornographic magazines to publish think pieces with titles like "Porn's Most Popular Perversion" (in *Screw*), "The Big Bondage Boom" (in *Adam*

Film World), "America Is Bullish on S/M" (in *High Society*), or "S-and-M: Porn's New Brand of Pleasure" (in *Porno Movie Girls*).[67] The first of these pieces explicitly tied the "kinky new S&M fad" to cultural legitimacy, linking hardcore titles like *The Naughty Victorians* (1975), *The Journey of O* (1976), and Jerry Damiano's *Story of Joanna* (1975), to the porn industry's ambitions to "gain . . . some respectability and a new, though possibly fleeting, audience of females." (The article also noted that both *O* and *Joanna* premiered in New York at "posh uptown locations"—the Baronet and the RKO 59th St. respectively—and went so far as to brand the S/M vogue a "whole new fashion in fuck films for females.")[68] The *High Society* article, meanwhile, noted with astonishment the mainstreaming of S/M in media on both sides of the Atlantic:

> The hottest box office attraction [of the recent spate of S/M films] is the legendary underground classic *The Story of O*. The movie was prefaced with a nationwide controversy in France, which received wide play in American news magazines. The French newsweekly *L'Express* carried the whip-marked star of *O*, Corinne Cléry on its cover and, to further boost reader interest, carried a serialization of the twenty-year-old book in subsequence editions. . . . *O* sold more tickets during its first two weeks in New York theatres than *M*A*S*H*, *Serpico* or *Murder on the Orient Express*. This happened despite internationally rotten reviews. Worse still, the panning uniformly complained that the movie *O* was simply not kinky enough! . . .
>
> Avoiding these pitfalls, director Gerard Damiano . . . released *The Story of Joanna* which scored the coveted "100 percent" on Al Goldstein's Peter-Meter with its "explicit, powerhouse S&M scenes" and its thesis of "sex as torture."[69]

As with the "bisexual chic" of *Score*, Metzger seems with *The Image* to have been capitalizing on sexual practices that were enjoying a "faddish" moment in the broader culture. Indeed, there is some irony in the fact that *The Image* would have been at the very forefront of the mid-1970s cycle of S/M films, had not Metzger's turn to hardcore delayed the film's release. As Metzger himself would later recall, "Between our acquisition of the book rights and the making of the film, *The Story of O* was released. It was very successful at the box office. . . . I preferred our film, but it suffered from being released at the same time."[70] In an alternate universe, an earlier release of *The Image* might have restored Metzger to the kind of tastemaker stature that directors like

Damiano, on the hardcore side, and Jaeckin, on the softcore, had since wrested from him. He might have been the doyen of a new front in the pursuit of erotic legitimacy, rather than the apparent bandwagon-jumper that the porno chic era was turning him into.

Yet insofar as S/M films thus existed on both sides of the hardcore/softcore divide, the sadomasochistic vogue of the mid-1970s actually obscures rather than clarifies the stakes of the Paris/Metzger dionym. The erotic capital of S/M was as evident in hardcore films like Damiano's *Story of Joanna* as it was in Metzger's *The Image*, and Metzger exploited the fad in his "Henry Paris" films too, in the bondage scenes that culminate both *Barbara Broadcast* and *Maraschino Cherry*.[71] S/M does not divide "Radley Metzger" from "Henry Paris" but is instead one of their points of contact.

3. Perhaps, then, the key issue is that *The Image* is simply *not* a hardcore film, inasmuch as it lacks the established generic signifiers of meat shots (close-ups of genital penetration) and money shots.[72] But it is difficult to maintain a line in the sand here, too. *The Image* troubled the softcore/hardcore distinction by including two scenes of unsimulated oral sex and one of explicit female urination, the latter of which goes far beyond what is described in the book and would have pushed boundaries even in hardcore.[73] (For example, Metzger's later *Barbara Broadcast* features a urination scene—no more or less explicit than in *The Image*—which was cut from VCA's 1989 VHS and 2000 DVD releases of the film, apparently deemed too perverse for a home audience.)[74] Metzger himself described *The Image* as the film in which he fully "relented" in the face of the hardcore boom, and a number of critics agreed: *Variety* described the film as "a Radley Metzger hardcore filmization [*sic*] of the Jean de Berg novel," and the adult magazine *After Dark* labeled it "openly hard core."[75] In his annual *Playboy* review of "Sex in Cinema," USC film scholar Arthur Knight paired *The Image* with *The Opening of Misty Beethoven* as "two triple-X films" by Radley Metzger.[76] Others, meanwhile, have considered *The Image* a more liminal or hybrid text—again, like *Score*, too explicit for softcore but not consistently explicit enough to be hard. No less an authority than Mr. Ten-and-a-Half himself, Marc Stevens, puzzled over the line that Metzger seemed to be drawing in a review of *The Image* in *Screw* magazine. Perhaps feeling burned that Metzger withheld his proper name from the films in which Stevens had performed, the actor held nothing back in a withering critique of the director's artistic affectations.[77] "What a fucking disappointment," he opined, lambasting Metzger for his "hypocritical horseshit." "Just because, in

The Image, the view of the chick's head is blocked while she's sucking cock . . . doesn't seem to me to be grounds for the difference between soft- and hardcore."[78] Archer Winsten of the *New York Post* responded more favorably, praising the film's "prying camera eye" for showing "just enough restraint to avoid the hard-core label."[79] More recently, porn scholar and historian Whitney Strub has described the film as "quasi-hardcore."[80]

It is worth mentioning that the "view of the woman's head" so desired by Stevens was actually *not* blocked in Metzger's original cut, although it does appear that the director prepared "hot" and "cold" versions of his film. According to one press report, a milder version was readied for international distribution and for conservative U.S. regions; according to another, a hardcore version was screened for critics in January 1976, but the film was recut as softcore for its actual release.[81] The latter report, if true, might explain why most critics noted an explicitness that Stevens, whose review came out weeks after the film's release, claimed not to be there. But it also demonstrates the extent to which the hardcore/softcore divide was, in practice, a leaky distinction that does not easily map onto the Paris/Metzger dionym. With *The Image*, Metzger was negotiating the market for hardcore film on his own terms; if those terms do not easily line up with formal generic categories, then we will want to look more closely at the films themselves with a view to questioning those categories.

"FORGIVE ME FOR I KNOW WHAT I DO": TABOO VS. THE CARNIVALESQUE

But there is one more hypothesis worth proposing, the most banal of all: *The Image* bears Metzger's name simply because it was shot before he had adopted the Henry Paris subterfuge and so could hardly have been conceived by him as anything *but* a Radley Metzger film. The reason for the film's delayed release, in this connection, bespoke no strategy of conscious product differentiation on Metzger's part, but was simply the same thing that led him to adopt the Henry Paris pseudonym in the first place: *Miller v. California*. "In the middle of shooting [*The Image*], the Supreme Court came down saying that you couldn't shoot erotic movies," Metzger later explained. "We were nervous because this was a film that was dealing with subject matter far more controversial than the typical erotic film. Nothing came from the decision, but we were held up. It took a little longer than the other films. In the meantime, we shot *The Private Afternoons of Pamela Mann*. We had to come back and finish *The Image*."[82]

This, at least, gives us the practical realities of the situation, yet at the high cost of absconding any further grounds beyond which *The Image* might be distinguished from the Henry Paris films. Yet the evidence is clear that Metzger *did* think of hardcore as fundamentally different from the kind of filmmaking to which he had previously attached his name. In a *Film Comment* interview published in January 1973—the very month Ralph Blumenthal coined the term "porno chic"—critic Richard Corliss invited Metzger to reflect on the growing market for hardcore. "This is [the] fundamental principle of hardcore," Metzger announced: "You have to go to a hard-core picture with the feeling that you're doing something illegal," although he added that the mainstream success of *Deep Throat* "may start a trend toward better production values." Later, asked whether the hardcore market was simply giving "the old soft-core audience . . . what it always wanted" or whether there was a "section of the old Audubon audience" that felt left out, Metzger reflected that both are "probably true," explaining: "I'm not sure that hard-core isn't more in the 'carnival' area, where you see stunts. I don't mean this as a put-down of hard-core, because I love it. Part of one's filmgoing should certainly include hard-core pornography, when it's done even reasonably well. But I think hard-core is designed less to turn you on and more to shock. I don't think it works you up."[83]

A sense of illegality and the ethos of carnival: together, these insights mark out a terrain in which sexual taboos are freely—indeed, ebulliently—disregarded, in defiance of what conventions permit. One is reminded perhaps of literary theorist Mikhail Bakhtin's celebrated concept of the "carnivalesque," first proposed in his 1968 study of medieval festivities, *Rabelais and His World*. Carnival, Bakhtin argued there, provided an important safety valve within the regimented social order of feudal Europe, a designated space of temporary release from social norms and convention: it "celebrated temporary liberation . . . from the established order" and "marked the suspension of all hierarchical rank, privileges, norms, and prohibitions."[84] Even more to the point, Bakhtin associated carnival with an exuberant celebration of the "bodily element." The carnivalesque body, he argued,

> is unfinished, outgrows itself, transgresses its own limits. The stress is laid on those parts of the body that are open to the outside world, that is, the

> parts through which the world enters the body or emerges from it, or through which the body itself goes out to meet the world. . . . The body discloses its essence as a principle of growth which exceeds its own limits only in copulation, pregnancy, childbirth, the throes of death, eating, drinking, or defecation.[85]

Within the study of popular film genres, the concept of the carnivalesque has most often been applied to comedy, but it is no stretch to see its application to the sphere of hardcore pornography: the clown and the porn star each "body forth" behaviors in defiance of normative conventions of comportment and restraint, albeit in self-evidently different ways. But might carnival also be the key for unlocking the Paris/Metzger dionym? Certainly the "Henry Paris" films are funny in a way that the "Radley Metzger" titles—with the single exception of *Score*—are not. Metzger approached his hardcore films *as* comedies (describing *Barbara Broadcast*, for example, as a "light comedy film") and the pictures were marketed accordingly: the trailer for *Naked Came the Stranger* sold the film as "The Turn-On Comedy of the Year," while radio spots described *Maraschino Cherry* as the "hardcore comedy hit of the year."[86] "The world of Henry Paris is the world of the running gag," summarizes the voiceover narrator of Metzger's compilation film *The World of Henry Paris*, which also describes the carnivalesque way in which "socially acceptable behavior and socially shocking behavior become interchangeable" in these films.[87]

Bawdy humor had been a feature of pornography since the earliest stag films, but, as Constance Penley notes, this had tended to drop out of the porno chic era, when aspirations to legitimation often resulted in a self-seriousness that mitigated against humor (at least of the intentional kind).[88] As critic Richard Milner declared in adult magazine *Stag*, most porn producers operated on the principle—a mistaken one, in Milner's opinion—that "you can't laugh and get hot at the same time."[89] Not so Metzger, though, whose more serious aspirations were safely parceled away in his orthonymic releases and who, in consequence, gave free rein in the Henry Paris films to a hitherto unsuspected predilection for punning dialog and wordplay. "I really wanted to keep alive the tradition of Borscht Belt humor," he explained of his hardcore scripts, penned under another pseudonym, Jake Barnes—which is itself a gag, albeit in rather poor taste, using the name of the impotent protagonist of Ernest Hemingway's 1926 novel *The Sun Also Rises*.[90] (It's worth noting that Metzger's puns are usually groaningly bad, as per this exchange between two women in *Maraschino Cherry*. "If they won't accept you as a lesbian, why do you go out with them?" "Well, if you can't join 'em, lick 'em.") Tellingly, when porn producer Bob Sumner argued that comedy ought to be embraced by adult filmmakers, rather than avoided, fully half of the six "successful X-film comedies" he pointed to were Henry Paris films: *The Private Afternoons of Pamela Mann*, *Naked Came the Stranger*, and *Misty Beethoven* (the others being *Deep Throat* and two of Sumner's own productions, *Take Off* [1978] and *Bon Appetit* [1980]).[91] Along similar lines, *Adam Film World* cited the Henry Paris films as a repudiation of the "old pet theory . . . that any injection of sexy humor detracts from the erotic arousal value of the sex action on screen."[92]

We will return to the comedic aspect of Metzger's Henry Paris films in the next chapter. For it is not only humor that matters here but also the different way taboo functions on either side of Paris/Metzger dionym. One way to think about hardcore pornography, after all, is as a form that lacks the pressure of taboo, which is the source of its anything-goes brazenness. (As scholar Joel Kovel nicely puts it, "One of the essential features of pornography is the Commandment: Thou shalt not be ashamed.")[93] This is less because the plots of hardcore films are necessarily about the *conquest* of shame—although they may be, as in the Mitchell Brothers' *Behind the Green Door*—but more commonly because the absence of shame is a de facto convention of the films' narrative worlds, which is the case with the Henry Paris films, too. The carnivalesque aspect of hardcore thus registers in the oft-derided license of the form in which, infamously, it is always bedtime, the men infinitely potent, the women inexhaustibly lusting.[94] But none of this really applies to Metzger's orthonymic films from the porno chic era, which tend to operate in a register for which taboo is more strongly inscribed and shame more strongly felt—whether dramatically, in the hesitancy and self-questioning that accompany sadomasochistic pleasure in *The Image*, or playfully, in the dumbstruck bewilderment of the younger couple during the spousal swapping of *Score*.

Taboo also played an important role in broader discussions of pornography's relation to art during this period, courtesy in large part of the writing of French philosopher Georges Bataille, whose work first entered into English translation in the mid-1950s. It had been Bataille's contention in his 1957 study *L'érotisme*, first published in English by City Lights in 1962, that taboo was the essential catalyst for eroticism: "Unless the taboo is observed with fear," Bataille wrote, "it lacks the counterpoise of desire which gives it its deepest signification."[95] Genuine eroticism, for Bataille, was not that which blithely ignores taboo but instead acknowledges it and is piqued by its shaming force. And it was Bataille to whom Susan Sontag had deferred in her essay on pornography, where she described him as the "writer who works with a darker sense of the erotic . . . than probably anyone." Sontag's defense of *L'image* and *Story of O* as artistic works that "push[ed] at intervals close to taboo and dangerous desires" simply could not have been made outside of her exposure to Bataille's thought.[96] What Bataille demonstrated was a way to reclaim certain "pornographic" works to a modernist aesthetic that brokered in extreme forms of human consciousness. His work suggested a new way of differentiating between works of adult literature, not in terms of their explicitness (as in the conventional softcore/hardcore binary), but rather in the way that sexual fantasy relates to taboo—the distinction, that is, between a "dangerous" and destabilizing Bataillean eroticism, on the one hand, and a blithely carnivalesque porn, on the other. Bataille had himself already anticipated something of this in *L'érotisme* when he differentiated the uniquely human experience of a of a "primary anguish bound up with sexual disturbance" from an animal sexuality that meets no barrier of resistance or shame, much as Sontag, in her essay, distinguished an erotic "art" that explores the "psychology of lust" from a pornographic "trash" that deals only in "tireless transactions" between sex organs.[97] Erotica, on this definition, is not necessarily a matter of tastefulness, nor does it necessarily lack "hard" imagery; rather, what defines it is the way fantasy gets braided around taboos whose power is accepted, rather than ignored.[98]

Historians of adult film have tended to be skittish around the kinds of distinctions that Sontag and Bataille invoke here, which have been fairly criticized as "vaguely subjective" and "leaky" (and thus hardly a basis for a soberly academic classification of adult materials).[99] But vague subjectivity is no fault when one is dealing with the forms of differentiation that are produced within a single artist's body of work, regardless of the labels used to describe them. The fact is that no other classification makes clearer sense of the Paris/Metzger dionym in terms of what distinguishes *The Image* from the Henry Paris films. To see this, it is enough to consider how taboo gets engaged in the former film. In its most basic form, the plot of *The Image* concerns a man's induction into S/M practice and, as such, is fundamentally *about* the confrontation with taboo. But the conceit of

3.6 Claire (Marilyn Roberts) inspects the submissive Anne (Mary Mendum) in a production still from *The Image*.
Source: Author's collection.

the narrative, as will become clear, is that this is not just the man's story, but one in which his experience acts as a catalyst for the taboo desires of others, each unlocking the next in a *matryoshka*-like process.

The opening scenes to *The Image* set these dynamics in motion. A writer, Jean (Carl Parker), meets an old acquaintance, Claire (Marilyn Roberts), at a literary soirée in Paris. Jean's voiceover informs us that, though he liked Claire, her impeccable manners and steely disposition were a turnoff. "I probably needed to feel that at least some little thing was vulnerable in order to arouse a desire in me to win her." Claire's younger friend, Anne (Mary Mendum, Metzger's then girlfriend), is by contrast vulnerability incarnate, as becomes clear the day after the party, when Jean joins the two of them for a tour of the Bagatelle Gardens. There Claire humiliates Anne, forcing her to raise her skirt in front of Jean and urinate on a rose. Claire, Jean learns, is in fact Anne's dominatrix, and she invites Jean to participate in the punishment she inflicts on Anne (figure 3.6).

3.7 Jean (Carl Parker) observing Anne's (Mary Mendum) humiliation. Screen captures from *The Image*.

Each of the film's three protagonists is, in different ways, locked into a state of unresolved desire that hesitates before fulfillment. The film's focus falls first on Jean's desire for Anne as the object of his nascent sadism. This is a desire that has to be taught: Claire instructs Jean in both the pleasure of dominating Anne and Anne's pleasure in being so dominated. "She likes doing that, you know," Claire explains at the rose garden. "I can prove it to you if you like. At the slightest provocation she gets all wet." For most of the film's first act, however, Jean remains in a state of mortified fascination, a spectator to Claire's cruelty, himself unwilling to take the step that would convert his own desire into action. "I can lend her to you, my dear, with no trouble at all," Claire explains after the incident at the rose garden. "You can make love to her if you're in that mood." "Thanks," Jean replies, "but I wouldn't know how to reciprocate." Jean's watching is less a matter of voyeuristic control than of a kind of hesitancy or disenfranchisement at taboo's threshold—an effect that Metzger underscores in framings that demote Jean to the rear plane of the image, uneasily looking upward or askance at the humiliating displays that Claire orchestrates from the foreground (figure 3.7).[100]

This kind of stalling of sexual affect, simultaneously awakened and arrested in a single act of perception, had been a hallmark of Metzger's representations of queer desire in films like *The Alley Cats* (1966), *Thérèse and Isabelle*, and *Score*. In *The Image*, however, it serves rather to interrupt the operations of a heterosexuality that in the Henry Paris films converts more smoothly into fulfillment and climax. Immobilized, Jean's desire is left to roil—memorably in a montage sequence in which his memories of Anne peeing are intercut with pluming

3.8 Jean assumes the controlling position in a turning-point scene. Screen captures from *The Image*.

Parisian fountains—until Claire eventually encourages him to be more than just an observer. In the film's turning-point scene, Claire forces Anne to undress before Jean and kneel between his legs while she first whips her and then, crouching down, chains her to his chair. Here Metzger's staging inverts his previous pattern to finally endow Jean's desire with a controlling force: it is Anne and Claire who now look upward at Jean, who converts affect into action, forcing Anne to take his penis in her mouth as he throws his head back, rejoicing (figure 3.8). From here on out the relation between the threesome changes: Jean now becomes a participant in Claire's sadistic games, not just their audience.

But *The Image* is more than a story about Jean's embrace of repressed sadism. The scene of Jean's conversion introduces another trajectory of desire that will braid uneasily with his own; namely, Anne's desire for her own ritual punishment. Throughout the film, Anne is, as Linda Williams puts it, a "cipher," a largely mute character who only once indicates a desire that is actively of her own making.[101] That moment occurs during her own passage through taboo, when, after first being whipped before Jean, she is commanded to choose the chain by which she will be bound to his chair. In one of Metzger's most exactingly conceived mirror shots, Anne's face is first seen in dim reflection, sobbing haltingly before the glass door of a cabinet containing S/M paraphernalia (figure 3.9). As she makes her choice and reaches into the cabinet, her reflection moves offscreen right, replaced by her hand, fingers outstretched, taking one of the chains down from its hook. The camera pans right to show her clutching the chain to her breast, but her sobs now shade into moans and her face hardens into a glowering smile. "Forgive me," she says firmly, her eyes meeting the camera. "For I know what I do."

1.3 Lobby card for *Sexus*.

Source: Author's collection.

1.8 Poster for *I, a Woman*.

Source: Author's collection.

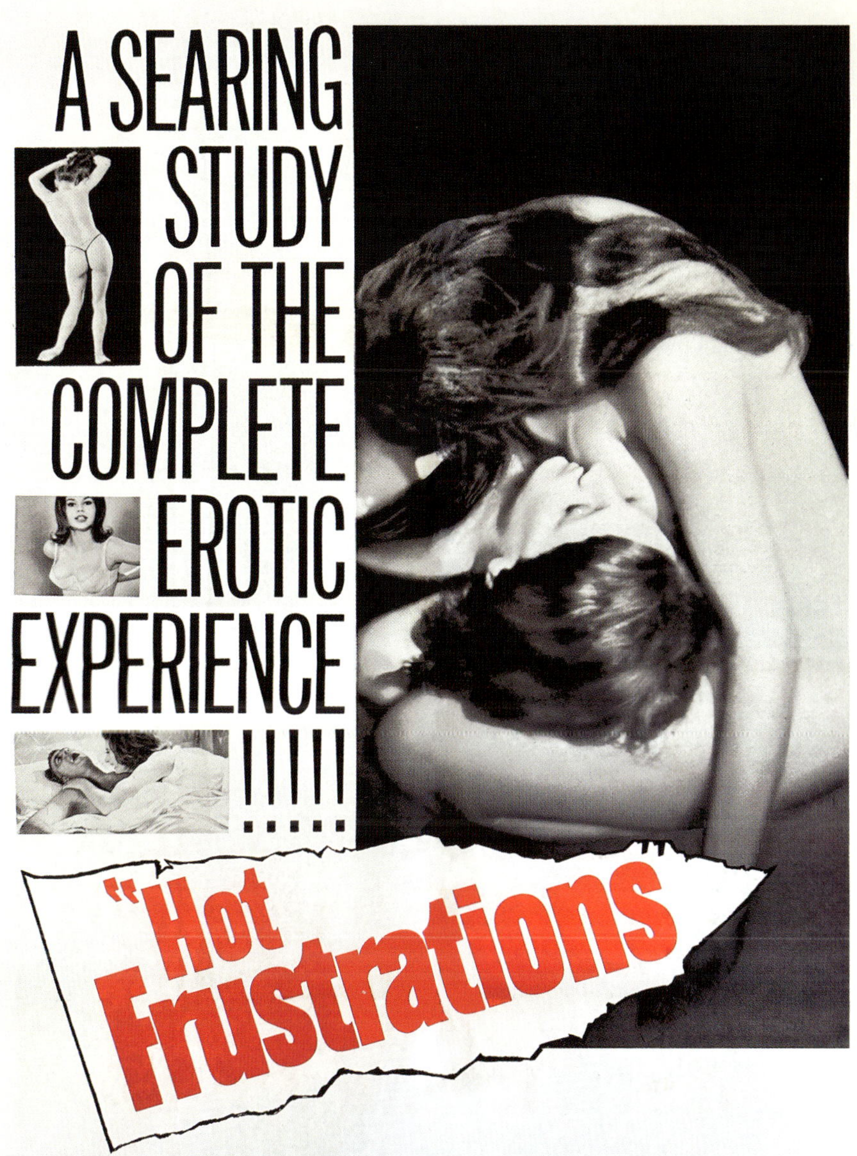

1.9 Audubon's new logo in the bottom-right corner of the poster for *Hot Frustrations*. Compare the cursive logo in figure 1.8.

Source: Author's collection.

1.14 Sex refracted through colored glasses in a single tracking shot. Screenshots from *Carmen, Baby*.

1.15 Poster for *Camille 2000*.

Source: Author's collection.

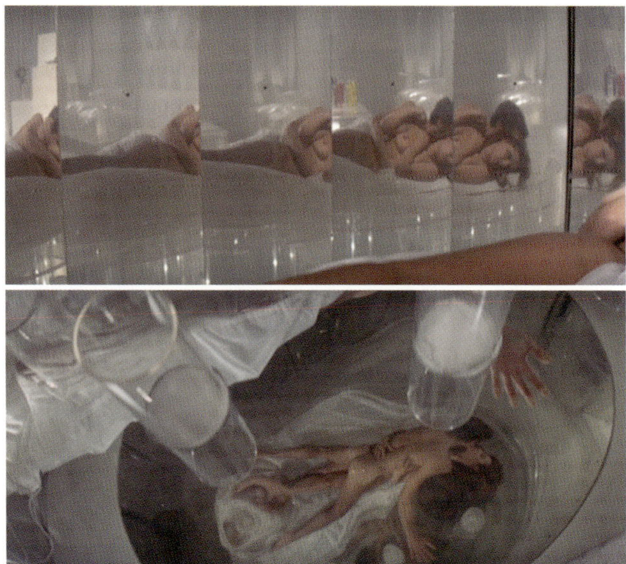

1.16 Mirrored reflections around a plastic bed. Screenshots from *Camille 2000*.

1.17 Racking focus between Camille in the background and a vase of camellias in the foreground. Screenshots from *Camille 2000*.

1.18 Cover of Audubon Books' *Collected Speeches of Spiro Agnew* (1971).

Source: Author's collection.

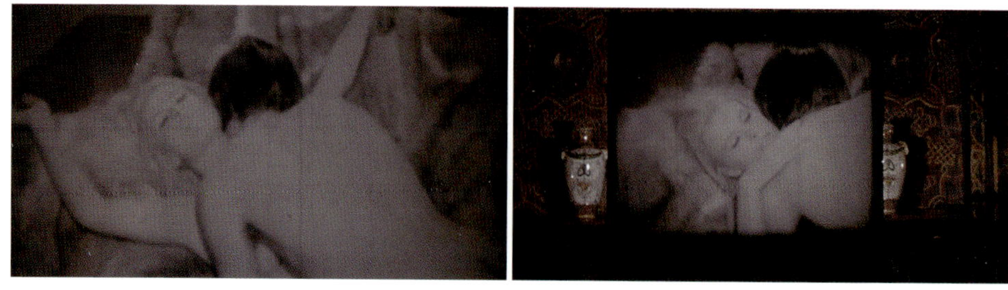

2.4 The opening shot reveals a film within the film. Screen captures from *The Lickerish Quartet*.

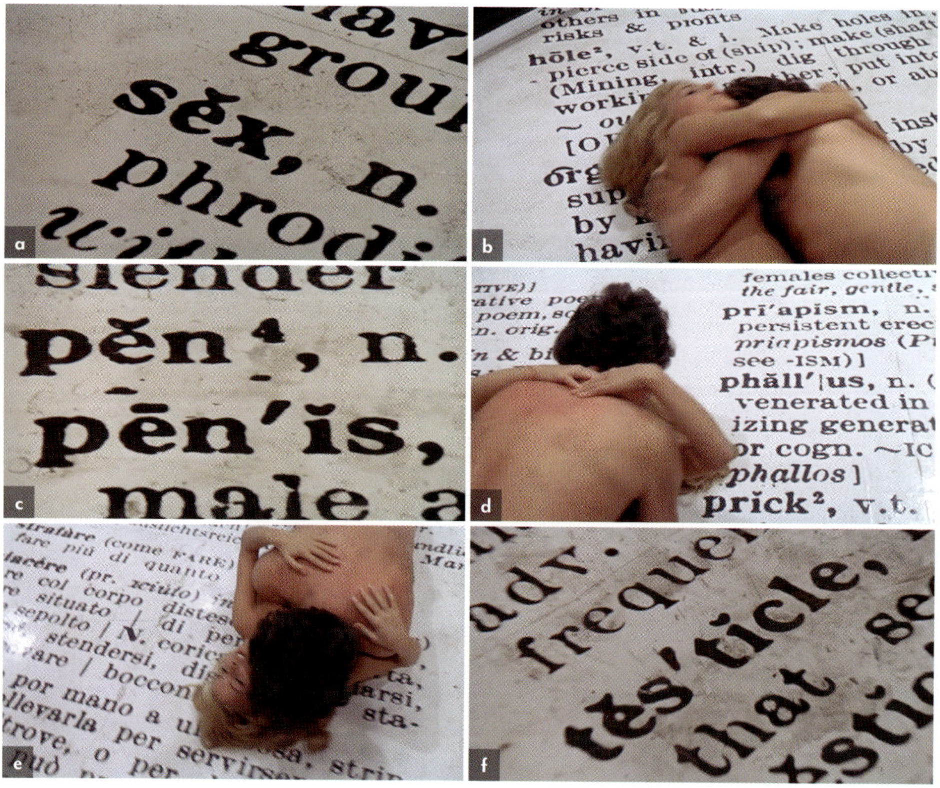

2.6 A montage sequence from the library sex scene. Screen captures from *The Lickerish Quartet*.

2.7 The long-take/long-shot style of the olive-grove sex scene. Screen captures from *The Lickerish Quartet*.

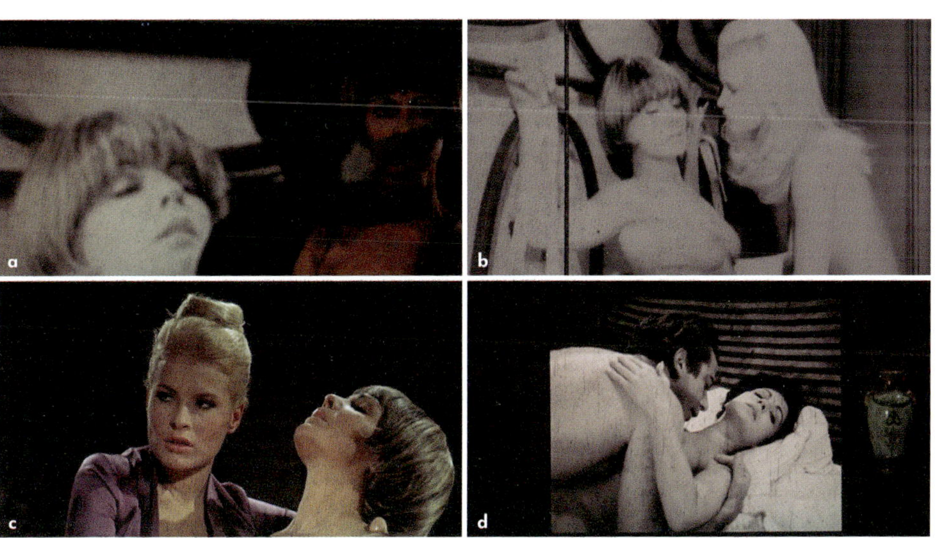

2.8 Discontinuity editing in the wife's seduction scene. Screen captures from *The Lickerish Quartet*.

2.11 Poster for *Little Mother*'s 1975 re-release as *Blood Queen*, on a double-bill with the similarly retitled *The Cop*.

Source: Author's collection.

2.12 A signature "glassy image." Screen capture from *Little Mother*.

2.13 *Little Mother* begins by demonstrating how political manipulation intercedes in the "liveness" of a television broadcast. Screen captures from *Little Mother*.

2.14 In the film's climax, Marina (Christiane Kruger) is killed while people watch her supposedly "live" Christmas television address. Screen captures from *Little Mother*.

3.2 A different type of sex film.

Source: Author's collection.

3.3 Pamela (Barbara Bourbon) and her husband (Alan Marlow) have sex while watching the filmed projection of her earlier sexual encounters. Screen capture from *The Private Afternoons of Pamela Mann.*

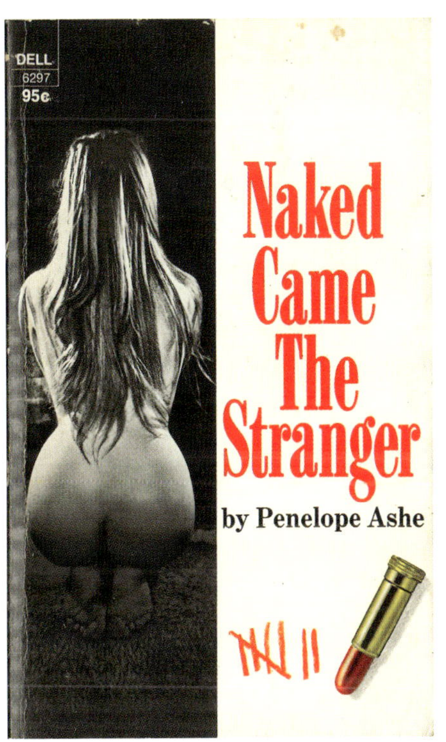

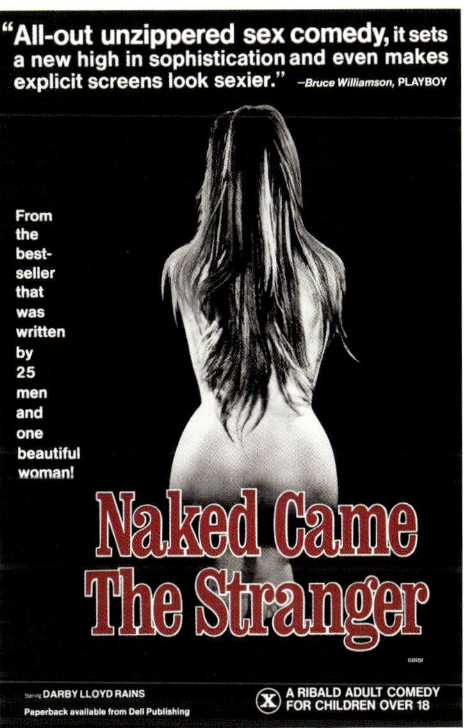

3.4 From book to film. Book cover (*left*) and poster (*right*) for *Naked Came the Stranger*.

Source: (*left*) Courtesy of Barricade Books; (*right*) Author's collection.

3.7 Jean (Carl Parker) observing Anne's (Mary Mendum) humiliation. Screen captures from *The Image*.

3.8 Jean assumes the controlling position in a turning-point scene. Screen captures from *The Image*.

3.9 "Forgive me, for I know what I do." Anne chooses the implement of her own punishment. Screen captures from *The Image*.

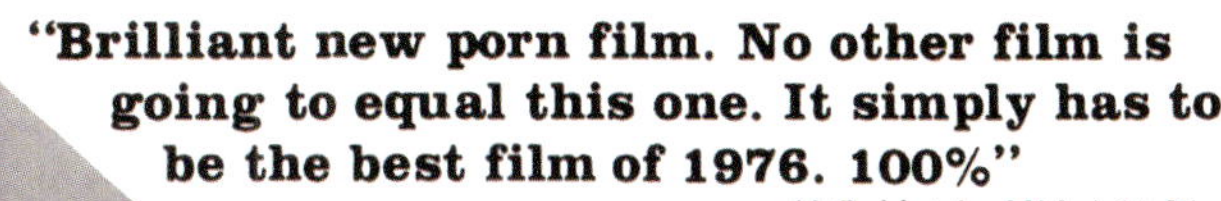

4.1 Poster for *The Opening of Misty Beethoven*.

Source: Author's collection.

4.2 The working title for *The Opening of Misty Beethoven* is visible on the clapperboard. Note how Radley Metzger avoided using his own name even here.

Source: Outtakes from author's collection.

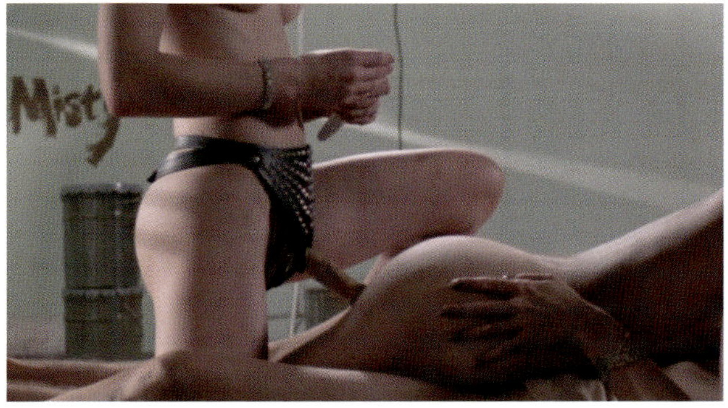

4.3 Misty (Constance Money) wields the phallus. Screen capture from *The Opening of Misty Beethoven*.

4.4 One of Radley Metzger's nomination cards from the Adult Film Association of America's first ever Annual Erotic Awards, in 1977.

Source: Courtesy of Steven Morowitz/Distribpix Inc.

4.5 Roberta (C. J. Laing) provocatively declares her sexual agency. Screen captures from *Barbara Broadcast*.

4.6 Barbara (Annette Haven) gazes at Roberta (C. J. Laing), while the faceless man (Jamie Gillis) serves as appendage to her desire. Screen capture from *Barbara Broadcast*.

5.2 Italian publicity falsely claimed that *The Cat and the Canary* was an Agatha Christie adaptation.

Source: Author's collection.

5.3 The icebox containing the reels of Cyrus West's will. Screen capture from *The Cat and the Canary*.

5.4 Past and present interact as Mrs. Pleasant (Beatrix Lehmann) appears to walk into, and then out of, the projected film. Screen captures from *The Cat and the Canary*.

Premium Erotica

"THE TALE OF TIFFANY LUST"

. . . a woman whose time has come

HENRY PARIS PRESENTS: "THE TALE OF TIFFANY LUST"
Introducing ARLENE MANHATTEN
with Misty • Desiree Cousteau • Veronica Hart • George Payne
Vanessa Del Rio • Merle Michaels • Marianne Flowers
A HENRY PARIS PRODUCTION • Directed by Gerald Kikoine

5.5 Poster for *The Tale of Tiffany Lust*.

Source: Author's collection.

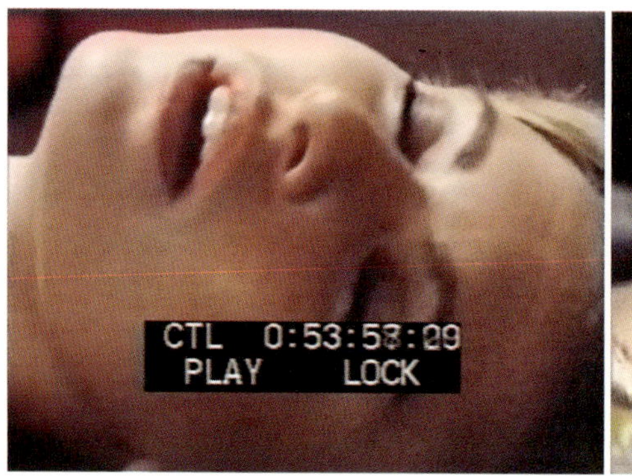

5.6 Sue (Sharon Moran, *left*) climaxes simultaneously with the woman (Crystal Sync, *right*) in Ilsa's film. Screen captures from *Love Standing Up*. (The burned-in timecode is an artifact of the VHS tape that contains one of the only known copies of the film.)

5.7 Radley Metzger at the 2014 Lincoln Center retrospective of his work.

Source: Courtesy of Dow Jones.

3.9 "Forgive me, for I know what I do." Anne chooses the implement of her own punishment. Screen captures from *The Image*.

It is through the act of making the choice, isolated here in the image of the hand that selects, that this remarkable sequence shot mediates between the two faces of Anne: one an obscure reflection, the other onscreen and incarnate; one riven by fear and trepidation, the other galvanized by the acknowledgment of her desire. It is as though the act of choosing brings Anne's will into focus rather than resulting from it. But what does Anne in fact choose in this moment? Anne's desire consists not in taking another as its object, neither Jean nor Claire, but in her submission to Claire as phallic mother, imaged here as a boot-clad leg that dominates the foreground as Anne returns, chain in hand. But this implies a fundamental incommensurability within the ménage à trois that Claire has created: Claire is using Anne to tease out Jean's sadistic desires, but Anne's pleasure exists only in relation to what Claire demands, irrespective of Jean's role. The terms have been set for the ultimate breakdown in the trio's relation when, in the film's climactic torture sequence, Jean wrests control of the action from Claire and gives his desire full rein, first by whipping Anne himself, then, for the only time in the film, having vaginal sex with her. Her mistreatment no longer authorized by Claire, Anne becomes simply inert. Claire meanwhile erupts with rage and whips the uncomprehending Jean out of the torture chamber.

Yet all along there has been a third desire at work that similarly hesitates before its fulfillment; namely, Claire's desire for Jean's sadistic attentions. Earlier in the film, this gets hinted at in an enigmatic scene that gives the original book its title. Alone with Jean, Claire shows him a series of strange photographs of Anne being punished, among which one image sticks out as not belonging to the others. Jean's voiceover explains:

> The last photo was very different from the others. For one thing, the body was completely cut off by the camera. For another, the pubic hair seemed darker. It was obvious to me that the model was no longer Anne but someone else. What gave me the final proof were the dark, polished fingernails of those two hands. I remembered that Anne left her fingernails natural. Claire became nervous, which was unlike her.

Accompanying this voiceover, which is assembled from bits and pieces from the original novel, a series of shot-reverse shots convey Jean's suspicion that the model is in fact Claire, who now breaks with her role as an icy dominatrix to become momentarily embarrassed, unable to meet Jean's inquiring eyes.[102]

In her essay on the original novel, Susan Sontag describes how this scene "insinuate[s] a mystery in what has been a brutally straightforward . . . situation."[103] Claire's efforts to model Jean's relation to Anne are here shown to contain an additional motive that remains obscure until the book's final chapter—and the film's final scene—when it is revealed that Claire has been using Anne, not as a plaything for Jean's sadism, but instead as her own avatar, to train him in how *she* wants to be treated. Her goal, that is, has been to use Anne to draw out Jean's sadism and then redirect that sadism onto herself. Arriving at Jean's apartment the day after the fight, Claire presents herself as a stand-in for the now absent Anne, dressed in one of Anne's outfits. Ordered to strip, she assumes one of Anne's submissive poses, kneeling with arms above her head, telling Jean he can do whatever he wants with her. "Have you ever been beaten?" Jean asks, before slapping her face and mounting her on the staircase. The camera pulls back to the accompaniment of Claire's gasps of pleasure and the film ends.

Réage's novel is in this way structured as a sadomasochistic *mise-en-abîme* in which a story of male sadism turns out to be housed within a story of female masochism, and in which the enactment of sadistic desire on Jean's part is preface to his recognition of masochistic intent on Claire's. As such, the narrative ends up hewing closer to a Freudian etiology in which masochism is understood as the inverse or complementary counterpart to sadism—the impulse to deflect onto one's self a "death instinct" that, in sadism, one directs outward at others—rather than a Deleuzian one, in which sadism and masochism are completely distinct.[104] More relevant to my purposes, though, is how this narrative, in Metzger's hands, gets dramatized through a series of interlocking character trajectories in which each protagonist is brought to—and then over—taboo's edge. Each character prevaricates in the unresolved gap that separates impulse from action: Jean in the face of Claire's humiliation of Anne at the rose garden, Anne before the cabinet of chains, and Claire in acknowledging her own masochism. Each character's passage through taboo enables the next character, in turn, to enact what shame should forbid: Anne's selection of the chain allows Jean to act upon his sadism, which in turn allows Claire to reveal her own submissive intent. And what Claire so carefully orchestrates out of this chain reaction (pun intended) is nothing less than her own unmasking. Anne's initial declaration of self-knowledge ("for I know what I do") in this way gets answered in Claire's culminating revelation of her own innermost sexual self as she presents herself, naked and unveiled, to Jean's control.

And so, as we delve into the enigma of Metzger's orthonymity in *The Image*, we find an unexpected corollary in the film itself, in the way its three protagonists, one after the other, also put masks aside. It is in the nature of a Bataillean erotica that the self is at stake in this way. Locked in a permanent dialectic with shame, erotic sexuality always operates *despite* one's everyday or social self; it necessarily involves a rending of masks, what Joel Kovel calls a "*dedifferentiating* [of] the socially constructed self," to reveal the "actual, soiled humanity" within.[105] Whereas carnivalesque liberty *requires* the mask as that which allows one to "reject . . .

conformity to oneself" (the words are Bakhtin's), erotic sexuality exists in the *failure* of the mask to cover over what, in desire, one cannot but conform to, even as one's self resists.[106]

What also gets uncovered in the Paris/Metzger dionym is, however, an alternate way of thinking about the "commonsense" or conventional categorizations of adult film into which Metzger's output has been misleadingly siloed. One of the paradoxes of Metzger scholarship is that it has usually favored one or other side of his output, in genre studies that either derive their definition of softcore from his "Radley Metzger" films or frame their model of hardcore in terms of Metzger's "Henry Paris" work, without either phase of Metzger's filmmaking being read in dialog with the other.[107] The problem with this way of framing Metzger's career is that it falsifies the record of his work in the mid-1970s when "Metzger" and "Paris" operated not only in tandem but also according to a principle that does not easily separate into a middlebrow softcore vs. its "low" hardcore other.

This is why I have dwelled on *The Image* in this chapter, because it suggests the need to think about the Paris/Metzger dionym outside of these hierarchies of "soft" and "hard." As we have seen in earlier chapters, scholars who have written on those distinctions have generally done so from the vantage point of a language of class habitus and distinction derived from the work of Pierre Bourdieu: the "low" genre of hardcore gets explained in terms of the class situation of the lower classes, while middlebrow softcore gets read in terms of middle-class status anxieties.[108] Yet in their sociologizing zeal, such arguments often overstate how distinctions in sexual taste separate out onto distinct class formations.[109] True, the same objection might be leveled against the porn/erotica dialectic, too, since works deemed "erotica" are typically defined in terms of a similarly Bourdieusian logic of taste hierarchy—that is, as having complex aesthetic intentions that presume a certain cultural capital on the part of their consumers. But in its further development through the work of Bataille and Bakhtin, as I have attempted here, the dialectic of pornography and erotica also takes on aspects of sexuality's relation to taboo that can only be correlated with class hierarchy at the risk of an absurd reductionism. The argument of porn scholar Susanna Paasonen applies here, namely that distinctions in the realm of explicit cinema engage affective and carnal registers that simply do not "fully translate into class allegory" and cannot be considered "simply an effect of social distinctions."[110] More so than any overt class orientation, it was the eroticism of taboo that fundamentally synthesized Metzger's orthonymic cinema of the mid-1970s—not just in the "quasi-hardcore"

S/M of *The Image* but in the unleashing of an unacknowledged queerness in the newlywed couple of *Score*, too—just as it was the absence of taboo's pressure that marked the more properly pornographic sensibility of the Henry Paris films.

To say all of this this is not to deny that sexual taste is "classed" in ways that are informed by distinct class-cultural formations, nor is it to ignore the fact that desire has a sociology as well as a psychology, nor, finally, is it to overlook the obvious class-aspirationalism of Metzger's passage through the 1960s, on which a Bourdieusian methodology sheds important light. Rather, it is to create a margin for understanding how the class dialectics that informed Metzger's early career no longer account quite as well for the Paris/Metzger dionym of the mid-1970s, which does not comfortably divide into a "hard" vs. a "soft" nor a "low" vs. a "high," but rather into the contrast between a pornography whose carnivalizing abandon is enabled beneath the security of false fronts and disguise (in *Pamela Mann* and *Naked*) and an erotica whose inducements of shame and humiliation require the self's unmasking (in *The Image*). Put another way, the division between the pseudonym and the orthonym, between the mask and its absence, ultimately exists in these texts not simply as alternate vectors for authorship but as alternate modes of sexual subjectivity: where *Pamela Mann* and *Naked* bespeak the sexual liberty that is secured through anonymity, *The Image* dramatizes subjects who are transformed by what desire brings to light. Note, though, how in both instances there is a kind of tension or opposition between sexual gratification and selfhood, the latter of which must be either hidden (in, e.g., *Pamela Mann*) or undone (in *The Image*) in the process of achieving the former. For his next film, Metzger would turn sex into a style of selfhood in its own right.

CHAPTER 4

"METZGER'S FUTURISTIC SOCIETY"

Pornotopia and the Public Sphere

What we had hoped to do was we wanted to blur the lines. We thought the idea of "adult entertainment" would disappear, that X-rated film as a separate genre [would disappear], that once the public got used to the idea they would get over the hysteria. . . . Because when you're making films or doing any artistic thing, it's like saying "You can compose this symphony but you can't use this octave. You can use anything else, but you can't play those notes." And I wanted to see people playing on a full keyboard.

—Kim Pope, 1970s adult-film star

The history of the porno chic era was marked by a persistent question: How did hardcore pornography relate to the mainstream of American cinema? Often the question was framed in more extreme ways: Would the distinction in question simply disappear? Was porn's success to be measured by the degree to which it willed itself into a kind of functional nonexistence, indistinguishable from a mainstream into which it would dissolve? For many of porn's defenders, the answer was an optimistic yes. William Rotsler, editor of the adult-film magazine *Adam Film World*, articulated the sentiment well when he wrote in 1973 that the "entire classification of erotic films as such will disappear, melting into movie-making as a whole, so that there will only be *cinema*, an artistic reflection of life as we know it, life as we wish it to be, and life in its rich complexity."[1] Gerard Damiano, whose *Deep Throat* (1972) catalyzed the porno chic era, was of similar mind, describing how "there will be no more fuck films because they will be incorporated into the everyday film."[2] In this anticipated future, not only would pornography as such vanish, but so too would the separation of porn stars from their mainstream counterparts. Marlon Brando's performance in Bernardo Bertolucci's *Last Tango in Paris* (1972) was a watershed in this respect, prompting Rotsler to imagine a time when mainstream actors would consider hardcore sex part of their craft. "It is a milestone film," he wrote, "not so much for its eroticism . . . but because an Oscar-winning major star chose to make it."[3]

To read the critics of the era is, in short, to be aware of a great excitement about the possibility that "real sex" would soon become a viable component of "real films." This, after all, was a period in which Damiano cheekily ran a full-page "for your consideration" ad in *Variety* for his 1974 hardcore film *Memories Within Miss Aggie*—not as a serious bid for mainstream Oscar success, to be sure, but certainly as a way to announce the enemy at the gates.[4] It was a period, too, in which *Screw* magazine could report the (false) rumor that Warren Beatty had been conscripted to star in "the first major motion picture studio hard-core production," and when a film like *The Devil in Miss Jones* could rank sixth in U.S. box-office grosses among *all* films released in 1973.[5] The infamous vision of Terry Southern's 1970 novel *Blue Movie*, about a high-budget pornographic film directed by a Stanley Kubrick–like auteur, seemed to many to be about to change from satire to prophesy.[6]

But it would equally be a mistake to imply any unanimity among hardcore's advocates on this issue. Some offered dissenting voices, arguing that porn's outlaw status was essential to its pleasures. "Porn is becoming so mainstream, so predictable in its plastic approach to human sexuality, that it stands ready to be subsumed into the greater mass of American plasticity," complained a critic in the *Erotic Film Guide*.[7] "Taking sex out of the gutter is the easiest way to kill it," agreed a writer for *Flick*.[8] Others expressed ambivalence, as was the case with adult star Jamie Gillis, who spoke plangently of the "heartbreaking struggle of porn film to get over the barrier": "So now the films are on [New York's] East Side," he noted. "But do they really belong on the East Side? . . . I want so much for this business to grow. At the same time, I don't want it to lose its constituency on Eighth Avenue."[9]

Pornographic culture of the mid-1970s was organized around this contradiction between gentrification and its dissidents, between filmmakers and films that sought to reconcile hardcore sex with the norms of "legitimate" film culture (in prestige porn films like *The Story of Joanna* or *Through the Looking Glass*, both

1976) and those that did not (as in director Shaun Costello's enema-themed *Water Power* of the same year). But in that contradiction was expressed not just a difference between types of film or filmmaking but also competing visions of the relations between sex and public culture: on the one hand, a vision in which sexual pleasure and license would be woven into the fabric of a normative social life; on the other, that of a sexual counterpublic that self-consciously operated outside of society's strictures of respectability. If the former crystallized in Gillis's nod to hardcore's tentative encroachment onto the Upper East Side—that is, into middle-class "safe spaces" like the East Eighty-Sixth Street Cinemas and the Trans-Lux at Eighty-Fifth Street, both of which eventually exhibited *Deep Throat*—then the latter was realized in the cultural imaginary of Eighth Avenue or Times Square as a space of socialization or "contact" (the term is Samuel Delany's) for a range of sexual subcultures.[10] Both entailed a repudiation of sex's confinement to the private sphere, but the consequences of that repudiation flowed in different directions: toward a democratizing of sexual pleasure within the existing frameworks of the liberal public sphere; and toward the growing visibility of alternative sexual publics that operated in various degrees of separation from, or even resistance to, those norms.

It will come as no surprise that "Henry Paris" was among the gentrifiers' most prominent luminaries. *The Private Afternoons of Pamela Mann* (1974) and *Naked Came the Stranger* (1975) had proven Metzger's ability to integrate hardcore sex into films with real production values. After their success, he recalled, he felt he could "walk on water."[11] Accordingly, for his next Henry Paris production, he upped the stakes dramatically and in the process created what has ever since been acknowledged as the gold standard of porno chic aspirationalism: *The Opening of Misty Beethoven* (1976) (figure 4.1). With a budget of around $250,000 the film was shot over a six-week schedule that encompassed studio work at the RKO soundstage on 106th Street—Metzger's stomping ground from his dubbing days—as well as locations in Paris and Rome. *Misty* went on to become the only porn film in history chosen as "best picture" by all of the institutions awarding such honors at the time—the Adult Film Association of America and the magazines *Adam Film World*, *Hustler*, and *Screw*—and was eventually crowned the top porno film of them all in Jim Holliday's 1982 guide, *The Top 100 X-Rated Films of All Time*.[12] The film became a proxy for widely voiced hopes for a major studio film with hardcore sequences: for Holliday, it was a "Hollywood film that contains explicit action"; for Al Goldstein, at *Screw*, it was "Hollywood-porn HERE . . .

4.1 Poster for *The Opening of Misty Beethoven*.

Source: Author's collection.

4.2 The working title for *The Opening of Misty Beethoven* is visible on the clapperboard. Note how Radley Metzger avoided using his own name even here.
Source: Outtakes from author's collection.

right now!"[13] But, I argue in this chapter, it was also Metzger's first and most fully realized vision of the kind of social world that such hopes implied, a film whose working title, not coincidentally, was *Society* (figure 4.2). The focus of my analysis, accordingly, will be not to defend or challenge *Misty*'s reputation as "the best" but to explore how Metzger's pursuit of gentrification resulted in a unique take on the intertwining of sex and public life—neither that of a sexual counterpublic, nor even of a sexual democracy, but instead a third, decidedly *antidemocratic* possibility: an aristocracy of sex.

"ALL HAIL THE GOLDEN ROD GIRL": *MISTY BEETHOVEN* AND THE ARISTOCRACY OF SEX

The relevant concept here is that of "pornotopia," coined by literary historian Steven Marcus to refer to the narrative worlds in which pornographic fiction takes place. In pornotopia, Marcus argues, everything matters only insofar as it motivates reasons to copulate: social relations between people are transformed into bodily relations between organs; settings exist only as places to have sex; and reality is sensualized at every level.[14] This is also, moreover, true of *Misty Beethoven*, as well as Metzger's two subsequent (and last) Henry Paris features, *Barbara Broadcast* (1977) and *Maraschino Cherry* (1978), all of which present worlds in which, on the one hand, only sexual transactions get included and, on the other, all nonsexual transactions get reimagined in sexual terms. Whether a matter of selecting items from a restaurant menu (in *Barbara Broadcast*) or paying for the dry cleaning (in *Maraschino Cherry*), the chief commodity on offer is always sex, and the only currency to pay for it is sex as well. This, for instance, is how you book a flight in the world of *Misty Beethoven*:

> **FLIGHT ATTENDANT:** I can confirm your return on that date.
> **MALE PASSENGER:** That's wonderful
> **ATTENDANT:** The destination is New York. And that's first-class?
> **PASSENGER:** Right.
> **ATTENDANT:** Which part of first-class? Sex or non-sex?
> **PASSENGER:** Sex.
> **ATTENDANT:** First-class. Sex. Nonsmoking or first-class sex smoking?
> **PASSENGER:** First-class sex nonsmoking.
> **ATTENDANT:** First-class sex nonsmoking. Adult film or first-class sex nonsmoking family film?
> **PASSENGER:** First-class sex nonsmoking adult film.
> **ATTENDANT:** First-class sex nonsmoking adult film. Vegetarian, kosher, or regular meal?
> **PASSENGER:** Regular meal.
> **ATTENDANT:** Are you a fucker or mostly just interested in a little head?
> **PASSENGER:** Just a little head.
> **ATTENDANT:** Very good.

Where Metzger's pornotopian vision departs from Marcus's template is in its relation to the public sphere. Marcus's definition presumes, after all, a kind of spatial and temporal seclusion that cordons off the real world: pornotopia, he writes, "may be said largely to exist at no place, and to take place in nowhere. The isolated castle on an inaccessible mountain top, the secluded country estate, set in the middle of a large park and surrounded by insurmountable walls, the mysterious town house in London or Paris . . . these are all the same place and are identically located."[15] But there are no borders in Metzger's final three Henry

Paris films, which turn away from the motifs of pretense and masquerade in *Pamela Mann* and *Naked Came the Stranger* to explore the fantasy of making sex public. Rather, these are films that, at least on the surface, appear to offer a hyperbolic vision of what Damon Young describes as the "liberal sexual subject"—the cultural fantasy, linked to the sexual revolution, of a "subject for whom sexual pleasure has been integrated into civic existence" and whose sexuality "assumes its significance in relation to . . . [the] public sphere."[16] First-class passengers in *Misty Beethoven* are openly fellated by flight attendants, while others complain that they're yet to receive their second blow job. The tableside salad-dressing service at the fancy restaurant in *Barbara Broadcast* features waiters ejaculating over the lettuce. *The Opening of Misty Beethoven* and its successors become, on this line of interpretation, the hardcore depictions of what Young already finds exemplified in Roger Vadim's softcore sci-fi film, *Barbarella* (1968): a world in which public culture and sexual culture become one and the same, and where sex is the literal and figural means through which society and social exchange is imagined.

That there was something of a science-fiction or, better, speculative aspect to Metzger's pornotopic imaginary becomes particularly clear in the case of *Misty Beethoven*, which merits extended attention here. "Like Fellini in *Satyricon*," wrote adult-film critic Reggie Danzig in his review of the film in *High Society*, "Metzger fashions his futuristic society—his own new world—by projecting what *could* happen if the sexual evolution continues to evolve."[17] In *Misty*'s case, however, this was owed less to a hitherto undetected vein of futurism on Metzger's part, than, paradoxically, to his characteristic orientation to the middlebrow literary past—specifically, his intent to make a hardcore version of George Bernard Shaw's 1913 play *Pygmalion*. "I remember going from my office into [Ava Leighton's]," Metzger later recalled, "and saying 'What do you say we do a modern version of the *Pygmalion* story, but instead of teaching her how to speak English we teach her how to make love, and'—this was all one sentence—'we'll call it *Society*.' "[18] What Metzger was proposing here was more than just a modern "updating" (in the spirit, say, of *Carmen, Baby* [1967] or *Camille 2000* [1969]), but a total reconceptualization of the social world that informed Shaw's source text: the original play's vision of a society in which distinction is coded by the markers of class membership ("proper" diction, etiquette, and so on) was to be rethought as a fantasy in which social hierarchy becomes a matter of sexual adventure. As Danzig astutely observed: "Whereas the characters in Shaw's play were part of a mosaic centering around a rigid Edwardian society in which language, poise and etiquette distinguished, often hypocritically, one social class from another, Metzger found it necessary to create a different milieu, one in which hedonism is the highest order mankind and womankind can reach."[19]

The question of how such a society would actually work is a moot one, though, since there is in fact no place *for* work in the world of *Misty Beethoven*, which was Metzger's deliberate intent. "I wanted to do it upscale because . . . if you want to do something comedic and light, you have to create a situation in which nobody thinks about how these people make a living."[20] What Metzger was committing to was a project on the scale of his pre–Henry Paris pictures: something that would use foreign locations (in this instance, a number of exterior scenes shot in Paris and Rome with actor Jamie Gillis, in the Professor Higgins role of noted sexologist "Dr. Seymour Love"), as well as the villas and chateaus of the wealthy (for which Metzger used the Mission-style Arcadia residence in Deal, New Jersey, doubling for the interiors of Dr. Love's supposedly "Italian" mansion).[21] He was also, however, committing not just to a depiction of *sex among the aristocrats*—long his preferred milieu—but to the new idea of a kind of *sexual aristocracy*, into which Misty Beethoven (Constance Money, in the Eliza Doolittle role) is initiated under Seymour's ministrations. As we will see, whatever surface similarities the film shares with the democratizing concept of the "liberal sexual subject" simply crumble under the weight of privilege and exclusivity in the world Metzger creates.

Misty's initiation provides the film's narrative framework, proceeding in a number of clearly defined stages, each of which motivates a variety of hardcore sequences. The story begins with Seymour's discovery of Misty, a cheap sex worker whom he spots giving a hand job to an old man dressed as Napoleon in a Parisian porno theater. Fascinated, he hires Misty to see her at work in a neighboring brothel, where she explains her uninspired sexual philosophy: "I do a straight fuck. I don't take it in the mouth. I don't take it in the ass." Within the social world of the film, Misty's commitment to the "straight fuck" (heterosexual vaginal sex) codes her as déclassé in contrast with the connoisseurship of Seymour Love, who vows proudly that he will transform her into the most desired sex worker of jet-set society, the "Golden Rod Girl." This in turn leads to Misty's training in Seymour's mansion, where, clad in a jogging suit, she is led through a montage of sexual workouts: she learns to "take it" in both the mouth and the ass with a series of plaster-cast dildos, and hones her ability to make three men cum simultaneously (with her two hands and mouth). With the training completed, the remainder of the film comprises a series of three seduction challenges, each one leading Misty further away from the standard phallocentrism of the "straight fuck."

One way of describing this narrative would be as an instance of what adult-film scholar Jeffrey Escoffier has dubbed pornography's "perverse dynamic," whose trajectory is always to push out into ever more outré sexual possibilities.[22] The first of the seduction scenes is the most conventional. Misty lures an Italian nobleman into the restroom of an opera house, where he fucks her from behind. The act brings her immediate notoriety: a montage shows a series of well-dressed elderly couples excitedly gossiping about the affair—what Metzger described as a kind of "Greek chorus" commenting on Misty's growing reputation.[23] For her second challenge, Seymour introduces Misty to the first in a series of what porn scholar Linda Williams describes as the film's "cross-gender identifications": Misty is tasked with taking the "masculine" role of sexual aggressor to seduce an impotent, queer art dealer (played by Cal Culver).[24] By way of preparation, Seymour stages an elaborate rehearsal of the proposed seduction in which his assistant, Geraldine (Jacqueline Beudet), plays the role of the art dealer, while Seymour's friend Tania (Terri Hall) takes on Misty's role as seducer—in effect, a lesbian run-through of what will eventually be a coupling between a straight woman and a gay man. It is, moreover, during this rehearsal that Seymour instructs Tania to repeat dialogue that Williams has described as "the most fascinating line in all of hard-core film pornography," namely: "I'm going to lick your cock like it's the inside of a ripe mango."[25] Williams's gloss on the line neatly captures the gender indeterminacies that are beginning to creep in: "A mango's 'inside' is not a particularly apt simile for an erect penis, in spite of the presence at its center of what in Spanish, at least, is called the 'bone.' But it is precisely this sexual ambivalence—between hard bone and soft flesh whose 'inside' is licked—that this entire rehearsal seems designed to express."[26] Paradoxically, given that Metzger stages the scene for straight male viewing pleasure, Seymour's lesson here would seem to be that sexual sophistication untethers from any necessary grounding in the specifics of gender and sexual identity: the spectacle of queer sex can be a pedagogy in straight seduction, genitalia can be dedifferentiated in the metaphor of a mango, and sexual pleasure becomes a value that transcends the gendered permutations that produce it.

This is a lesson that Misty applies well to her final challenge: the conquest of Lawrence Layman (Ras Kean), a foppish and vain adult-magazine editor and

4.3 Misty (Constance Money) wields the phallus. Screen capture from *The Opening of Misty Beethoven*.

film producer, at a wrap party for his latest picture. Making a beeline for Layman through the party guests, Misty declares her intentions immediately, telling his partner, Barbara (Gloria Leonard): "I'm going to get your old man off." "You don't think I'll let him make that perilous journey alone?" Barbara replies, and what ensues is a remarkable three-way in which Lawrence penetrates Barbara vaginally while Misty dons a strap-on dildo and penetrates Larry anally.[27] Misty not only wields the phallus, but *is* the phallus, kneeling, erect, over the supine bodies of Layman and Barbara (figure 4.3). Nor are Metzger's directing choices here governed by the pleasure of straight male viewers, as in the earlier rehearsal scene: the presumptive heterosexuality of hardcore cinema is queered by a decoupage in which the only meat shots are of Misty's dildo entering Layman's anus.

To be sure, the scene was unexpected enough to have raised eyebrows at the time, even among reviewers well accustomed to the hardcore beat. *Screw* magazine's Larry Wichman balked at it, protesting somewhat too much by dismissing the scene as a "tedious bit of titillation," while Bordon Scott at *After Dark* described it as "unusually bizarre."[28] Even in an article celebrating the film's "Great Sex Scenes," *Adam Film World* tactically obfuscated the specifics of the action between Misty and Layman, referring simply to a "wild scene of cunts, huge cock, and hungry mouths" in which "Misty is set upon by superstud Ras [Keane]."[29] The scene was also cut from subsequent home video release in the 1980s as part of what adult-film historian Whitney Strub describes as the adult video industry's retroactive "sanitizing" of the porno chic era's erotic imaginary in the wake of the anti-porn Meese Commission report.[30] (Even the film itself seems to walk back its own perversity in the film's coda, in which Misty and Seymour are reunited in a loving heteronormative fuck.)[31] Yet the pegging scene remains the most striking consequence of a social conception in which distinction is measured by degrees of remove from the meat-and-potatoes of a "straight fuck." "All hail the Golden Rod Girl," Misty accordingly declares after the act, when she returns to the guests at Layman's party, and the film then cuts to another Greek chorus scene in which her sexual/social climbing is celebrated on the streets of Rome. "Misty Beethoven made quite the hit at Lawrence Layman's party," comments an elderly woman. "Really? I always thought she was the best," answers another.

Scholars have noted how Seymour Love's aspiration to combine sensual pursuits with social distinction mirrored Metzger's own aesthetic aims.[32] But it is also this aspirationalism that, in the end, drives a wedge between *Misty*'s pornotopic vision and other theorizations of sex and the public sphere. Young's "liberal sexual subject," for instance, bespeaks the ideal of a civic existence in which sexual pleasure and sexuality are included under liberal principles of democratic equality and reciprocity. More famously, perhaps, Herbert Marcuse's 1955 *Eros and Civilization* proposed a "non-repressive society" in which humanity's sensuous faculties (or "Eros") would be reconciled with the values of reason and civilization ("Logos"), resulting in the disintegration of the repressive institutions in which "private interpersonal relations have [heretofore] been organized, particularly the monogamic and patriarchal family."[33] By contrast, Metzger's film simply proposes sexual derring-do as a substitute for class relations as the basis of a new hierarchy: the world in which Misty moves ignores questions of labor to substitute sexual adventure as the only true basis for social distinction. It is as though property relations get replaced by relations of promiscuity in a pornotopia that is decidedly *not* for all. What we get instead is a kind of trickle-down version of the sexual revolution in which the ripest fruits of sexual democracy are reserved for the connoisseurs. Everyone else just gets to watch.

Those who watched seemed happy enough, though: the film was a sensation. *Misty Beethoven* debuted on March 18, 1976, at the Times Square World Theatre, where, according to *Box Office* magazine's metrics, it outperformed every other film in New York City in its first three weeks, eventually clocking in with a mighty six-month run that grossed over $500,000.[34] (The film was ultimately replaced at the World in September with another landmark in prestige porn, Jonas Middleton's *Through the Looking Glass*.) The film also chalked up impressive runs in more mainstream theaters, too, running for some sixty weeks in the Santikos theater chain in San Antonio, and over a hundred weeks at the shopping-mall theater the Shirley Duke 3 in Alexandria, Virginia (breaking an area record of ninety-seven weeks previously held by *The Sound of Music* [1965]!). Critical reception in the adult press was meanwhile adulatory, with the film variously described as "the filmic erotica of the century" (*Hustler*), "decadence for the masses" (*Screw*), and "[being] to porn filmmaking what Pelé is to soccer" (*After Dark*).[35] The film would go on to dominate at the Adult Film Association of America's first ever Annual Erotic Awards, held in July 1977 at the Wilshire Ebell in Los Angeles, where Jamie Gillis won for best actor and "Henry Paris" for best director, screenplay, and editor, making him the top individual winner of the occasion (figure 4.4).[36] Summarizing the occasion, *Adam Film World* declared Henry Paris "a latter-day Orson Welles as writer, director, and editor of *Misty*."[37]

Certificate of Award

THIS CERTIFIES THAT

Henry Paris

HAS BEEN NOMINATED FOR

Best Screenplay ■ Opening of Misty Beethoven

FOR OUTSTANDING CONTRIBUTIONS, AND IS A FINALIST

IN THE

1977 EROTIC AWARDS

JULY 14, 1977

Virginia Ann Perry

PRESIDENT

afaa ADULT FILM ASSOCIATION OF AMERICA

4.4 One of Radley Metzger's nomination cards from the Adult Film Association of America's first ever Annual Erotic Awards, in 1977.

Source: Courtesy of Steven Morowitz/Distribpix Inc.

Metzger had never enjoyed this measure of acclaim, but, true to form, remained ambivalent about its validity. "I always wonder," he once mused on *Misty*'s reputation as porno chic's gold standard, "is that an absolute judgment or a relative judgment?"[38] His youthful fantasies of being "Orson Welles on the inside" (see the introduction) had been returned to him as if in a fun-house mirror. Preferring to protect his pseudonym rather than receive the awards, he did not attend the ceremony.

By this time, though, Metzger may well have begun to sour on the film, which was beginning to drag him into what would become a bitter legal dispute with *Misty*'s star, Constance Money. Money's experience on the set had been a profoundly upsetting one, beginning with her first sex scene with Jamie Gillis, shot two weeks into filming, on October 20, 1975.[39] Forebodingly described as a "rape" in a handwritten script breakdown, the scene in question—not used in the final cut—featured a naked Misty chained spread-eagled to the floor while Dr. Love gives her a primer in BDSM.[40] Gillis, however, had a reputation for pushing the envelope of consent with his female scene partners and, in this case, took advantage of Money's shackled immobility.[41] As she later recalled:

> I thought for sure I was in a snuff film, I did. I thought I was dead. I thought I was going to be killed. I had not a clue. . . . Anything Jamie did was fine. That's his thing, and let him do what he wants, as long as he doesn't hurt anybody. You know, when it's not consensual and you're hurting somebody, then it's wrong. But the problem was, Jamie got off on crossing that line. That's what he enjoyed was crossing that line, and that's what I didn't agree with. And people have to agree to what they're doing, or it crosses into something else—the big "R" word.[42]

Her on-set safety so brutally compromised, Money experienced the rest of the shoot as a compounding series of disparagements, wrongs, and affronts. She alleged that Metzger slighted her acting ability and sex appeal when she couldn't keep gay actor Cal Culver erect in her scene with him (filmed on October 27); that Metzger didn't pay her for an additional three days of shooting; and that he stole over a thousand dollars' worth of her personal belongings while filming on location in New Jersey. "I try to psychologize Radley Metzger," she later mused, "but I don't know. I think he had a thing about me being a WASP."[43]

Some of these allegations would only fully surface later. Even at the time, however, Money publicly hinted at difficulties in a *Playboy* interview, noting how she "wasn't charmed by Radley Metzger" and felt "broken down and degraded" during the shoot.[44] For his part, Metzger acknowledged in private what he euphemistically described as "the trouble she had with Jamie" and attempted to settle Money's complaints over loss of property and unpaid overtime with paltry payments of $150 and $250, respectively (the former amount being little more than a tenth of what Money was asking for, the latter considerably lower than her contracted day rate of $150).[45] But the trouble was only just beginning. When Money had first signed with Metzger she had actually agreed to appear in two films, *Society* (as *Misty* was originally titled) and a mysterious *Project 175* (which eventually became *Maraschino Cherry*); but she only ever approved a release for her work on the first of these.[46] The problem here was that at least two of the scenes that Metzger had filmed with Money were intended for *Project 175*—specifically, a scene beginning at the Central Park model boat pond and ending in an apartment (shot on October 7, the first day of shooting, and November 3) and a group sex scene with a matador (shot October 8). Metzger also hoped to include the unused S/M scene with Gillis in *Barbara Broadcast*, which was planned for a July 1977 release. Accordingly, in May of that year, Metzger's business partner Ava Leighton contacted Money in an attempt to secure permission for the use of these scenes by paying again for her overtime days, this time with a check for $450, accurately reflecting Money's rate.[47] Money's response this time, however, was to lawyer up. When Metzger went ahead and released *Barbara Broadcast* and *Maraschino Cherry* with the footage anyway, Money's legal threat materialized in the form of a $2,250,000 claim for damages and a request for a permanent injunction preventing the distribution of the latter film. "By reasons of defendants' intentional, malicious and unlawful actions herein," the legal documents read, "plaintiff has sustained injury to her business and reputation and defendants have been unjustly enriched."[48]

But this, in turn, had the effect of producing *another* lawsuit against Metzger, this time from the financial backers of *Maraschino Cherry* itself. Previous to that film, all of Metzger's hardcore titles had been produced in-house, for Audubon Films (albeit hidden behind a variety of shell companies, such as Hudson Valley Properties, for *The Private Afternoons of Pamela Mann*, and Stranger Associates, for *Naked Came the Stranger*). But, in the summer of 1976, he had entered into an agreement with Sam Lake and Bob Sumner to produce a film for their Mature Pictures for which Metzger would be paid $105,000.[49] Sumner initially shrugged at the threat of Money's legal action ("That could be the handle we were looking for," he reportedly replied to Metzger over lunch, enthusiastic for the unpaid publicity). But he changed his tune when the lawsuit actually materialized, and in May 1978 filed suit to have Metzger's $105,000 fee returned if *Maraschino Cherry* was indeed subject to injunction.[50]

As film historian Ashley West observes in his remarkable archival reconstruction of the case—from which almost all the preceding information is drawn—Metzger's "main concern" in fighting the lawsuit "was that he didn't want to set a precedent" that would encourage other actors to pursue porn producers for similar reasons.[51] In this respect, Metzger succeeded: the court's first decision went his way—the injunction on *Maraschino Cherry* was refused—and Money and her lawyers backed off, agreeing to settle things out of court for the largely gestural amount of just $4,750.[52] Money's anger at Metzger never abated, though, and for the rest of her adult career, she rarely missed an opportunity to remind interviewers how Metzger had exploited her. "I think the man is real sick," she told *Adult Video News* in promotion for her last adult film, *A Taste of Money* (1983). "He's the only man in my life I've ever felt like that about."[53]

A crucial addendum: Metzger may well have been the only man to stir such feelings in Money, but she was far from the only woman whose dealings with Metzger ended in bad blood. His one-time girlfriend Mary Mendum—Anne from *The Image* (1976)—recalled him as a manipulative partner who abruptly discarded their relationship when he fathered a child with a French production assistant.[54] "I've always been taught that if you have nothing positive to say about someone, you shouldn't say anything at all," Mendum said when asked about her experience with the filmmaker in later years.[55] Another of his girlfriends, meanwhile, described him as a commitment-phobic "conman."[56] None of these claims can be independently verified, but they certainly jar with key aspects of Metzger's critical reputation. One of the most frequent claims about Metzger's work concerns its ostensible progressivism on matters of gender: then as now, Metzger's career-long preference for female-centered narratives has been framed as a commitment to women's "full erotic expression" and the "workings of female desire," according to some recent assessments.[57] But if so, this was a commitment Metzger freely contravened off-camera, where the only sexual autonomy he respected seems to have been his own.

"THE EVENTS OF THIS FILM ARE BASED ON AN AUTHENTIC FANTASY": PORNOTOPIA AND NARRATIVE FORM IN *BARBARA BROADCAST*

Attentive readers will recall from the introduction how the magazine *Gentlemen's Quarterly* once described Metzger as the very opposite of the cliché of the sleazy adult filmmaker. ("Radley Metzger, according to stereotype, should be loud-mouthed, crude and lecherous. . . . Actually, he's more Prince Hamlet than King Leer.")[58] But the fallout from *Misty Beethoven* suggests that the shoe eventually fit after all. The Metzger that Money experienced was the very worst type of "King Leer": a filmmaker at best indifferent to consent, willing to exploit his nineteen-year-old female star, and happy to slap together pornographic features out of leftover sex scenes. Just as surprising is the return of filmmaking practices from Metzger's early days with Audubon, when he would happily cut in titillating sequences (usually stripteases) on flimsy narrative pretexts.[59] *The Opening of Misty Beethoven* may have marked a highpoint in the porn industry's aspirations for Hollywood-style production and story values, but the film's very success resulted in a perceptible slackening in Metzger's ambitions on his subsequent hardcore films. Even aside from their shared use of leftover footage of *Misty*'s star, both *Barbara Broadcast* and *Maraschino Cherry* have reputations as merely "loop carriers"—that is, films that are structured less in story terms than as a thinly narrativized assemblage of sex scenes, in keeping with the industry's ungentrified origins in the 8mm "loops" in peep-show machines. It is as though the alleged criminal negligence of his onset behavior on *Misty* kickstarted a creative regression, too. The question, then, is how to explain this narrative deterioration in a filmmaker whose previous Henry Paris films had been acclaimed as models of hardcore aspirationalism?

The first answer is the most pragmatic: Metzger had exhausted himself. *Misty Beethoven* had been, in his words, "the most difficult thing I'd ever done," and his next film, *Barbara Broadcast*, was deliberately planned as a "reaction to that, a relaxation."[60] "I think the operative word was a *simpler* film," he explained. "It was a much more confined film."[61] Whereas *Misty* had involved a six-week shooting schedule across two continents, with an additional twelve weeks of post-production, *Barbara Broadcast* was shot over consecutive nights during a single week in August 1976 and at a single location: New York City's Royal Manhattan Hotel at Forty-Fourth Street and Eighth Avenue. (The hotel was then in the process of being sold, so Metzger struck a deal with the owners to shoot at night while the hotel's furnishings were being auctioned off by day.)[62] Narratively, the film at first sight offers nothing more ambitious than a "day in the life" of the titular protagonist (played by Annette Haven), a former high-class prostitute and author of a best-selling memoir—a character obviously based on Xaviera Hollander—who is interviewed at a restaurant where sex is literally on the menu. Ditto *Maraschino Cherry*, whose plot, such as it is, features a high-class madame (Gloria Leonard) who introduces her younger sister Penny (Jenny Baxter) to the tricks of her trade, illustrated by a series of flashback sex scenes as she recalls the various peccadilloes of her girls' clients. The shoot for that film was, if anything, even more drastically pared back, since *all* of the flashback hardcore scenes were discards from Metzger's previous Henry Paris shoots. (In addition to the matador and Central Park scenes featuring Constance Money, the film includes a pair of sequences with Annette Haven—one at a piano bar, the other a basement S/M sequence with C. J. Laing—that had been taken during the *Barbara Broadcast* shoot.) Filmed in a luxury apartment in the spring of 1978, the only new footage was for framing scenes at the cathouse that forms the film's backdrop.[63]

Although both films were largely praised in the adult press—indeed, *Screw* magazine named *Barbara Broadcast* the best film of 1977, as it had *Pamela Mann* and *Misty Beethoven* for both 1974 and 1976, respectively—their relatively plotless structure inspired a notably different style of review.[64] Whereas critics of the earlier films had celebrated them as broadsides in the porn industry's bid for legitimacy, reviews of *Barbara Broadcast* and *Maraschino Cherry* settled instead for a recounting of sexual scenes, in a tone reminiscent of historian Steven Marcus's description of the enumerative quality of literary pornography ("parts of bodies, limbs, and organs . . . diagrammatic schema for sexual ballets").[65] Contrast, for instance, *High Society* critic Reggie Danzig's earlier quoted review of *Misty Beethoven*, which he discussed insightfully in relation to Shaw's *Pygmalion*, with the same writer's fervid praise of the "clit-licking good treat" that was *Barbara Broadcast*:

> Barbara, a whore-turned-writer, continues to practice the oldest profession. Hell, practice? This fuckable feline is letter-perfect. When she's around, all the other women on the screen are inspired to open their hearts, their thighs, their throats, and their asses. Take Roberta (C. J. Laing), for example. (Anyone would take Roberta given half a chance.) Roberta is a roving reporter who is lunching with Barbara—and later, *on* Barbara. Roberta is anxious to secure an eye-opening, leg-opening interview with the best-selling writer. The interview is so inspirational that when Barbara dashes off to sit on the cock of a paying customer, Roberta blindly heads for the restaurant-kitchen—which in her frenzied state she mistakes for a john. After taking a spectacular leak, a virile dishwasher decides to plug her plumbing—front and rear.[66]

Or consider the criteria of evaluation mobilized in the case of *Maraschino Cherry*, whose star, Gloria Leonard, had risen from her adult-film debut in *Misty Beethoven* to become the celebrity publisher of *High Society* as well as a porn star in her own right.[67] This is how Leonard's own publication described the film:

> Any film that opens with our own Gloria Leonard wrapping her expert tongue around Wade Nichols' well-hung member can't help but be hot. . . . The sexual capers are all perfect to ejaculate to. In one, Ms. Cherry flirts with a bored housewife (Annette Haven) in a piano bar. With the wink of an eye, the housewife is lying nude on the piano, getting eaten by our starving Gloria and then fucked by a passer-by. In a following sequence that rivals Hitchcock's shower scene, a masochist (played superbly by doe-eyed C. J. Laing) is forced to balance a glass of expensive scotch on each of her outstretched hands. . . . For a little more tension, a huge dildo is pushed in and out of her asshole. This scene had me sitting on the edge of my seat—as you'll probably be, too. By the end of the film, Ms. Cherry's sister is handling two dongs at once by herself, thus proving *Maraschino Cherry* is a fruit to be swallowed whole.[68]

Along similar lines, *Adam Film World* in 1978 summarized the appeal of *Barbara Broadcast* in eighteen choice words: "Some hot scenes and some kinky ones—Laing pisses into a dish and is ass-fucked by the dishwasher."[69]

The striking tonal shift in the reception of Metzger's Henry Paris films points to a second context for understanding *Barbara Broadcast* and *Maraschino Cherry*:

namely, a kind of gentrification fatigue that began to settle onto the porn industry in the second half of the 1970s (what Whitney Strub and Peter Alilunas have wittily described as the period of hardcore's "Jimmy Carter-era malaise").[70] The porn scholar Peter Lehman has argued that, despite the aspirations of many filmmakers earlier in the decade, "porn may never have been suited fully to the feature format," creating disillusionment among those who had hoped otherwise.[71] *Contra* Lehman, however, this realization did not only await the advent of the video era, as he contends, but was already being voiced in the late 1970s by a growing chorus of critics and observers who were frustrated by films that continued to emphasize narrative values as the royal road to pornographic success. "It appears that a serious reorientation of priorities is necessary for skin flick producers," wrote reviewer Mark Adamsbaum in exasperation in 1977. "Speaking for myself, I go to fuck films because they are just that: *fuck* films. I enjoy a good plot if it enhances the film's sexual content. That's fucking with a plot. As soon as this gets turned around (that is, a plot with fucking) the emphasis is on the wrong elements."[72] Even those who, like Al Goldstein and Gerard Damiano, once envisioned a future in which hardcore would simply dissolve into the mainstream of American narrative cinema, began walking back those expectations. By 1975 Damiano was vociferously refusing the idea that adult film needed any "redeeming" qualities at all, arguing that his more or less plotless *Portrait* (1974) was made to show "that the last step to our awareness of our sexual freedom is to say that we do not have to justify—that we are, that we exist, that we should be allowed to do anything that turns us on so long as we are consenting adults."[73] Meanwhile, the Al Goldstein who had optimistically celebrated *Misty Beethoven* as "Hollywood-porn HERE . . . right now!" ended the decade by acknowledging that his hopes had been misplaced: "When I started reviewing fuck films 10 years ago, I honestly hoped that the business would dramatically improve to the point where the only difference between Hollywood output and blue-film output would simply be the explicitness of the sexual activity. This has generally not come to pass."[74] *Playboy* magazine raised this same issue in a review of *Barbara Broadcast* itself, openly wondering whether the film testified to Metzger's "utter boredom with the task of pretending that sex movies are actually something else."[75] The initial wave of excitement that colored the first phase of the porno chic era had evidently ebbed by this time, prompting industry insiders like Marc Stevens to wonder why the industry had seemingly regressed back to "those early days of filming in beds that stunk of stale come."[76]

That's not a description that would quite apply to Metzger's films, of course, and there remains a third hypothesis that would explain the peculiarities of *Barbara Broadcast* and *Maraschino Cherry* in less dismal fashion: namely, that the films are extrapolations of the pornotopic project begun in *Misty Beethoven*. Such, for instance, is suggested by the relative position that the films' titular characters occupy within their respective sexual utopias. If *Misty* gives viewers the story of a woman's induction into the sexual aristocracy, then Metzger's next two films revolve around women who have *already been* inducted. Both Barbara Broadcast and Maraschino ("Mara") Cherry are in a sense simply continuations of what Misty has become by the end of her film. But this, in turn, offers a new light from which to consider the narrative stalling that marks the latter two films. Put simply, an achieved utopia is a narrative dead end, at least for its inhabitants. As Fredric Jameson notes in a study of utopian science fiction, the only "story" that an achieved utopia suggests is that of the visit, in which a utopian "explainer" introduces a tourist-outsider figure to their world. To quote Jameson: "nothing but the guided tour can really happen," as evidenced by utopian science-fiction novels from Edward Bellamy's *Looking Backward* (1888) and William Morris's *News from Nowhere* (1890) to B. F. Skinner's *Walden Two* (1948) and Ursula K. Le Guin's *Always Coming Home* (1985).[77] Ditto, though, for Metzger's final Henry Paris films. Pornotopia has already been realized for each film's lead protagonist; all that remains is for it to be shown, which is the task that Barbara and Mara—the films' respective "explainers"—perform for the journalist Roberta and Mara's sister, Penny, respectively.

That much is clear from *Barbara Broadcast*'s introductory title card: "The events in this film are based on an authentic fantasy. Only the names have been changed to protect the guilty," which is to say that the film's primary concern will be less to tell a story than to display a fantasy. Once again, the fantasy is that of a world for which public sex is a mode of social distinction for the well-to-do, here realized in the form of an upscale Manhattan restaurant whose business model is close cousin to that of *Misty Beethoven*'s airline. The tone is triple-X Ophülsian: to the soundtrack accompaniment of Strauss's "The Blue Danube," the film begins with languorous handheld tracking shots following the maître d' (Bobby Astyr) through the restaurant, with cut-ins to various scenes of hardcore action among the diners. A bearded gentleman (played by the legendary Zebedy Colt) beckons a waitress over: she takes his order, hoists up her skirt, and sits down on the table, legs apart. A woman can't find her waiter and so calls another over: she unzips his pants and deep-throats him on the restaurant stairs. At the center of it all is Barbara Broadcast herself, whose interview with Roberta is repeatedly interrupted by admirers who ask her for autographs and blow jobs, both of which she obligingly provides. In pornotopia, it would seem, there is no desire, only sex.

Nor is there any meaningful relation to historical time, either; rather, the film's action exists in a kind of posthistory of the sexual revolution in which fantasies of a fully sexualized public sphere have magically come to pass. We learn briefly that Barbara was once deported—a brief nod to Xaviera Hollander's life story—but that is all the prehistory the film can sustain lest its social vision implode under the weight of having to explain itself. This is one reason, in fact, why *Barbara Broadcast* is so nicely illustrative of what Linda Williams has identified as one of the major narrative templates of adult films—the "dissolved utopia," which Williams explores through an analysis of Marilyn Chambers' *Insatiable* (1980). What typifies "dissolved" hardcore, on Williams's reading, is that pornotopia is no longer a state to be attained through the resolution of a narrative (as is the case, say, for Misty in *Misty Beethoven*); rather, "pornotopia is *already* achieved" as the premise of the film's action.[78] There is no longer any obstacle to be overcome, nor any antinomy to be worked through, with the result that the film's narrative trajectory and its hardcore "numbers" simply collapse onto one another: the narrative *is* the numbers.

Yet if the world of the film is, by definition, problem-free, then it follows that sex should be uncontaminated by gendered imbalances of power: "the dissolved utopianism of the film," Williams writes of *Insatiable*, "lies in part in its banishment of the ill effects of power in a pursuit of cheerful pleasure."[79] For Metzger, this registers primarily in the way his later Henry Paris films often run against the grain of straight hardcore's heterosexist conventions. To the extent to which there is a developing trajectory at all in the final Henry Paris films, it is found in the assertion of a specifically female agency on the part of the tourist-outsider figure, whose own sexual pleasure gets charted against a growing anonymization and depersonalization of the men from whom it is taken. In *Barbara Broadcast*, that trajectory begins when Barbara leaves the interview for an appointment with a businessman, advising Roberta to make sure she gives her compliments to the chef. What next occurs is one of the most sensational—indeed, infamous—declarations of female sexual intent from the porno chic era. Roberta wanders off into the kitchen, where she spots a chiseled, shirtless dishwasher (Wade Nichols). Smiling, she kicks a kitchen pot out in front of her,

4.5 Roberta (C. J. Laing) provocatively declares her sexual agency. Screen captures from *Barbara Broadcast*.

hoists up her skirt, squats over the pot, and urinates. Roberta's bold overture is punctuated by a series of shot-reverse shot edits as the two protagonists lock eyes, the urine still tinkling into the pot: the beefcake dishwasher's initial look of bewilderment fades slowly into a smile of recognition as Roberta throws her head back, laughs, and walks over to him (figure 4.5).

A decade after the film's release, porn chronicler Jim Holliday would select the ensuing action as the top anal scene in hardcore history.[80] But the specific orifices involved are perhaps less relevant to the scene's impact than the way in which Roberta's opening gambit has the effect of reconfiguring the conventions of sexual agency in hardcore film. (Like the pegging scene in *Misty Beethoven*, the urination sequence demonstrates how Metzger's departures from porn's normative phallocentrism often ran into censorship trouble: the action was cut in nearly every state as well as in early home video versions.) What happens in the kitchen is that the act of anal sex, often coded as a pinnacle of female submission in straight porn, is instead taken over by the unmistakable agency of Roberta, whose purpose, inspired by her interview with Barbara, is her own pursuit of sexual adventure. Nor is this a one-off. The film redeploys the same pattern in its very next hardcore scene, when Barbara and Roberta reunite at the hotel's nightclub. Once again, the sequence is orchestrated around the representation of female sexual agency, here in what begins as a lesbian scene between Barbara and Roberta on the dancefloor but soon develops into a three-way with a faceless man. And once again the representation of straight, penetrative sex (during the threesome) is untethered from the conventional coordinates of male initiative and pleasure. Metzger's depreciation of masculinity is here foreshadowed by a series of comical cutaways to a pair of musclebound men arm-wrestling at a nearby table, their empty show of machismo completely blinding them to the sexual action right next to them. But it becomes even more pronounced once the unidentified man joins the action, penetrating Roberta from behind while she goes down on Barbara. His face never visible, the man exists in the scene *only* as a penis, which is seen in close-up meat shots and, subsequently, in an oral scene in which Roberta deep-throats him while Barbara stares meaningfully into her eyes (figure 4.6). Put another way, the penis enters the film's representation primarily as an appendage to Barbara and Roberta's pleasure, rather than the man's. The act of heterosexual sex, both vaginal and oral, is stripped from the agency of the male participant to instead finds its purpose as a term of the two women's sexual enjoyment of each other.

This, in fact, is another reason why Metzger's decision to include the Money-Gillis S/M sequence from the *Misty* shoot sounds such a sour note, even aside from its problematic legal and ethical implications: put simply, the S/M action—which follows the dancefloor sequence—entirely upsets the gendered terms of the film's pornotopia. The narrative motivation for the inclusion of the S/M sequence is beyond flimsy. The dancefloor sex over, the faceless man is finally revealed: actor Jamie Gillis, in the role of Barbara's friend, Curly, who, we learn, had previously helped Barbara with one of her "girls." "We had a little PAP," Barbara explains to Roberta. "A Protestant-American Princess," Curly adds (a play on the antisemitic acronym JAP, *Jewish*-American Princess). "Yes," Barbara adds, "we had this little PAP working for us. And to set her straight, we let Curly at her." And, with that, a film whose pornotopia has so far been explored as an arena of female sexual

4.6 Barbara (Annette Haven) gazes at Roberta (C. J. Laing), while the faceless man (Jamie Gillis) serves as appendage to her desire. Screen capture from *Barbara Broadcast*.

autonomy introduces the spectacle of Constance Money chained to a bathroom floor, subject to the sadistic administrations of a man who will "set her straight." Nor is this the only way in which the sequence upsets the framework of the film's previous action. One of the odd aspects of *Barbara Broadcast*, for instance, is that it largely withholds the display of the nude female body: "almost all of the fucking and sucking takes place fully or semi-clothed," noted the reviewer for *Screw*—except, that is, for the S/M sequence, in which "Curly" has his way with a fully naked Money.[81] Then, too, there is the abrupt way in which the film quickly ends after this scene—returning briefly to Roberta and Barbara who promise to meet again tomorrow, same time, same place—with no attempt to repair the narrative and thematic disturbance that the scene introduces.

Viewed in terms of Metzger's disputes with Money, there is a strange spitefulness that hangs over these slapdash formal choices, as though the need for any textual integrity has been overridden by Metzger's own ill will regarding his former star. The abuse that Money encountered on the set of *Misty* here gets extended metatextually into another film, in which it is now reframed as a diegetic "punishment" inflicted on a woman who needs to be "set straight," even at the cost of that film's overall cohesion. Certainly, the odd ethno-religious framing of the S/M sequence—the punishment of a "PAP" at the hands of a Jewish actor (Gillis), filmed by a Jewish director (Metzger)—jibes uncomfortably with Money's claim that the filmmaker "had a thing about me being a WASP." Has the ethnic resentment that seems to have simmered between Metzger and Money during the production of *Misty Beethoven* returned to intrude upon the pornotopia of *Barbara Broadcast*? Perhaps. But we do not need to hypothesize some kind of ethnic friction as the snake in this hardcore Eden to identify how Metzger's Jewishness may have played a role in the pornotopic social imaginary of his final Henry Paris films. We need also to attend to their humor.

"WE ALL HAVE OUR CROSSES TO SCHLEP": *MARASCHINO CHERRY* AS BORSCHT BELT PORN

The porn industry's ethnic affiliations are, by stereotype, Italianate, given the extent of Mafia control over the distribution of adult film during the porno chic era.[82] On any given porn set, however, the demographics would more likely have tilted Jewish, at least in terms of the performers and filmmakers. There is a passage in novelist Samuel Delany's memoir of Times Square porn theaters, *Times Square Red, Times Square Blue*, in which the author describes how "a good number of the working technicians, writers, and actors were the disaffected brothers and sisters and cousins and aunts and uncles of the Jewish New Left."[83] Others, meanwhile, have suggested that the same radical energies that led secular Jewish immigrants to the New Left also placed them at the vanguard of the sexual revolution in the 1960s and after.[84] Whatever the reason, it remains the case that Metzger's own time in hardcore saw him lean more heavily into his Jewish identity than ever before. A good number of the performers and technicians with whom he chose to work were Jewish: actors Jamie Gillis, C. J. Laing, Gloria Leonard, David Savage, and Marc Stevens—many of whom were represented by agent Dorothy Palmer—as well as his cinematographer, Paul Glickman, and editor, Doris Toumarkine. But we should also recall, in this context, Metzger's ambition "to keep alive the tradition of Borscht Belt humor" in his adult work—touched on in the previous chapter—which helped to make his two final Henry Paris films the most culturally Jewish movies he ever made.[85] Again, the jokes are not very good; but they *are* explicit in their cultural references. "That chopped-liver cock's gorgeous! It must have been done by the sculptor Horowitz," notes a customer at the buffet display in *Barbara Broadcast*. "That couldn't be Horowitz's work," her friend corrects her. "Horowitz only works in Halvah"—which is, admittedly, less a punchline per se than a Jewish in-joke in place of one. That dialog is immediately followed by a scene in which actor Alan Marlow propositions a woman played by Shirley Peters, the only black adult performer in Metzger's filmography.[86] "Are you circumcised?" she replies to the man, because "I don't want you to think I'm not interested in you as a person"—which doesn't quite land either, because nobody really expects the inhabitants of pornotopia to be interested in each other "as people" anyway. More successful, at least in formal terms, is Penny's throwaway aside in *Maraschino Cherry*, after she blithely comes out as gay: "Well, we all have our crosses to schlep." The point here is not, of course, that Metzger had previously hidden his Jewishness. Rather, it is that the disparaged genre of hardcore porn seems to have given Metzger license to engage a bawdy, subaltern dimension of his identity that his earlier auteurist pretensions had bracketed off.

But this has important implications for Metzger's pornotopic social imaginary. For one thing, the emphasis on Jewish cultural identity raises questions about the broader dynamics of inclusion and exclusion in these films, particularly in terms of racial representation. Does the pronounced Jewishness of Metzger's hardcore universe account for the general absence of black bodies in these films? Perhaps, although any claim along these lines would need to be leveraged against the simple fact that black/white interracial scenes only really became common in the 1980s.[87] For another, Metzger's carnivalizing approach—again, touched on in the last chapter—means a commitment to a topsy-turvy model of social interaction, what Mikhail Bakhtin, in his discussion of medieval carnival, described as "liberation from the prevailing truth," and what Metzger, in his script for the compilation film *The World of Henry Paris* (1981), summarized as "people living in a realistic world behaving in a make-believe way."[88] It means a commitment to the logic of the "world upside down"; for Metzger, a vision of the public sphere in which all social exchange is managed in sexual terms. What needs to be added, though, is the way this social conception harbors an immanent comicality. It was the great anthropologist Mary Douglas who argued that jokes, in upending our normative inferences and conventional expectations, typically thrive within social worlds in which norms and conventions are also being upended. If jokes thrive in *Misty Beethoven* and *Barbara Broadcast*, then one reason is that their social worlds are similarly upended, with sexual pluck substituted for class hierarchy as the basis of social existence.

With *Maraschino Cherry*, however, Metzger would take a step further by making a film whose overall structure put at least one reviewer in mind of sketch comedy: a "surreal sexual circus," in the words of a *Playboy* writer, "as loosely organized as *Laugh-In*."[89] Hardcore scenes, in *Maraschino Cherry*, are structured as much as gags or skits as for their carnal appeal. Consider, as an initial salvo, a sex scene between actors Michael Gaunt and Susan McBain early in the framing action at Mara's brothel. "Do you think I could get VD from a toilet seat?" the man asks at the scene's beginning. "No," the woman answers. "That's a fallacy. Medical science has proven that. Really. It's perfectly safe." "Okay," the man smiles in relief, then sits down on a toilet seat and beckons the woman over for sex. The operative principle here is not that of narrative causality, as though the hardcore action that ensues can plausibly be understood as a narrative effect of the opening conversation; rather, action relates to conversation primarily as punchline to setup. The scene is, after all, nothing more than the literalization of the old joke in which someone explains that they got a venereal disease from a toilet seat. "That's a very unusual place to have sex!" is the traditional laughline.[90] In all its versions, the joke works by exploiting a buried ambiguity in the idea of catching an STD "from" a toilet seat. "From," in this context, humorously juggles meanings, suggesting both "due to contact with" and "during the act of sitting on," which, in the context of the scene in *Maraschino Cherry*, allows the man to make the absurd leap from hygiene myth to a foolish assumption of sexual protection. Gag form substitutes for narrative motivation as the scene's orchestrating principle.

A more sustained example comes in the matador sequence that Metzger borrowed from the *Misty* shoot. The dialog that sets up the hardcore scene again takes the form of a gag, in which a soft-spoken man (Marc Valentine) explains his sexual hangups to Mara:

> **MAN:** Actually, I have a problem communicating with women, trying to feel a rapport with them, trying to understand them.
>
> **MARA:** What do you do for a living?
>
> **MAN:** I'm a gynecologist.

The humor here is simple incongruity: incompetence with women at one level is laughably paired with medical expertise at another. But this is only the beginning of a metonymic chain of incongruities, in which each absurdist twist gets remobilized as gag set-up for another. For instance, noticing that the man has been admiring a matador's outfit in her office, Mara next encourages a little cosplay:

"I suggest you begin thinking of yourself as a more dominant male figure. . . . The bravest bullfighter of them all! Who uses women like marionettes! Think about it." Mara's suggestion motivates the matador footage that now follows—a fantasy sequence in which the man daydreams himself as a bullfighter embarking on a hardcore *corrida* with Money—even as it renders the footage utterly comedic, the overwrought macho fantasy of a gynophobic gynecologist. (Even within the man's own daydream, Money is unable to take his virile posturings seriously: "Have you seen the new movie about the bullfighter?" she asks. "He got into the S&M scene in Fire Island. It's called *Blood and Sand*"—the title of a 1922 bullfighting melodrama starring Rudolph Valentino, but more wittily a reference to Wakefield Poole's queer landmark *Boys in the Sand* [1971], itself shot on Fire Island.)[91] But this daydream sequence in turn becomes the setup for a closing punchline. Disturbed from his reveries by a woman's entry into the room, the man attempts to apply his bullfighter's machismo to the real world, commanding the woman to "get your sister and suck her off." In response, she slaps him in the face, and he falls whimpering to the floor. "Who does he think he is, a gynecologist?" offers an onlooker. The series of incongruity gags here comes full circle, each one ping-ponging between incompatible models of masculinity: the man who cannot communicate with women is a nebbish gynecologist; the nebbish gynecologist is a swaggering matador; the swaggering matador is a sniveling wreck, dropped by a woman's slap; and the sniveling wreck is a nebbish gynecologist.

If we leave our analysis there, however, we miss the way in which Metzger's "Borscht Belt" hardcore style is bookended in *Maraschino Cherry* by journeys from and to America's Protestant heartland. Penny has come to Manhattan from a place called Poplar Springs on a mission to convince Mara to return to help her parents, who have recently lost the family farm. The scene in which Penny explains all this parodies the kind of *Leave It to Beaver* pastoralism that a name like "Poplar Springs" evokes: "Mara," Penny drawls, "it would have done your heart good to see Ma and Pa when your mail arrived from New York." And how to solve the family's economic problems? By bringing the Jewish cathouse to the *goyim*. "Poplar Springs is right in the middle of a strongly religious and God-fearing area of the country," Penny explains. "So, we thought it would be a natural for a middle-income whore house. And we thought you could tell us something about *your* operations." Accordingly, at film's end, having trained Penny to manage the business in her absence, Mara dutifully begins her journey home, hailing a yellow cab and telling the driver "I think you go left at St. Louis." Metzger's Borscht

Belt hardcore is, in this way, wrapped in the flimsy framework of an outdated Protestant sentimentalism that, paradoxically, needs New York more than New York needs it: the farm in Poplar Springs can survive only through the incursion of Mara's moral economy—urban Jewish and hardcore carnivalesque.

Of course, we never get to see what Poplar Springs' renewal would actually look like, just as, in *Misty Beethoven*, no meaningful attention is given to the question of how a society ordered around sexual virtuosity would actually work. Yet, it should be clear that this question asks more of Metzger's pornotopia than it is willing to give, which is, in the end, less a social program than a depiction of the pleasures that might result from one—a hedonistic superstructure with no glimpse of a determining base. If Metzger's pornotopic social vision may fitly be described as carnivalesque, then this is in the end not only because of its humor, nor because of its topsy-turvy depiction of a sexualized public sphere, but because the carnivalesque is not a viable mode of social belonging in the first place. In his study of utopian fiction, Jameson has described Bakhtin's notion of carnival as a "vanishing mediator," a moment of freedom that exists only in the interstices between periods of social order, or in the transition from one social system to another, but which cannot coalesce as a self-subsistent utopia in its own right.[92] Something similar applies to Metzger's pornotopic imaginary. In contradistinction to those theorists of the sexual public sphere who have called for a "world-making project" that would dissolve the repressive structures in which sexual intimacy is enmeshed, Metzger's pornotopia exists as a state of exception that cannot be reliably depended upon to "make" a world but can only be passed along.[93] The pornotopic narrative in Metzger is, accordingly, not just a narrative of entry—the "tourist" introduced to a garden of earthly delights—but one of exit too, a fleeting stage of existence through which its inhabitants pass. In the closing minutes of *Misty*, the social calendar comes full circle, bringing another contender for the title of "Golden Rod Girl" as elderly gossips struggle to remember the name of the last one. "Who was the *last* Golden Rod Girl?" asks one. "Misty, uh, *Mozart*," replies another. "Now nobody knows where she is. Last I heard she was writing a book." Barbara, in *Barbara Broadcast*, has meanwhile already written that book and, having introduced Roberta to her world, ends the film considering her own passage out of it. "Who knows," she muses in the voiceover that closes out the "cool" version of the film. "Maybe I'll learn to be a reporter."[94] And then there is Mara, who trains her sister to be her own replacement before returning to Poplar Springs to ply her trade in her old hometown.

Pornotopia is never a destination in these films but only a lay-by, its pleasures bought at the cost of their own ephemerality. But this means that the question of the social is never a really serious one but a scaffold onto which carnivalesque alternatives can be temporarily hoisted, with no clue as to where they might lead. Any claim regarding pornography's supposed sexual utopianism must be qualified in the case of the Henry Paris films, whose pornotopias are only ever short-term propositions for their transient inhabitants.[95]

All this would be mirrored in Metzger's own professional journey; for he, too, had been preparing his departure from the realm of pornotopia. Shortly after wrapping *Barbara Broadcast* in the summer of 1976, Metzger left the country for the United Kingdom to direct *The Cat and the Canary*, his first "straight" (that is, non-sex) feature since *Dark Odyssey*. As the next chapter explores, the film would be his last bid for a legitimacy that was now further away than ever.

CHAPTER 5

"CULT PORN IDOL GONE STRAIGHT?"

The Return(s) of Radley Metzger

The Argentine writer Jorge Luis Borges once wrote that an author is always the "other one," separate from and not the same as the living, breathing person.[1] The author, in this formulation, is not exactly the person who writes, but rather something like an effect of the writing, a figure that the act of writing itself brings into being. At the same time, the notion of the author as "other one" suggests a certain foreignness, as though the author has a life or persona of its own that the writer can neither fully know nor control. The point would become something of a commonplace in poststructuralist thought from the late 1960s onward, when continental theorists Roland Barthes and Michel Foucault both announced the "death of the author," challenging the notion of the author as the singular and authoritative creator of an artwork's meaning.[2] But few actual authors can be said to have lived these paradoxes quite as directly as Radley Metzger, who over the course of the 1970s had divided himself into two distinct authorial personas: "Radley Metzger," Audubon's softcore impresario, and "Henry Paris," the hardcore industry's ace in the hole. What is more, the vicissitudes of Metzger's passage through the late 1970s and into the 1980s—his last period as an active filmmaker—would see this masquerade multiply in dizzying fashion in a vain effort to bring these personas under his control: on the one hand, a series of failed ventures to reclaim the Radley Metzger mantle; on the other, and punctuating these, the dissolution of Henry Paris into further pseudonymous and heteronymous fronts: "Gérard Kikoïne," "Gene Borey," "Peter Wolfe," and "Stanley Paul." Authorship, in this final phase of his filmmaking career, existed for Metzger simultaneously as something to be rehabilitated and something to be buried. This is what happens when the man of taste puts himself in his own discriminating crosshairs.

Not that Metzger really needed to complicate matters for himself at this stage. The period in question was already turbulent and transformative enough for those in the field of adult filmmaking. The Golden Age of adult film in the early to mid-1970s had represented the zenith of the public exhibition of pornography in the United States, peaking at just under eight hundred theaters nationwide playing 35mm adult films.[3] But the advent of the home-video market for pornography quickly wrought an epochal shift. By the mid-1980s, there were only around 250 such theaters left in business, and the subdistributors on which adult film depended were going bankrupt. Over the same period, however, the X-rated video market grew to around a hundred million weekly rentals—the same number as admissions to adult theaters at the start of the decade—most of which were of films produced quickly and on the cheap. As adult-film historian Chuck Kleinhans notes, "a budgeting rule of thumb assumed two video features could be made for about $15,000, and that involved a two-day shoot, including cast and crew salaries, equipment rental, and postproduction editing costs."[4] Perhaps this explains why the transition to video has traditionally been framed as a narrative of pornography's decline, since it brought an end to the gentrifying ambitions that had sought to make pornography part of the mainstream of cinematic culture.

The validity of that narrative is debatable. In a recent account of the adult video boom, Peter Alilunas suggests that video likely *saved* the porn industry, given the economic downturn of the late 1970s.[5] We also saw in the previous chapter how the impetus driving porn's gentrification was already on the wane from the mid-1970s onward—that is to say, *prior* to video's full impact.[6] Less open to revision, however, is the way that adult home video partook in a much broader change in the place and visibility of sex within the public sphere. The move to video was concurrent with other shifts in the sociopolitical environment, including changes in sexual practices and ideologies due to the AIDS crisis, as well as conservative moral panic over porn's supposedly harmful effects, fueled by Attorney General Edwin Meese's Commission on Pornography in 1986. It was not video—or not video alone—that killed the porno chic era, but the broader collapse of pornotopian social imaginaries, rendered untenable in the years of Reagan and AIDS.

How, then, to negotiate those shifts? To clarify Metzger's strategies, it will be helpful to return to Gérard Genette's essay "The Name of the Author," to the passage where Genette identifies the three conditions under which the name of an author can appear: "Either the author 'signs' . . . with his legal name," Genette writes, "or he signs with a false name, borrowed or invented . . . or he does not sign at all"—a series of options corresponding to the conditions of orthonymity, pseudonymity, and anonymity, in that order.[7] Each of these can help frame the various steps taken by Metzger during this period. For one thing, Metzger would seek to reclaim his orthonymic authorship, first in attempting a mainstream horror-mystery film, *The Cat and the Canary* (1978), next in an ill-fated attempt to restore his late 1960s softcore style in the made-for-cable *The Princess and the Call Girl* (1983), both released under his own name. He would also take steps to extricate himself from his "Henry Paris" pseudonym, even to the extent of calling time on his alter ego with the release of a "best of" compilation film *The World of Henry Paris* (1981). Yet, despite these moves, he would still on occasion dabble in hardcore when the opportunity or money was right, which now required him to invent further pseudonyms for his work. Just as Metzger had had cause to invent "Henry Paris" in the early 1970s to distinguish his hardcore work from his "Radley Metzger" films, so too did the "Henry Paris" films now need similar curatorial protection. The very last feature film he directed, *Love Standing Up* (1984), would fittingly involve a plot that insists on the right of the adult filmmaker to remain anonymous and unknown.

Of course, Metzger's most recognizable trademark as a director had always been this need to draw distinctions; but that impulse would eventually cannibalize and dismantle the conditions of his own authorship, fracturing his oeuvre across a variety of silos in a way that turned his hoped-for return into a disappearing act instead. As Genette drolly notes, the "pseudonym habit is very much like the drug habit, quickly leading to increased use, abuse, even overdose."[8] If the name of the author can be thought of as an invitation to reading, then Metzger might fairly be criticized for micromanaging his invite list. Radley Metzger, the person, and "Radley Metzger," the authorial brand, became terms that could no longer be easily made to coincide. It would take the efforts of others, less concerned than he was with such discriminations, to reconnect them in later years.

"THE TIMING WAS OFF": METZGER'S LAST ORTHONYMIC FILMS

First announced in the fall of 1976, with a four-week UK location shoot scheduled to start on November 22, *The Cat and the Canary* proved to be Metzger's last

5.1 Radley Metzger (*left*) directing Edward Fox in *The Cat and the Canary*.
Source: Photofest.

opportunity to "go straight" after some fifteen years in the sex film business, and his first non-adult film since *Dark Odyssey*.[9] It was, as *Variety* opined, Metzger's endeavor to finally "make the hump into non-sex pix," or, as *Life* put it more forthrightly, a case of the "cult porn idol . . . gone straight."[10] The finished film was also quite warmly received by critics who praised its "cracking cast"—consisting largely of British stalwarts of stage and screen like Wilfred Hyde-White, Dame Wendy Hiller, Edward Fox, and Honor Blackman, plus American actors Carol Lynley and Michael Callan—and even highlighted Metzger's "crisp direction" (figure 5.1).[11] Other hardcore filmmakers similarly pivoted to horror as the market for theatrical porn dried up, among them William Lustig, who went from directing films like *The Violation of Claudia* (1977) to the slasher film that made his name, *Maniac* (1980), and Roberta Findlay, who switched her attention to horror with a series of films in the mid-1980s. But few had the kind of talent and production values that Metzger could conjure.[12] Why, then, did *The Cat and the Canary* fail to yield the breakthrough that Metzger hoped for?

The answer: an unworkable combination of opportunism and bad timing. *The Cat and the Canary* had its origins in a successful 1922 stage play of the same name by American playwright John Willard, which had already been adapted for film multiple times before Metzger's attempt: a 1927 silent version directed by expatriate German filmmaker Paul Leni for Universal; a 1930 sound remake (under the title *The Cat Creeps*), also for Universal, with an accompanying Spanish-language version; and Paramount Pictures' more comedic 1939 variation, starring Bob Hope and Paulette Goddard. Following Willard's passing in 1942, his wife, actor Roberta Arnold, had prevented subsequent adaptations—at least until *her* death in 1966, at which point the film rights were picked up by Raymond Rohauer, an infamous film collector with a habit of acquiring rights to the work of dead artists.[13] A decade later, British producer Richard Gordon secured adaptation rights from Rohauer, a friend of his, with a view to capitalizing on the recent success of mystery novelist Agatha Christie adaptations.

This was the opportunism. As Gordon later recalled: "I was impressed with the revival of interest in Agatha Christie's stories and the success of films like *Murder on the Orient Express* [1974] and *Death on the Nile* [1978]. . . . I began to think that a remake with an all-star cast like the Agatha Christie pictures would appeal to the same kind of audience." To write the screenplay and direct, Gordon approached Metzger, whom he had known since the early 1960s when Metzger supervised the dubbing for Gordon's import of a 1959 German film, *Verbrechen nach Schulschluß* (released as *Crime After School* in the United States). "I used to talk to him often about the possibility that one day we might do something together," Gordon remembered. "When I decided that I would like to make *The Cat and the Canary*, I mentioned it to him and he reacted very enthusiastically."[14]

Aside from the opportunity to break into the mainstream, one of the likely appeals of the property, for Metzger, was the occasion it offered to once again position his work within a preexisting cinematic lineage. Just as *Carmen, Baby* (1967) had been promoted as the thirteenth film adaptation of Prosper Mérimée's story, and just as *Camille 2000* (1969) presented itself as an alternative to MGM's 1936 take on Dumas's original, so Metzger's version of *The Cat and the Canary* was promoted as the "fifth screen reincarnation" of Willard's play (counting the Spanish-language version of *The Cat Creeps*), for which Metzger claimed, as he always did, that he had "stuck closely to the original version [i.e., the play]."[15] At the same time, Metzger's ongoing concern with brand management meant that he avoided obvious links to his Audubon label: although Metzger and Leighton's company was involved in a coproduction capacity, the film was identified solely under Gordon's Grenadier Films shingle, with UK distribution handled by Gala Film Distributors and international distribution by Gordon Films, Inc.[16] As for the film's U.S. distributor, Gordon approached a number of the major studios—all of which passed—before settling on an independent company called Cinema Shares.[17]

This was the bad timing. Cinema Shares first screened *The Cat and the Canary* in the United States in November 1978 at the Miami Film Festival, where the film received the Special Jury Gold award.[18] But Cinema Shares then failed to meet its contractual obligation to put the film into theatrical release by December 31, which led Metzger to take the company to court in order to win back distribution rights. "I think it was a fun picture," Metzger later commented, "but the litigation involved was horrendous. The distributor chose not to honor the contract. We sued, and it is very difficult to be the aggressor in a law suit. After all those years of defending myself in censorship cases in which we never lost, there I was trying to create a case on the other side. It took a very long time. We won the suit because it was an obvious breach."[19]

But this meant that by the time the film eventually saw U.S. release in 1981, the Agatha Christie cycle was on the wane.[20] Despite earlier reviews that foresaw the film as a shoo-in for the "mystery afficionados who have been flocking to those Christie thrillers," *The Cat and the Canary* ended up missing its moment in the U.S. market, where it proved a dud.[21] "The timing was off," Metzger himself acknowledged.[22] Frustrating evidence of what might have been was meanwhile provided by the country where the film was first released—Italy, in September 1978—and where *The Cat and the Canary* was marketed as an *actual* Agatha Christie adaptation: the film slowly climbed to rank among the country's top ten box-office hits for two weeks the following March, even besting Michael Cimino's *The Deer Hunter* (1978) at the Italian box office (figure 5.2).[23] "That got it off to a very good start, and immediately created tremendous interest in France and Germany and elsewhere," Gordon recalled, even though that enthusiasm failed to buoy the film's deferred American debut.[24]

The Cat and the Canary was hardly a bust, then, even if it failed to become the breakout success that might have led Metzger to more mainstream gigs. It also gave some evidence of how Metzger's more modernist leanings could profitably be applied outside the realm of adult film. To gauge this, we can compare the various film versions' handling of one of the cornerstone set pieces of Willard's play,

5.2 Italian publicity falsely claimed that *The Cat and the Canary* was an Agatha Christie adaptation.
Source: Author's collection.

the scene of the will reading, in which the relatives of the late Cyrus West learn that he has left two wills, the second of which to be read out the following day if the inheritor named in the first fails to survive the night.

Leni's take on the scene exemplifies the subjective stylization for which silent-era German cinema was known: a dolly in to an extreme close-up of the will reader's mouth, a character's distorted reflection in a piece of silverware, the mechanism of a ticking clock superimposed over the action, and so forth. Paramount's horror-comedy version offsets Bob Hope's irrepressible one-liners against the housekeeper's ghostly warnings. Metzger, meanwhile, uses the scene to indulge his more reflexive leanings, as well as his cinephilia: he borrows a detail from the 1934 George Arliss film *The Last Gentleman*, in which a dead man reads out his own will to his survivors via a prerecorded film. The will of Cyrus West, in Metzger's hands, is stored not in an envelope—as in all prior versions—but on reels of film, preserved in a coffinlike icebox, bound in heavy chains (figure 5.3). The will-reading scene accordingly involves a portable screen at one end of a dining table and a projector at the other, so that the late West appears to be phantasmatically "joining" his relatives for the will reading over dinner. Within this setup, West's filmed image gives commands from beyond the grave, instructing his housekeeper, Mrs. Pleasant, to serve the wine while he harangues and abuses his greedy descendants. At one point, Mrs. Pleasant walks behind the screen at the exact same moment that she appears onscreen in the film recorded years earlier, as though she has somehow jumped through time from present reality into the past (figure 5.4). "That was entirely Radley's idea," Gordon later acknowledged, "and I think he staged it brilliantly. It's one of the highlights of the movie."[25] It also picks up threads in Metzger's corpus from more or less exactly where he had left off prior to his Henry Paris hiatus. As we saw in an earlier chapter, Metzger's *The Lickerish Quartet* (1970) had been inspired in part by the Czech multimedia group Laterna Magika, whose shows involved fluid interactions between live dramatic action and film projection.[26] In *The Lickerish Quartet*, that influence had registered in the way the screen-within-the-screen functions as a surface of sexual fantasy into which the protagonists eventually project themselves. In *The Cat and the Canary*, the influence registers again, albeit here in a more studied effort to replicate the "trick" effect of seamlessness in which the Czech group specialized. Nor is it quite right, as Linda Williams has

5.3 The icebox containing the reels of Cyrus West's will. Screen capture from *The Cat and the Canary*.

5.4 Past and present interact as Mrs. Pleasant (Beatrix Lehmann) appears to walk into, and then out of, the projected film. Screen captures from *The Cat and the Canary*.

suggested, to see Metzger's use of the device in *The Cat and the Canary* as a mere "gag" in comparison with the thematic complexity of the earlier movie.[27] The motif strikingly captures the past's spectral grip on the living. The celluloid image here becomes a way to cheat death's finality—what film theorist André Bazin described as cinema's "mummy complex," its ability to give the semblance of life even to the dead—so that West can toy with his descendants from beyond the grave.[28] Once again, then, Metzger finds in the apparatus of cinema a material metaphor for his story—albeit, in this instance, one linked not to a context of memory and sexual fantasy, as in *Lickerish*, but to the more horror-appropriate theme of the dead's continued hold on the living.

Metzger's second shot at orthonymity was no less plagued by poor timing, only this time the filmmaker opted to try his hand within the rapidly growing mediascape of nontheatrical adult film. As Metzger himself put it in a 1994 interview with *Psychotronic Video*, "After *Cat*, it was a question of going into video production or TV production. . . . I just think that things had changed to the point that the [theatrical] audience wasn't there. The couples market was gone and everything had shifted."[29]

One of these changes was cable television's emergence as a new venue for the kind of softcore content with which Metzger had first established himself. The growth of the hardcore industry a decade earlier had decimated theatrical demand for the tamer product in which Audubon and Metzger had formerly specialized, but the advent of cable threw out a potential lifesaver: on the one hand, sexually explicit material was, by the late 1970s, an established route for cable channels seeking to differentiate themselves from broadcast television; on the other, federal obscenity law meant that cable providers were nonetheless wary of content that was *too* explicit. One of Metzger's Henry Paris films demonstrates the fine line that cable providers had to walk. In 1976 HBO briefly flirted with a possible deal with Robert Sumner's Mature Pictures to screen hardcore material at 1:00 a.m. on Sunday mornings in the Manhattan market, with *Naked Came the Stranger* (1975) floated as the film to launch the series. The experiment was ultimately abandoned, though, when HBO program chief Harlan Kleiman decided that hardcore material presented "too many problems."[30] With hardcore a dicey proposition, the stage was set for a cable-fueled resurgence in softcore product, what film historian David Andrews describes as softcore's "second Golden Era," which would ultimately crest in the 1990s with the late-night programming associated with Showtime's "After Hours" and Cinemax's "After Dark" blocks and series like *Red Shoe Diaries* (1992–97), *Erotic Confessions* (1992–96), and *Hot Line* (1995–96).[31] Metzger's work had played a catalyzing role in the first of these Golden Eras (the 1960s); might he find a new toehold in the second?

Initial signs were good. By the late 1970s, a small number of cable operators were offering softcore titles as pay-per-view options, and there were several nationally available subscription channels devoted exclusively to such content, with names like Private Screenings, the Pleasure Channel, and Adults Only, although most of these were short-lived.[32] Metzger had long anticipated television as an eventual destination for his films: almost a decade earlier, during post-production on *The Lickerish Quartet*, Metzger had described how, as "television becomes more candid, the chances [become] more favorable for a pickup of my films on the late or late, late picture programs."[33] In 1981 those hopes were formalized as a reality when Metzger struck a deal with the Escapade cable network for exclusive long-term rights for seven of his pictures, including *Camille 2000* and *The Lickerish Quartet*.[34] What Metzger could not have foretold, though, was how that deal would open the door for his return to the director's chair. In 1982 Hugh Hefner's *Playboy* magazine made a partnership arrangement with Escapade's parent company, Rainbow Programming Services, to take over and rebrand the channel as the Playboy Channel, in the process inheriting Escapade's existing subscriber base.[35] As announced in *Playboy*, initial programming was to include "music and comedy specials, in-depth interviews, lifestyle documentaries, game shows and, of course, specially selected adult films."[36] Early series on the channel indeed ran the gamut, including a sitcom (*Four Play*), a talk show (*Women on Sex*), an investigative documentary series (*The Friday Files*), the monthly "video centerfolds," as well as music specials from the Newport Jazz Festival, among other shows. The films, meanwhile, would include "no X fare" and initially consisted of "theatrical-release movies" and "R-rated cinema classics" (such as *Emmanuelle II* [1975] and the Joan Collins–starring *The Stud* [1978]). Soon, however, the channel began experimenting with an in-house model for its features, signing established adult-film directors like Chuck Vincent and Lem Amero to produce movies exclusively for cable exhibition.[37]

This was the context in which Radley Metzger made his second return as "Radley Metzger": *The Princess and the Call Girl* (1983), which he directed as part of the "Playboy Premiere" series released simultaneously on the Playboy Channel and on MGM/UA videocassette.[38] For the project, Metzger was given considerable creative leeway—"They gave me *carte blanche*," he recalled, "I could do anything I wanted"—and the result was, in many respects, typical pre-Henry-Paris Metzger, albeit on a slighter scale. Based on another "classic" literary source, here Mark Twain's *The Prince and the Pauper* (1881), the film gave Metzger one last opportunity to shoot in the stomping grounds of the jet set: in Metzger's version of Twain's story, the "princess" is a New York socialite who swaps roles with an identical call girl (both played by Carol Levy) who plies her trade in the French Riviera. The end credits practically boast of each and every locale in which the film was shot: "the Principality of Monaco, Nice, Antibes, Beausoleil, and Rocquebrune." Yet, for all that, there remains a change in how the film relates to those locations: the action of *The Princess and the Call Girl* takes place in the hotel rooms and seafront cafés of the Côte d'Azur, not its villas, opera houses, or ballrooms. Which is to say, Metzger's Europhilic sensibilities here run closer to the ethos of a tourist than to that of the jet set itself. In part this was a symptom of production circumstances that constrained Metzger to the straight and narrow. For the first time in his work in adult film, he was employed as nothing more than a director for hire: although budget information for *The Princess and the Call Girl* is not available, Metzger was evidently careful to avoid extravagance. Despite his claims to creative *carte blanche*, Metzger chose not to "take advantage of that" and "didn't want to give [Playboy] something they couldn't easily market."[39]

Perhaps this is why Metzger's characteristic authorial tropes come off largely as garnish in his Playboy film, sundered from the ambitions of his previous work. The sustained self-reflexivity of films like *The Lickerish Quartet* now surfaces only in occasional one-liner references to *The Princess and the Call Girl*'s media of distribution (e.g., "Andrew, I know it isn't this way in the movies or on videocassettes"; or "Oh, I don't have HBO" to a character who reports having recently watched a "dirty movie"). The cinephiliac play of *Naked Came the Stranger* is meanwhile channeled into a single scene in which the titular "princess" seduces a man by suggestively reciting the names of studio-era film stars (Richard *Dix*, Anna May *Wong*, and the like). And Metzger's peekaboo softcore style gets curtailed to the most rudimentary and ready-to-hand of resources, such as a disco ball throwing dappled patterns of light over naked bodies or a sex scene framed to emphasize shadows on a wall. In attempting to provide something that Playboy could "easily market," Metzger ended up making a film that reduced his authorship to a surface effect: unlike *The Cat and the Canary*, which offered glimpses of what could have been, *The Princess and the Call Girl* was a bric-a-brac version of something Metzger had already done.

When the film played at the Cannes Film Market in the spring of 1984, it predictably failed to impress, particularly among those cognizant of Metzger's broader career. *Variety*, for instance, pulled no punches, declaring that Metzger's typically "glossy" style had, in this case, produced a mere "snooze-producer . . . for unfussy sexpo fans only."[40] Metzger may have been at fault in attempting to recreate his old softcore style, especially when compared to somebody like Chuck Vincent, say, who took the opportunity at Playboy to reinvent himself with a more warmly reviewed *Porky*'s knock-off, *Preppies* (1984), which even bagged a theatrical release. In comparison, Metzger's film debuted on the channel's July 1984 programming only to quickly disappear, eventually resurfacing five years later in a handful of showings in the "After Dark" slot at Cinemax. This was not quite the end of Metzger's association with Playboy, as we will see, although it did mark the closing of an opportunity. Shortly after Metzger laid his egg, the Playboy Channel went into significant retrenchment. Despite an overall growth in the cable market, Playboy's subscriber base was lagging far behind predictions, forcing the channel to cut back on in-house features and turn instead to what one journalist described as "third-rate, poorly dubbed European sex films."[41] Even Vincent's deal with Playboy sputtered after *Preppies*.[42] Radley Metzger, meanwhile, would never again make a feature film under his own name.

"NOT TO BE ASSOCIATED WITH MY OTHER WORK": METZGER VS. "METZGER"

During the delays that beset *The Cat and the Canary*'s uneven distribution, Metzger continued to receive offers to return to hardcore, which he summarily rejected lest he sabotage any further shot at a mainstream career. But one offer broke his resolve. In early 1980 the French producer Wilfred Dodd approached Metzger to make a hardcore film with financing from the German firm Ribu Video, on the understanding that Metzger's name would in no way be connected to the project. Although Metzger agreed to script the production, his primary on-set involvement would be as an advisor to French filmmaker Gérard Kikoïne, who received sole directing credit. (Kikoïne later described the film as "codirected" by Metzger and himself, with Metzger in charge of communicating with the actors and Kikoïne responsible for shot selection and framing.)[43] While the film would still be publicized in connection with Metzger's "Henry Paris" moniker, this would be at one remove, as a "Henry Paris Presents" production as opposed to "Directed by." The crew would be French—including cinematographer Gérard Lobeau, whom Metzger would subsequently hire for the French location work on *The Princess and the Call Girl*—as was the female lead, Dominique Saint Claire, appearing under the pseudonym Arlene Manhatten [*sic*]. For the rest of the onscreen roles Metzger assembled what was indubitably the strongest lineup of hardcore stars he had ever worked with—including George Payne, Veronica Hart, Vanessa Del Rio, Desiree Cousteau, Samantha Fox, and Ron Jeremy—for a week-long shoot that took place in New York in early May 1980, prior to the film's 1981 release under the eventual title *The Tale of Tiffany Lust* (figure 5.5).[44] The following year,

5.5 Poster for *The Tale of Tiffany Lust*.

Source: Author's collection.

the same filmmakers—and many of the same stars—regrouped for a follow-up "Henry Paris Presents" film, *Aphrodesia's Diary* (1983), which, as per Metzger's established practice at this point, included unused footage from the *Tiffany Lust* shoot as a flashback sequence.

Uncertainties of attribution have hounded these two pictures ever since their release. Most reports on *Tiffany Lust* at the time simply ignored Kikoïne's credit and treated the picture as another Henry Paris film. Others took the credit line at face value and made no mention of Paris at all. Only one reviewer was savvy enough to join the dots all the way to Metzger himself—adult performer Sue Feele, whose review in *Adult Cinema Review* described *Tiffany Lust* as "Radley Metzger's new screen gem."[45] Extant production stills discovered by adult-film historian Ashley West confirm Metzger's active role in the *Tiffany Lust* shoot, where he is seen blocking scenes with actors, checking light meters, and the like.[46] At the textual level, too, *Tiffany Lust* bears the hallmarks of Metzger's hardcore authorship: thematically, it extends Metzger's reflexive preoccupation with media, this time radio, in a plot that uses a sex-talk radio show as a formal basis for interweaving the various sexual escapades of its listeners; and the script is replete with Metzger's usual dreadful puns ("How do I know so much about crabs? I learned about them from scratch").[47] None of these features distinguish *Aphrodesia's Diary*, though, and Metzger is conspicuously absent from extant set photos from the latter film. It would seem, then, that Metzger's deal with Dodd was to use the French crew initially in something of an apprentice role, before handing over the reins to the French filmmakers entirely for the second feature.

The "Henry Paris Presents" strategy effectively elevated Metzger's pseudonym to the same kind of brand identity or trademark status that had once defined "Radley Metzger" at Audubon. Even as Metzger sought to extricate himself from Henry Paris as an active filmmaking persona, he allowed his alter ego to be abstracted into something like a sexual sensibility or ambience that could at times exceed the specifics of individual authorship. We see this too in the "best of" compilation film *The World of Henry Paris*, which Metzger cut for VHS and cable release in 1981. Consisting of a series of sex scenes accompanied by a husky female voiceover, *The World of Henry Paris* conceptualizes Paris's authorship entirely as a matter of mood and atmosphere, which the opening narration summarizes through the ideas of "sophistication," "humor," and "luxury." "The world of Henry Paris," we are told, is variously "a world of fantasy and gratification," "a realistic world [in which people] behave in a make-believe way," and a world "where all desires are satisfied and dreams come true," each claim serving as setup for the sex scenes that follow. The voiceover's rhetorical structure is that of metonymy, the "world of" trope serving as a way to enumerate the qualities for which "Henry Paris" becomes a placeholder. Authorship here is less a matter of the individualizing markers of, say, a visual style than it is of a generalized sexual ethos, one whose name others could be allowed to share, like Gérard Kikoïne, but from which Metzger now seemed almost willfully to be cutting himself off.

That, at least, would be the lesson of the final, most mystifying item in Metzger's adult filmography, dating from the period of his brief association with Playboy. Neither a "Henry Paris" film, insofar as it was not hardcore, nor a "Radley Metzger" film, insofar as it didn't meet his own orthonymic standards, the film in question was credited to director "Stanley Paul," writer "Gene Borey," and producer "Peter Wolfe," all of which were fronts for Metzger.[48] "Just as I didn't want Henry Paris to be associated with the films I'd made with my real name in the 1960s," Metzger later explained, "I didn't want this film to be associated with any of my other work."[49] Doubts even exist surrounding the name of the film itself, which began life under the working title of *The Iris Movie* before being prepared for release as *The Sins of Ilsa*, and then limping onto the Playboy Channel under uncertain conditions three years later as *Love Standing Up*. As such, the film, which I will call by its eventual release name, becomes a kind of vanishing point for authorial analysis: not only was this Metzger-directed picture not a "Radley Metzger" film, but, as we will see, it also covertly incorporated two decade-old short films that Metzger had created during his Henry Paris phase as test material for *The Opening of Misty Beethoven* (1976), in a plot that is explicitly about anonymity in adult film. A condition of authorial nonattribution thus pervades the film at all levels: the buried secret of Metzger's filmography, *Love Standing Up* buries secrets of its own, as we will see.

Adult-film historian Ashley West's interviews with Metzger allow us to reconstruct the film's production history. The project was proposed to Metzger in 1984, at a point when he had retired his "Henry Paris" brand and twice faltered in his efforts to relaunch "Radley Metzger." Money, it seems, was the leading factor in his decision to take on the film: "The money was attractive," he remembered. "Not in terms of the overall budget—which was fairly low—but in terms of what I was being offered." As he had done so often before, he chose to base his script on an already existing literary property: the film's working title, Metzger explained, reflected the script's indebtedness to an Iris Murdoch novel. Although he did not indicate which one, the source seems to have been Murdoch's 1954 debut, *Under the Net*, which tells the story of a struggling young writer, Jake, who finds his literary calling by reconnecting with an old acquaintance who now runs a film studio. *The Iris Movie*, accordingly, tells the story of a struggling New York journalist (initially called Joanie, later changed to Sue), who finds her literary calling by researching an article on a former adult-film star (Iris) who has retired into obscurity. Before filming began, Metzger tried to juice the picture's commercial prospects by taking advantage of the name recognition of the 1970s *Ilsa* exploitation series, retitling the film and renaming its porn star protagonist. ("Richard [Gordon] and I were discussing film franchises that had been successful," he later remembered. "And we were both marveling at the enduring success of the *Ilsa* series, which had done so well.")[50] The picture was subsequently shot over just seven days, from December 14 to December 20, 1984, with additional exteriors filmed in Paris the following April.

This limited schedule provided practical motivation for Metzger to include the two unreleased Henry Paris shorts, which feature in the film's centerpiece scene in which Ilsa (played by porn actress Helga Sven) shows the journalist some of her self-directed work. Yet, intentionally or not, the decision also generates intriguing effects by implicating Metzger's own filmography into the plot of *Love Standing Up*: it creates a hidden link, as it were, between Ilsa and Metzger himself as the two "directors" of the footage, one within the world of the film's fiction, one without. The film even winkingly gestures toward the double attribution when Sue praises Ilsa's direction in terms that were often applied to Metzger himself. "Ilsa had a particular touch directing women," she comments in voiceover. "At the time, I didn't know why." In terms of the film's diegesis, what explains Ilsa's "particular touch" will be the discovery that Ilsa is bisexual, which Sue soon learns when Ilsa seduces her in a jacuzzi. But at another level the "touch" in question is also explained by what the fiction itself cannot acknowledge: that the two shorts were actually shot by Radley Metzger, a filmmaker with a long-established reputation for the self-same "particular touch." Knowledge of Metzger's authorship—both of *Love Standing Up* and of the short films themselves—here becomes what Gérard Genette would call a "paratextual element" that creates a different set of readings that unfold alongside and interrogate the meanings that the film itself creates.[51]

As for the shorts themselves, the first of these is introduced by Ilsa with the title *The Scarf*: it had in fact been shot by Metzger over two days in September 1975 as test footage for Béatrice Harnois, a star of the French hardcore film, *Le sexe qui parle* (a.k.a. *Pussy Talk*, 1975), whom Metzger had flown over from France to audition for the lead in *Misty Beethoven*.[52] Within the terms of *Love Standing Up*, *The Scarf* is presented as Ilsa's first real fruition as a filmmaker: as Sue's voiceover explains, "This film looked like it was going to be much better" than the crude loops Ilsa earlier showed her. Viewed from the perspective of Metzger's secret authorship, however, it is as though Metzger attributes to Ilsa an alternate-universe version of his hardcore masterpiece, *Misty Beethoven*, featuring the actress that Metzger himself passed on.[53] The second short film, meanwhile, is given no title, but derives from the same 1975 shoot, albeit minus Harnois. Importantly, it is while this short is playing, on television from a VCR copy, that Ilsa seduces Sue. Both the woman on the television screen (porn star Crystal Sync) and Sue in the jacuzzi achieve climax simultaneously, the film cutting between close-ups of Sync's face on television and identically composed close-ups of Sue (figure 5.6). Within the framework of the film itself the scene could be read as a self-reflexive demonstration of pornography's operations as what Linda Williams calls a "body genre"—the way in which, in watching porn, the spectator's body becomes riven with an excitation that mirrors that of the bodies of the performers on screen.[54] From the perspective of Metzger's direction, however, the scene gives a remarkable autobiographic spin to one of the key tropes of his oeuvre: cinema's capacity for collapsing present and past, here realized in a scene that resurrects Metzger's filmmaking past within the framework of his filmmaking present. *Love Standing Up* is in this sense less a resting place for Metzger's unreleased Henry Paris work than the site for its secret reanimation, its erotic potential unleashed as a source for Sue's pleasure.

But how much of a secret did *Love Standing Up* remain? In his interviews with Ashley West, Metzger claimed that the film was never released. Having prepared a final cut under the *Sins of Ilsa* title, he reportedly spent much of 1986 schlepping the film to home-entertainment companies like Vestron Video only to find no takers. Nobody wanted the film unless Metzger was willing to put his name on it, which he steadfastly refused to do.[55] But Metzger's memory was faulty here. Existing television listings prove that the film in fact showed up on the Playboy Channel in March 1987 under the title of *Love Standing Up*, which, within the film, is the title of the article that Sue's editor proposes to her.[56] The film's screening on the Playboy Channel might suggest that Playboy was itself the

5.6 Sue (Sharon Moran, *left*) climaxes simultaneously with the woman (Crystal Sync, *right*) in Ilsa's film. Screen captures from *Love Standing Up*. (The burned-in timecode is an artifact of the VHS tape that contains one of the only known copies of the film.)

entity behind the film, although no archival records exist to confirm this. In any case, the two years separating the production of *Love Standing Up* from its release suggest otherwise, since there would be no reason for a delay if the film's broadcast destination was already secured. More likely is that having failed to land a deal for a home-video release, Metzger simply sold the film to Playboy, where it screened as the unremarked and unacknowledged finale to his career in adult film. But *Love Standing Up* seems to have foreshadowed this fate within the terms of its own plot. Sue writes Ilsa's life story but at the last minute withholds it from publication lest she bring Ilsa unwillingly out of anonymity. "There's no story," she tells her furious editor. "You know how the modern world is. Does anybody know anybody anymore?" It is as though the film has been pervaded by a kind of authorial death wish that would eventually envelope the entire production. Ilsa's story becomes the unknown secret of an unpublished article in a film that served as the unmarked tomb of one of porn's most storied directors. With *Love Standing Up*, Metzger had built a labyrinth for authorship to lose its way.

"YOU GET OUT OF THEM WHAT YOU PUT INTO THEM": RADLEY METZGER, POST-PORN AUTEUR?

By the time Metzger returned from hardcore to reclaim his earlier authorial identity, the class politics of explicit material had changed dramatically from those that had shaped his pre–Henry Paris career. With the collapse of obscenity prohibition, sexual explicitness no longer carried the avant-garde charge it had enjoyed in the late 1960s. The unstable alliance between pornography and artistic experiment that fueled films like *The Lickerish Quartet* had simply dissolved, just as the lifestyle modernism represented by Hugh Hefner's *Playboy* or Barney Rosset's Grove Press had fallen from cultural prominence. Instead, the class politics of pornography shifted toward the spirit of a working-class carnivalesque best represented by publishers like Larry Flynt of *Hustler* magazine, what scholar Constance Penley felicitously describes as the "white trashing of porn."[57] There was simply no place for the kind of cultural project that the name "Radley Metzger" had once stood for.

And Metzger was being forgotten. In early 1986, the adult-film industry's lead journal *Adult Video News* misremembered which of the Radley Metzger/Henry Paris pairing was the real person and which the pseudonym, describing "Radley Metzger" as the moniker under which "Henry Paris" worked.[58] The next year, *Adam Film World* published a special issue on porn's best directors from which both Paris and Metzger were entirely absent, despite the inclusion of other founding figures like Gerard Damiano and Alex de Renzy.[59] And then, on August 27, 1987, Metzger's longtime business partner, Ava Leighton, died of cancer following a long illness. Audubon's slowing business meant that Metzger and Leighton had not been working closely together for some time. Although she remained the company's vice president, Leighton had in recent years taken up organizational roles within the Adult Film Association of America and had even established her own cable distribution company, Bonavision.[60] But Metzger's bereavement was profound nevertheless, and he decided to redirect his creative attention to the topic of alternative health care. "Because of my relationship with Ava, and a close-up exposure to illness, I felt that . . . people needed more information on an intelligent approach to health and disease—that they needed to know about alleviating guilt. That was my emphasis."[61] As a result, Metzger's last completed work would be a five-part video series *Conversations on Homeopathy*, released in 1990. Whatever trepidation Metzger had once felt about the use of his own name vanished with the loss of his partner: he is credited in the opening titles as the series' writer and producer and appears throughout as an on-camera narrator and interviewer. By this point, though, the naming was irrelevant. Radley Metzger may have directed these videos, but "Radley Metzger" had long since been finessed into nothingness. The man of taste had disappeared under the force of his own powers of distinction.

This book has told the story of a filmmaker who defined his authorship through the exercise of taste and the cultural politics that implied. It has been the tale of an erotic artist who helped set in motion historical forces in the field of explicit film that eventually overtook him. And it has explored the various ways in which eroticism defers against taboo, across the related fields of cultural value and social hierarchy (chapter 1), medium ontology (chapter 2), and psychosexual desire (chapter 3). Yet the difficulties Metzger faced in in the last phase of his career point to a closing theme: namely, how eroticism raises dilemmas for authorship in the first place. If the erotic is indeed a structure of deferral, then erotic authorship is necessarily defined by the internal boundaries it establishes with respect to taboo, that is, to what can or cannot be shown. But this implies only two possible trajectories of development for the erotic auteur: the continual relocation of those boundaries, which Metzger attempted with the greater explicitness of *Score* (1973) and *The Image* (1976); or their transgression, at which point the authorship in question ceases to be erotic *strictu senso* but passes into the realm of the pornographic. Put another way, erotic authorship cannot be sustained beyond the point of taboo, which is why Metzger's passage into hardcore necessitated the ever-multiplying pseudonyms of his later career (chapters 3 and 4). No doubt all authorship can, at some level, be understood as an exercise of sensibility; in Metzger's case, however, the enmeshing of his authorial name ("Radley Metzger") with a particular taste sensibility (the "erotic") came at the cost of any broader authorial coherence across his body of work, requiring that he instead fracture his identity as a filmmaker into multiple different personas.

This is where the dilemmas of adult-film historiography assert themselves. In his 2016 study of vintage pornography *Disposable Passions*, film scholar David Church argues that the corpus of adult film is subject to the twin pressures of concealment and revelation. "Concealment" here refers to the obscurity to which the history of pornography, a disparaged genre to begin with, has been largely consigned; "revelation" to the efforts of preservationists, historians, and home video distributors to restore that corpus. (As Church notes, essentially "complete" versions of around 40 percent of all heterosexual softcore and hardcore films are currently lost, with a higher rate of around 75 percent for all-male films. Of the films that do survive, moreover, the under-the-radar status of surviving business records and widespread practices of recutting and retitling make it difficult to discern what should count as the original or "true" text.)[62] What makes Metzger distinctive, within this framework, is the intent with which he himself, while an active filmmaker, established the conditions of his *own* obscurity, with the result that it would be left to others, after the fact, to restore and reincorporate what Metzger had once so carefully buried. What further complicates things is that these efforts at restoration in turn produced a new "Radley Metzger" that, in incorporating what Metzger had so carefully disavowed, was inevitably quite different from Metzger's own "Metzger": the curatorial care with which Metzger managed his authorial self-image would be outmatched by the completionist agenda of his later fans and historians.

That restoration proceeded in two stages. The first began in earnest in the late 1990s, with the rediscovery of *Score* in the context of the "New Queer Cinema" that had emerged within the American indie film scene in the wake of the AIDS crisis.[63] In 1997 New York's Cinema Village brought Metzger's film back as a historical precursor for a twenty-fifth anniversary screening. The theater may have been off by one year, but the film's rerelease brought Metzger long-absent visibility courtesy of an accompanying profile in the pages of *Time Out New York*.[64] A renewed interest in *Score* led to a career-survey interview in *Filmmaker Magazine* a few months later, "The Libertine: Stephen Gallagher on *Score*'s Radley Metzger," followed by a 1998 think piece in *Bright Lights Film Journal* similarly stressing his queer-themed films.[65] That year would also see Metzger's first career retrospectives, one at San Francisco's Castro Theater and another at Los Angeles' Nuart, followed in 1999 by the first DVD releases of his orthonymic titles by Image Entertainment.[66] This initial phase of Metzger's reappraisal was, then, led primarily by a resurgent interest in the archive of queer representations in film, with Metzger reassessed as one of the "few of porn's pioneers [who] took the sexual revolution seriously and [brought] more authentic gay and bi imagery into their 'straight films,' " to quote Gary Morris in *Bright Lights*.[67] The Metzger that emerged here was a filmmaker who, himself straight, might nonetheless be considered ahead of his time in treating the categories of sexual orientation as social constructs: "Seduction is universal," he told *Time Out*. "I think *we* break it down and say, 'This is straight, this is gay.' "[68]

Metzger's rediscovery as a pioneer in the archives of queer representation is, perhaps, an unexpected turn in our story, but not an unexplainable or mistaken one. Writing in 2019, porn scholar Whitney Strub referred to the "queer-tending sexuality" of Metzger's hardcore films, as explored in the previous chapter's discussion of *Misty Beethoven*.[69] A few years earlier, Elena Gorfinkel had associated Metzger's softcore films with the camp sensibilities of queer audiences, noting how his films' mannered style and aristocratic leanings inevitably invite a "camp reading" for present-day spectators.[70] Closer to the time of Metzger's active filmmaking, *Variety* critic and Metzger enthusiast Addison Verrill was openly gay, known for holding court in New York City's leather bars before his untimely death.[71] In 1978, in fact, San Francisco's Strand Theatre programmed a double bill of Metzger's *Thérèse and Isabelle* (1968) and *Camille 2000* as part of a festival for queer audiences that also included titles like John Waters's *Pink Flamingos* (1968) and Robert Aldrich's lesbian drama *The Killing of Sister George* (1968)—perhaps the first time, aside from the initial release of *Score*, that Metzger's work was explicitly situated for nonheteronormative appeal.[72] Of course, such screenings speak only to the possibility of queer *pleasure* in Metzger's films, not to his supposed role as a pioneer of queer *representations*, which was how he was rediscovered in the 1990s. Regardless, Metzger was happy to welcome new audiences on whatever terms he could get. Of the interest in his work that the 1990s rerelease of *Score* inspired, Metzger remained winkingly noncommittal: "It's like what someone once said about brassieres: You get out of them what you put into them. Or maybe I should say jocks."[73]

But this was not quite the image of Metzger that would accompany a second phase of his reappraisal, when, beginning in the 2010s, his films started to be restored for "collector's edition" DVD and Blu-ray release. This time, Metzger would be the beneficiary of what Jacques Boyreau has called the "post-porn rise of the pornoisseur"—a new fan-scholarly paradigm that began to reclaim Golden Age pornography from its cultural demonization to treat it as an object deserving of meticulous historiographic restoration in its own right.[74] Examples of this "post-porn" paradigm are provided by a number of initiatives from the early 2010s: Joe Rubin's Vinegar Syndrome DVD/Blu-ray brand (founded 2012), the "In the Flesh" vintage porn screenings at New York's prestigious Anthology Film Archives (beginning 2013), and, above all, the *Rialto Report* website (also launched 2013), where Metzger was a subject of repeated articles thanks to a close friendship with the site's founders, Ashley West and April Hall.[75] In this context, the second restoration of Radley Metzger would inevitably include—in fact, arguably, *prioritize*—the Henry Paris titles. Metzger's softcore work admittedly came first: in 2011, *Camille 2000*, *The Lickerish Quartet*, *Score*, and *The Image* were all rereleased in special editions by the CAV-distributed labels Cult Epics (which handled the first three, all with director commentaries) and Synapse Films (which handled *The Image*, lacking a commentary). But the hardcore films were soon folded in, when Stephen Morowitz of adult-film label Distribpix, Inc., approached Metzger with the idea of crowdfunding restorations of his Henry Paris titles. Between 2011 and 2014, *The Private Afternoons of Pamela Mann* (1974), *Naked Came the Stranger*, *The Opening of Misty Beethoven*, and *Barbara Broadcast* (1977) were all released in 2K Blu-ray restorations with 5.1 digital surround sound and Metzger commentary tracks for each of them. For all of these releases—both the orthonymic and pseudonymous titles—Metzger opened his own collection to supply print materials for deleted scenes, alternate (hot/cold) versions, clippings, and behind-the-scenes featurettes. Another round of retrospectives and revivals followed: the "Radley Metzger" films were shown in "Smooth Operator: The Opulent Eroticism of Radley Metzger" at UCLA's Billy Wilder Theater in 2011 and "This Is Softcore: The Art Cinema Erotica of Radley Metzger" at New York's Film Society at Lincoln Center in 2014, while two of the "Henry Paris" films—*The Private Afternoons of Pamela Mann* and *Naked Came the Stranger*—featured in the "Erotic City" retrospective at New York's Quad Cinema in 2017 (figure 5.7). During the same period, Metzger's work would be profiled in dozens of painstakingly researched posts on the *Rialto Report*, with the most substantive archival effort devoted to the Henry Paris titles. Buoyed by his late-career rediscovery, Metzger even completed one final script in October 2015—*The Heat of the Midnight Sun*, based on Toni Bentley's 2005 erotic memoir about anal sex, *The Surrender*—which he planned to direct, even to the point of beginning casting, before getting cold feet.[76] Eighteen months later he was dead.

True, the Paris/Metzger distinction remained in play during this second restoration, courtesy of the fact that his films tended still to screen in different venues and were distributed on different labels; but, for several years now, both the "Radley Metzger" and "Henry Paris" have circulated visibly alongside one another as part of a single—and singular—corpus. And yet . . . Metzger has arguably remained as much a fiction as ever. The hardcore titles may have been reclaimed, but at the cost of their "post-porn" evaluation as objects of a primarily aesthetic and historical interest, freed from their condemnation as merely masturbatory aids. (David Church cites as a telling symptom of change one of Anthology's "In the Flesh" screenings, from which a male viewer was kicked out for masturbating. Anthology may have been willing to screen the films that once played at Times Square's The World, but it would not tolerate the filmgoing practices that

5.7 Radley Metzger at the 2014 Lincoln Center retrospective of his work. *Source*: Courtesy of Dow Jones.

had originally accompanied them.)[77] It is as though Henry Paris could be resurrected only after his films had wriggled free of the framework of moralizing opprobrium that had necessitated his existence in the first place.

But this is not the only way in which a certain belatedness colors the terms of Metzger's recent rehabilitation: if the cultural present has seen the emergence of "post-porn," then it is also no less an era of what has been called "post-taste."[78] What I have in mind here is not the degree to which taste has been algorithmically atomized and personalized by subscription streaming services and online recommendation systems—a process that is, in any case, yet to really sink its teeth into Metzger's corpus.[79] More to the point are the changing ways in which distinction in matters of taste is today exercised. Writing at the end of the last millennium, American sociologists Richard Peterson and Roger Kern suggested that the "highbrow" taste model had begun to change from one of "snobbish exclusion" to that of "omnivorous appropriation," whereby distinction is today won by the ability of the well-educated to "code switch" in their hopscotching expertise across the entire spectrum of cultural value, from vintage video games to the cinema of Céline Sciamma, from *Mad Magazine* to free jazz.[80] The "man of taste" today would not be like Metzger, in his aspirational commitment to a Europhilic model of art cinema, but they would possibly be a fan *of* Metzger as a filmmaker whose work requires cultural competence in the seemingly opposed codes of both art cinema and hardcore porn. In such a context, it makes sense that the Henry Paris titles constituted the bleeding edge of his late-career reappraisal, insofar as a familiarity with triple-X pornography represents a limit case of sorts for omnivorousness. It also makes sense that Metzger's orthonymic work might, in comparison, begin to appear as the less challenging standard-bearers of an older model of taste that the omnivore now disregards—Metzger as the "lava lamp of screen sex," in Bart Testa's witty putdown.[81] In an astounding reversal, it is arguably *Misty Beethoven* more than *Camille 2000* that today answers to the politics of taste distinction.

This book joins that history as a symptom of those changes. For it is only in the passage beyond the man of taste, and the taste practices that he adhered to, that the various phases of Metzger's career can be brought equally before the scholar's purview. Perhaps that is one reason why adult film's past is doomed to remain at some level a "lost object," always just beyond our grasp.[82] The historian who studies vintage pornography must, to some degree, demur from and suspend the judgments of taste—of the licit and the illicit, the proper and the improper—that imbued these texts with their frisson in the first place. And so there is no happily ever after in which "Radley Metzger" and "Henry Paris" can be made whole again. We can get to know them both better, of course, but only when we stop believing in the kind of distinctions that Metzger's career embodied.

ACKNOWLEDGMENTS

This might seem an unexpected book for me to have written. In truth, no other has seemed as predestined. The pathway toward *Man of Taste* began with my first full-time teaching job at the University of Toronto in 2007. My office neighbor, Bart Testa, introduced me to Metzger's work, courtesy of Bart's exceptional article on the director's career. The next step came five years later after I moved to Columbia University, where my colleague Hilary Brougher introduced me to Radley himself. Thereafter, he became a regular guest in my class on Cult Cinema and Exploitation. The year after Radley's 2017 passing , Frank Kelleter, visiting from the John F. Kennedy Institute in Berlin, asked if I wanted to catch a tribute screening of *The Opening of Misty Beethoven* (1976) at New York's Quad Cinema. Over drinks afterward, Frank suggested I write the book that you're now reading. Thanks to all, but especially Radley, for shepherding me to a memorable period in my scholarly career.

But Fate's hand was nowhere more evident than when I chanced upon the contents of Radley's storage unit on eBay, a couple of years after his death. I duly swept up everything I could and in the process created a private archive of Metzger memorabilia that includes many treasures: video tapes of unused footage, behind-the-scenes material, and even a full version of his difficult-to-see last feature, *Love Standing Up*. Thanks, then, are also owed to ace eBay seller Joe Grispino (aka original-picker1), who showed me that pandemic-era online browsing could have its upside, as well as to Madeleine Mendell, Elizabeth Resko, Michael Cacioppo Belantara, and Peter Vaughn, who organized the digital transfers and scans of Metzger's many video tapes, mini DVs, posters, lobby cards, and other miscellany. (Once this book is out of my system, I will be donating much of this material to Columbia University's Rare Book & Manuscript Library to establish a small Radley Metzger collection for future researchers.)

Scholarship in adult film often requires building a personal archive along these lines, given the frequent absence of any "official" records. But that's not to say that no traditional archives were involved in my research. I'm grateful to Eisha Neely, who helped me navigate Cornell University's Human Sexuality Collection, and to Ashley Swinnerton at the Museum of Modern Art, as well as to the many librarians at New York Public Library, none of whom ever batted an eyelid when I needed their help loading up microfilms of *Screw* magazine. I am also indebted to Steven Morowitz at Distribpix for help with permissions, as well as to Ashley West and April Hall, whose extraordinary website *The Rialto Report* has become the equivalent of the Media History Digital Library for researchers in adult film. Ashley in particular responded with patience and grace to my many queries, even as he was preparing his own book on Radley (which will be an essential read).

Since this book was largely written during the COVID-19 lockdowns, very little of its argument has seen the light of day. Whit Strub and Elena Gorfinkel offered incisive feedback on an early version of chapter 3 at the 2019 Society of Cinema and Media Studies conference in Seattle. Ann Douglas gave sage advice for rewriting the book's introduction and first chapter. The three anonymous readers for Columbia University Press provided spot-on critiques of this book's first draft, and Gregory McNamee judiciously copyedited the final manuscript. All raised my game. My editor at Columbia, Philip Leventhal, has meanwhile been a model of good-humored encouragement ever since I first cold-called him with a completed draft three years ago. I look forward to working with him again. And thanks also to Ava Witonsky, who brought the project home by creating the index.

It can be tricky to square researching explicit film with the demands of family life. My partner, Inie Park, gave her consent both to the project and to the many eBay purchases it entailed, although goodness knows what she'll make of the finished book. Her bemused tolerance of my outré film enthusiasms has long been a gift, which, I'm happy to say, survived this particular stress test undamaged. I am also thankful that my children, Samantha and Sullivan, have remained ignorant of what I've been up to, although I know the day will come when they figure out that their dad wrote a book on porn. Sorry about that, kids. Ideally my next project won't require me to hide my research materials at the top of a closet.

It's also difficult to figure out to whom a book like this should be dedicated. But there's really only one answer: Radley himself. By the time I knew him, his remembrances of his career had been smoothed over into a seemingly inexhaustible series of anecdotes and one-liners that made talking to him an addictive experience. (The first time I met him, he told me that he wasn't able to complete his master's degree at Columbia "because of my uncle." "Oh?" I replied, confused. "Uncle Sam," he answered, in smirking reference to his military service during the Korean War.) Those anecdotes, many of which can still be heard in the numerous DVD and Blu-ray commentaries he recorded toward the end of his life, were his way of historicizing his own life. But now that Radley's gone, we need new ways of telling that story. I hope he'd have enjoyed this one.

NOTES

INTRODUCTION

1. Ron Alexander, "I, a Filmmaker," *Gentlemen's Quarterly*, Winter 1969–70, Radley Metzger clippings file, Museum of Modern Art, New York (hereafter MoMA).
2. David Andrews, *Theorizing Art Cinemas: Foreign, Cult, Avant-Garde, and Beyond* (Austin: University of Texas Press, 2013), 10, 112.
3. Richard Brown, "Radley Metzger: Auteur of the Erotic," *Today's Filmmaker*, August 1971, 28, Radley Metzger clippings file, MoMA; Jim Holliday, *The Top 100 X-Rated Films of All Time* (Hollywood, CA: WWV, 1982), 7.
4. "Cinema Score-Broad," *Screw*, October 27, 1969. The review is of Metzger's *Camille 2000* (1969).
5. "Journey to the end of taste" is the subtitle of Carl Wilson's celebrated study of Celine Dion, *Let's Talk About Love* (New York: Bloomsbury, 2007), a major inspiration for this book.
6. Erik Jackson, "What's the *Score*?," *Time Out New York*, n.d. (ca. 1997), 75, *Score* clippings file, New York Public Library (hereafter NYPL).
7. The interviewer was John Bartholomew Tucker for the show *AM New York* on WABC. The audio from this undated show, ca. early 1971, is available at "Radley Metzger 1971," *The Rialto Report*, September 24, 2017, https://www.therialtoreport.com/2017/09/24/radley-metzger-3.
8. Don Vaillancourt, "Producing Works of Art or Obscenity?," *Newark Sunday News*, February 28, 1971, Radley Metzger clippings file, NYPL.
9. Aesthetic categories, Sianne Ngai writes, are both "the judgement we utter, a way of speaking" and "the form we perceive, a way of seeing," both "sutured by affect into a spontaneous experience." Sianne Ngai, *Theory of the Gimmick: Aesthetic Judgment and Capitalist Form* (Cambridge, MA: Harvard University Press, 2020), 1.
10. Walter Kendrick, *The Secret Museum: Pornography in Modern Culture* (Berkeley: University of California Press, 1996 [1987]), 244.
11. Kendrick, *The Secret Museum*, xiii.
12. Steinem quoted in Andrew Ross, *No Respect: Intellectuals and Popular Culture* (New York: Routledge, 1989), 185.

13. Lynda Nead puts the point well: "if pornography is the domain of forbidden sexual representation, then erotic art must always carry the traces of this possibility in order to retain its distinctive identity and not simply be absorbed into the realm of art." Nead, " 'Above the Pulp-line': The Cultural Significance of Erotic Art," in *More Dirty Looks: Gender, Pornography and Power*, 2nd ed., ed. Pamela Church Gibson (London: BFI, 2004), 217.
14. Steven Marcus, *The Other Victorians: A Study of Sexuality and Pornography in Mid-Nineteenth-Century England* (New York: Basic Books, 1966), 36n2.
15. Hollis Alpert, no title, *Saturday Review*, May 25, 1968, Radley Metzger clippings file, MoMA.
16. George Melly, "The Swamps of Porn," *Observer*, October 24, 1971, *Camille 2000* clippings file, NYPL.
17. Joel Doerfler, "Radley Metzger: Let 'Em See Skin," *Boston After Dark*, February 9, 1971, Radley Metzger clippings file, NYPL.
18. Rex Reed, no title, *New York Daily News*, January 19, 1973, *Little Mother* clippings file, MoMA.
19. Information on Metzger's upbringing, here and in what follows, is collated from a number of sources accessed through AncestryLibrary.com, including its online database of U.S. School Records, 1900–1999, and the U.S. Federal Census Records for 1930 and 1940.
20. On the Jewish garment trade in New York, see Moses Rischin, *The Promised City: New York's Jews, 1870–1914* (Cambridge, MA: Harvard University Press, 1962), 51–52.
21. Brown, "Radley Metzger," 27.
22. Metzger quoted in "Radley Metzger's Beginnings: The Audubon Ballroom," *The Rialto Report*, April 6, 2017, https://www.therialtoreport.com/2017/04/06/audubon-ballroom.
23. Pierre Bourdieu, *Distinction: A Social Critique of the Judgement of Taste*, trans. Richard Nice (Cambridge, MA: Harvard University Press, 1984), 67.
24. Metzger's viewing statistics are taken from claims in Alexander, "I, A Filmmaker," and Brown, "Radley Metzger," 27.
25. Information on Metzger's instruction at City College is taken from Brown, "Radley Metzger," 27.
26. Russell Lynes, "Highbrow, Lowbrow, Middlebrow," *Harper's Magazine*, February 1949, 19. On postwar taste culture, see Jordan S. Carroll, *Reading the Obscene: Transgressive Editors and the Class Politics of US Literature* (Stanford, CA: Stanford University Press, 2021); Barbara Wilinsky, *Sure Seaters: The Emergence of Art House Cinema* (Minneapolis: University of Minnesota Press, 2001); and T. J. Jackson Lears, "A Matter of Taste: Corporate Cultural Hegemony in a Mass-Consumption Society," in *Recasting America: Culture and Politics in the Age of Cold War*, ed. Lary May (Chicago: University of Chicago Press, 1989), 38–57.
27. Steven Lowenstein, "The German-Jewish Community of Washington Heights," in *American Jewish Life, 1920–1990*, ed. Jeffrey S. Gurock (New York: Routledge, 1998), 51, 53.
28. Metzger quoted in Brown, "Radley Metzger."
29. Bosley Crowther, "The Screen in Review," *New York Times*, July 7, 1953.
30. Howard Thompson, "By Way of Report," *New York Times*, September 21, 1958; "New Acting Talent Development Not Matched by Similar Interest in Tomorrow's Directors, Writers?," *Variety*, August 16, 1961.

31. I am using "analogy" in the precise sense suggested by Raymond Williams, who contrasts it with its sibling term "homology" as follows: " 'Homology' is correspondence in origin and development, 'analogy' in appearance and function." Williams, *Marxism and Literature* (New York: Oxford University Press, 1977), 105.
32. Another film on which Metzger is credited as editor is the cult-favorite monster movie, *The Flesh Eaters* (1964), directed by Jack Curtis. However, in a 2002 interview in the horror magazine *Fangoria*, the film's writer and coproducer, Arnold Drake, attributed the editing to Curtis himself. On Drake's account, Metzger was involved only in arranging the film's preview screening during the brief period when he operated the Charles Theater in 1963. "We knew a fellow named Radley Metzger who owned The Charles, a theater on Avenue B and 12th Street in the East Village where he was showing art films and old American classic films, and he offered us the theater for a sneak preview. 'Oh, goody!' we thought—that's not easy to get. So we did a sneak preview at Radley's theater and we came away with about an 80 or 85 percent approval in the reviews we got back from the audience." Tom Weaver, "Flesh Eaters and Fantasy," *Fangoria* 219 (2002): 75, 82. How, then, did Metzger end up with the editing credit when *The Flesh Eaters* eventually went into release the following year? Two speculative possibilities suggest themselves, either that Metzger did some reediting on the film following the preview or that he received the credit as thanks for his early support of the picture.
33. The largest Greek neighborhood in New York at that time ran up Eighth Avenue between Fourteenth and Forty-Fifth Streets, long before Astoria in Queens became the city's default "Greektown." Chelly Wilson, meanwhile, would become a major figure within the New York adult-film market of the 1970s as the founder of Avon Films and owner of many of the city's gay porn theaters.
34. Howard Thompson, "Screen: 'Dark Odyssey,' " *New York Times*, June 26, 1961.
35. DVD commentary, *Score* (Cult Epics, 2010).
36. Josh Lambert, *Unclean Lips: Obscenity, Jews, and American Culture* (New York: New York University Press, 2013). On the "speaker's benefit," see Michel Foucault, *History of Sexuality, vol. 1: An Introduction* (New York: Pantheon, 1978), 7.
37. Robert J. Stoller, *Observing the Erotic Imagination* (New Haven, CT: Yale University Press, 1985), 33.
38. A useful reference here would be to what Martin Heidegger meant by the idea of the *ontological*, which refers to the underlying structures and categories that govern reality and consciousness, and which the philosopher distinguished from the *ontic*, which signifies the specific things that occupy those structuring positions or categories within any given society or ideology. The distinction is central to Heidegger's 1927 *Being and Time*, where the ontological refers to the "being-ness" (*Dasein*) of any being and the ontic to the specific qualities of any given being in its particularity.
39. This framing of the erotic as "gap" is partly informed by Jacques Lacan's theorization of sex as that which eludes symbolic representation. As articulated in his infamous claim that "there is no sexual relationship," sex for Lacan is what is missing from the Symbolic Order, the negativity around which all signification orbits. Jacques Lacan, "L'étourdit," trans. C. Gallagher, *The Letter* 41 (2009 [1973]): 31–80.
40. Brown, "Radley Metzger."

41. For example, Metzger's *The Opening of Misty Beethoven* is the central case study for Linda Williams's influential argument equating the generic operations of hardcore porn with those of the Hollywood musical. See Williams, *Hard Core: Power, Pleasure, and the "Frenzy of the Visible"* (Berkeley: University of California Press, 1989), 120–52. David Andrews's definition of softcore as a middlebrow form is meanwhile grounded in a close discussion of Metzger's pre–Henry Paris career. See Andrews, *Soft in the Middle: The Contemporary Softcore Feature in Its Contexts* (Columbus: Ohio State University Press, 2006), 23–44.
42. Elena Gorfinkel, *Lewd Looks: American Sexploitation Cinema in the 1960s* (Minneapolis: University of Minnesota Press, 2017), 214.
43. DVD commentary, *Score*.
44. Unless otherwise indicated, years given for Audubon titles are for the films' U.S. release dates.
45. Marshall McLuhan and Harley Parker, *Through the Vanishing Point: Space in Poetry and Painting* (New York: Harper & Row, 1968), 213.
46. Bourdieu, *Distinction*, 56.

1. "TO CREATE THE KIND OF FILMS HE HAD FORMERLY ONLY PURCHASED"

1. Leighton and Metzger's relationship has long provoked speculation, although there is nothing to suggest anything beyond a professionalism that developed into deep friendship. Leighton was already married, in 1940 to Sebastian Sparacino, with whom she remained until her death.
2. Perhaps surprisingly, Metzger had not been all that impressed by the Bardot film, although he was an admirer of its director Roger Vadim's horror film *Blood and Roses* (1960), which includes a scene in which a vampire's bite turns into a lesbian kiss. Describing that scene in a later interview, Metzger asserted that it had "probably had a greater effect on filmmaking than anything since *The Great Train Robbery*. Nobody ever talks about it, strangely enough, and yet the impact is there." Douglas Brode, "Radley Metzger: Master of the Erotic on Film," *Show*, September 1971.
3. One might imagine that *Mademoiselle Strip-Tease* was suggestive enough not to need retitling. Ironically, however, the title had already been used for the U.S. release of the Brigitte Bardot film *En effeuillant la marguerite* (1956).
4. Richard Brown, "Radley Metzger: Auteur of the Erotic," *Today's Filmmaker*, August 1971, Radley Metzger clippings file, MoMA.
5. Kenneth Turan and Stephen F. Zito, *Sinema: American Pornographic Films and the People Who Make Them* (New York: Praeger, 1974), 72.
6. Brown, "Radley Metzger."
7. Richard Corliss, "Radley Metzger: Aristocrat of the Erotic," *Film Comment*, January–February 1973.
8. "An Evening with Radley Metzger," Museum of Modern Art Program Notes, January 26, 1971, Radley Metzger clippings file, MoMA.
9. Kevin Thomas, " 'Laughing Woman' New Radley Metzger Film," *Los Angeles Times*, August 7, 1970; Arthur Knight and Hollis Alpert, "Sex in Cinema 1969," *Playboy*, November 1969.

10. Elena Gorfinkel, *Lewd Looks: American Sexploitation Cinema in the 1960s* (Minneapolis: University of Minnesota Press, 2017), 218.
11. I derive the concept of "erotic capital" from Adam Isaiah Green's essay "The Social Organization of Desire: The Sexual Fields Approach," *Sociological Theory* 26, no. 1 (March 2008): 25–50.
12. James English, *The Economy of Prestige: Prizes, Awards, and the Circulation of Cultural Value* (Cambridge, MA: Harvard University Press, 2005), 12–13.
13. Eric Schaefer, "Pandering to the 'Goon Trade': Framing the Sexploitation Audience through Advertising," in *Sleaze Artists: Cinema at the Margins of Taste, Style, and Politics*, ed. Jeffrey Sconce (Durham, NC: Duke University Press, 2007), 24.
14. Andrew Sarris, "Why the Foreign Film Has Lost Its Cachet," *New York Times*, May 2, 1999. On the foreign film's ambiguous status as both "art" and "sex," see David Andrews, *Theorizing Art Cinemas: Foreign, Cult, Avant-Garde, and Beyond* (Austin: University of Texas Press, 2013), chap. 3, from which I derive the Sarris quote (58).
15. Barbara Wilinsky, *Sure Seaters: The Emergence of Art House Cinema* (Minneapolis: University of Minnesota Press, 2001), 15.
16. Eric Schaefer, *"Bold! Daring! Shocking! True!": A History of Exploitation Films, 1919–1959* (Durham, NC: Duke University Press, 1999), 332.
17. Figures cited in Wilinsky, *Sure Seaters*, 73.
18. Frank Thistle, "Ingmar Bergman: Cinema Sultan of the Sex Shockers," *Adam Film Quarterly*, November 1967. On *Adam Film Quarterly/World*, see David Church, *Disposable Passions: Vintage Pornography and the Material Legacies of Adult Cinema* (New York: Bloomsbury, 2016), chap. 2.
19. Elena Gorfinkel, "Radley Metzger's 'Elegant Arousal': Taste, Aesthetic Distinction and Sexploitation," in *Underground U.S.A.: Filmmaking Beyond the Hollywood Canon*, ed. Xavier Mendik and Steven Jay Schneider (London: Wallflower, 2003), 28–29.
20. Corliss, "Radley Metzger."
21. Brown, "Radley Metzger."
22. Corliss, "Radley Metzger." The source novel for *I Spit on Your Grave* was written by Boris Vian under the pen name of Vernon Sullivan. Vian was strongly opposed to the book's adaptation by director Michel Gast and died of a heart attack while yelling at the screen during a showing of the film.
23. Brown, "Radley Metzger."
24. See Schaefer, *"Bold! Daring! Shocking! True!,"* chap. 2.
25. For example, Doris Wishman's *Playgirls International* (1963) and *Behind the Nudist Curtain* (1964) were each built out of scenes from a European travelogue, into which Wishman spliced the requisite nudist footage. See Michael J. Bowen, "Embodiment and Realization: The Many Film-Bodies of Doris Wishman," *Wide Angle* 19, no. 3 (July 1997): 72. Michael Findlay's *Satan's Bed* (1965), meanwhile, consisted of footage lifted from *Judas City*, which featured a young Yoko Ono, and newly shot scenes of dope fiends and criminals. See Whitney Strub and Peter Alilunas, "Introduction: Sleazy Honesty," in *ReFocus: The Films of Roberta Findlay*, ed. Peter Alilunas and Whitney Strub (Edinburgh: Edinburgh University Press, 2023), 4.
26. Brown, "Radley Metzger."
27. "Open 'Grave' to Big Biz in Providence," *Variety*, August 21, 1962; Vincent Canby, "Wider Public for Sexy Films," *Variety*, February 10, 1965. Two years later, in April 1967, Ava

Leighton reported that the film's total rentals had increased to $750,000. "Ava Leighton Sees 'I, A Woman' Rents at $1-Mil by Fall," *Variety*, April 5, 1967.

28. Corliss, "Radley Metzger."
29. Also worth noting in this connection is the later career of director Roberta Findlay, who transitioned into distribution in 1979 when she cofounded Reeltime Distributing with Walter Sear.
30. Ralph Zucker, "Indie Films on Spot," *Back Stage*, December 23, 1966.
31. "Ohio Authorities and Theatres Feud; 'Plot' Felony Rap vs. Edward Wads," *Variety*, February 21, 1962; "Audubon Films' Victory in Censorship Action," *Box Office*, March 19, 1962.
32. "Prosecutor Chided for Grab of Prints," *Variety*, April 11, 1962.
33. "Appeal Virginia Ban on Audubon's 'Grave,'" *Variety*, October 31, 1962; "Virginia Censor Lifts Ban on 'Your Grave,'" *Variety*, January 2, 1963.
34. "'Censor Substitutes His Judgment' As to Art: New Pitch Versus State," *Variety*, May 9, 1962; "'Twilight Girls' Held Licensable," *Variety*, July 8, 1964. See also Elena Gorfinkel's detailed summary of the case in her *Lewd Looks*, 52–55.
35. *Roth v United States*, 354 U.S. 476 (1957). For a concise summary of these issues, see Kimberly A. Harchuck, "Pornography and the First Amendment Right to Free Speech," in *New Views of Pornography, Politics, and the Law*, ed. Lynn Comella and Shira Tarrant (Santa Barbara, CA: Praeger, 2015), 9–36.
36. Brown, "Radley Metzger."
37. "'Daniella by Night' OK'd by Board of Regents, Cite 'Twilight Girls,'" *Variety*, September 2, 1964. Although Audubon acquired *Daniella by Night* for U.S. distribution, the film was one of two pictures that the company sold off to Lee Hessel's Cambist Films. The other was the Spanish film *Juventud a la intemperie* (1961), released in the United States as *The Unsatisfied*.
38. Jay Kay Lorentz, "The Erotic World of Radley Metzger: Interview by Jay Kay Lorentz," *Psychotronic Video* 17 (Winter 1994): 30.
39. "Musmanno's Death as Aftermath; Was He Instigator and Judge, Too in Ban of 'Theresa and Isabelle?,'" *Variety*, October 16, 1968.
40. "Appeals Admonished Pittsburgh's Duggan as to 'Harassment,'" *Variety*, March 11, 1970.
41. On "hot" vs. "cold" versions, see Schaefer, *"Bold! Daring! Shocking! True!"* 73–75.
42. Corliss, "Radley Metzger."
43. On Grove Press, see Loren Glass, *Counter-Culture Colophon: Grove Press, the Evergreen Review, and the Incorporation of the Avant-Garde* (Stanford, CA: Stanford University Press, 2013).
44. On art cinema and its distinction from classical film narrative, see David Bordwell's essay, "The Art Cinema as a Mode of Film Practice," *Film Criticism* 4, no. 1 (Fall 1979): 56–64.
45. Dan Shocket, "The Roots of Reel Raunch: Coming Home," *Starlet*, September–October 1981.
46. Eric Schaefer, "'I'll Take Sweden': The Shifting Discourse of the 'Sexy Nation' in Sexploitation Films," in Schaefer, ed., *Sex Scene: Media and the Sexual Revolution* (Durham, NC: Duke University Press, 2014), 207–34.
47. Brown, "Radley Metzger."

48. On subtitling vs. dubbing in postwar art theaters, see Wilinsky, *Sure Seaters*, 35–36.
49. Corliss, "Radley Metzger."
50. As usual with Audubon, all legal cases against the film and its exhibitors were eventually overturned, with Kentucky being the slowest state to reach that conclusion (in 1970). See: "Objectionable, But Legal: Ruling on 'I, a Woman,'" *Variety*, February 8, 1967; "'Woman' Wins Again," *Box Office*, March 13, 1967; "Memphis Negro Judge Upheld in 2 'Smut' Rulings, One 'Olga' Trailer," *Variety*, March 29, 1967; "It's We, Some of Columbus, O., against Imported 'I, a Woman,'" *Variety*, April 19, 1967; "Third Print Unreels after 'Woman' Raid(s)," *Variety*, June 14, 1967; "Jury Frees Nitz Pair for Showing 'I, a Woman,'" *Variety*, July 12, 1967; "Jury Finds 'I, a Woman' Obscene; Recommends $1,500 for Mgr.," *Variety*, August 16, 1967; "Chi Seizes Film Not Censored as City Had Ordered," *Variety*, October 9, 1967; "Latest on 'Woman,'" *Variety*, October 18, 1967; "'Chi Censor Version' at Issue in Counties Fighting 'I, a Woman,'" *Variety*, November 1, 1967; "Courts of Appeals Support Judge in 'Woman' Rebuke," *Variety*, December 6, 1967; "Fed Court Rulings on 'Woman' May Cripple Indiana's Obscenity Statute," *Variety*, December 12, 1967; "Teitel-Audubon Attorneys Win Move Re Chi Censors Holding 'Woman' Prints," *Variety*, January 31, 1968; "Appeals Supports Restraint on 'I,'" *Variety*, May 1, 1968; "U.S. Court Again Slams Ind. Laws vs. Obscene Pix," *Variety*, May 8, 1968; "Court Orders Illinois Release Film It Seized," *Variety*, July 3, 1968; "Appeals in 7–0 Support, Holding 'Woman' Obscene," *Variety*, February 19, 1969; "Censorship Cauldron Boils Over on All Levels," *Independent Film Journal*, April 1, 1970.
51. "Re-Totaled U.S. Take of 'I, a Woman'; March 31 Shows $3,120,000 So Far," *Variety*, May 1, 1968.
52. Calculated from box-office figures in Larry Michie, "Audubon in SEC Plea Reveals Its Profits, Pic by Pic," *Variety*, August 28, 1969. Audubon's previous highest-grossing year had been 1965, with $542,250.
53. Arthur Knight and Hollis Alpert, "Sex in Cinema 1969," *Playboy*, November 1969.
54. United States Commission on Obscenity and Pornography, *The Report* (Washington, DC: U.S. Government Print Office, 1970), 85.
55. Andrews, *Theorizing Art Cinema*, esp. chap. 10, "Art Cinema, the Distribution Theory."
56. "Most Imported Sexploitationers Fail in U.S.; Audubon's Rad Metzger's Slants on 'Nymphomaniacal' Theme," *Variety*, June 14, 1967.
57. The "run-zone-clearance" system was one of the primary ways in which the "Big Five" major studios (Paramount, Loew's-MGM, Warner Bros., Twentieth Century-Fox, and RKO) had controlled the distribution of their films. According to this model the national market was divided into geographical "zones" within which films would move from first-run down to final-run venues. Each run, moreover, was separated from the next by a "clearance" period in which the film was temporarily taken off the market. The practice was outlawed with the passing of the Paramount decision in 1948. For a detailed exploration of this system, as well as its eventual ban, see Thomas Schatz, *Boom and Bust: The American Cinema in the 1940s* (New York: Scribner's, 1997), chaps. 3 and 9.
58. On the Trans-Lux's battles over *A Stranger Knocks*, see Christine Grenz, *Trans-Lux: Biography of a Corporation* (Norwalk, CT: Trans-Lux Corporation, 1982), 56–58.
59. "New Type of Theatre for Newsreels Opens," *New York Times*, March 16, 1931.

60. Kathleen Carroll, " 'Woman' One More Good Gal Gone Bad," *New York Daily News*, October 12, 1966, *I, a Woman* clippings file, NYPL; Vincent Canby, " 'I, a Woman' a Hit and It's a Surprise," *New York Times*, August 10, 1967.
61. Archer Winsten, "Swedish 'I, a Woman' at Trans-Lux, Rialto," *New York Post*, October 12, 1966, *I, a Woman* clippings file, NYPL.
62. DVD commentary, *Score* (Cult Epics, 2010).
63. The release print of *Hot Frustrations* does not appear to be extant, although the original French film is. The likely addition of striptease inserts is nonetheless indicated by Audubon's poster for the film, which includes a photo of a woman in a thong that appears nowhere in the French original (see figure 1.9). Metzger's more moderate editorial approach, post–*I, a Woman*, is meanwhile demonstrated by the example of *La Matriarca* (1968), released by Audubon in 1969 as *The Libertine*: Metzger's version differs from the Italian version only in the restoration of a few brief shots of frontal nudity which the Italian film board had excised. Nucleus Films' 2020 Blu-ray release of *The Libertine* includes both the original Italian and Audubon versions of the film, together with extra features collecting outtakes and censor cuts.
64. "Most Imported Sexploitationers Fail in U.S."
65. As scholar Bart Testa describes the film: Ahlberg's "expedients [are] simple: implant erotic experience in the subjectivity of its protagonist and use art-film narrational procedures to de-linearize the plot." Bart Testa, "Soft-Shaft Opportunism: Radley Metzger's Erotic Kitsch," *Spectator* 19, no. 2 (Spring–Summer 1999): 47–48.
66. "Audubon to Produce New 'Carmen' Film in Europe," *Box Office*, October 17, 1966. Not all of Audubon's post–*I, a Woman* output was of a piece, of course, and the company continued, on occasion, to release titles that were throwbacks to its earlier output, such as *Hot Frustrations*, which Metzger had acquired before *Woman*'s release, and director Henry Jacques's 1967 *Sexy Gang*, which Audubon released as *Michelle* in 1968.
67. Glass, *Counter-Culture Colophon*, esp. 120–28.
68. See J. Hoberman, "Vulgar Modernism," *Artforum* 20, no. 6 (February 1982): 71–76.
69. Glass, *Counter-Culture Colophon*, 128.
70. Ron Alexander, "I, a Filmmaker," *Gentlemen's Quarterly*, Winter 1969–70, Radley Metzger clippings file, MoMA.
71. " 'The Laughing Woman' at Showcase Theaters," *New York Post*, May 21, 1970, *The Laughing Woman* clippings file, NYPL.
72. Untitled article, *New Leader*, June 9, 1969, *The Libertine* clippings file, NYPL.
73. All quotes from *The Radley Metzger Trailers* (First Run Features, 1999).
74. Mark Jancovich, "Naked Ambitions: Pornography, Taste and the Problem of the Middlebrow," *Scope* 20 (2001), https://www.nottingham.ac.uk/scope/documents/2001/june-2001/jancovich.pdf.
75. Barbara Ehrenreich, *The Hearts of Men: American Dreams and the Flight from Commitment* (New York: Anchor Press, 1983), 108. The developments tracked in this paragraph and the next help explain why many historians have denied that the sexual revolution was really a "revolution" in any meaningful sense. Historian of sexuality Steven Seidman argues that the 1960s demarcates a period of "sexual liberalization" rather than revolution, insofar as all of its major terms—rising rates of divorce and nonmarital sex, the

growing visibility of queer subcultures, and so on—represent processes already in motion from before the war. Porn scholar Jeffrey Escoffier similarly suggests that the decade in question was less defined by any change in sexual *behavior* than by the evolving *social framework* within which sex took place. Further, to the extent to which a "sexual revolution" can be said to have occurred at all in the postwar period, this was primarily a matter of the courtroom battles over obscenity that began in the late 1950s. See Steven Seidman, *Embattled Eros: Sexual Politics and Ethics in Twentieth-Century America* (New York: Routledge, 1992), chap. 1, and Jeffrey Escoffier, *Sex, Society, and the Making of Pornography: The Pornographic Object of Knowledge* (New Brunswick, NJ: Rutgers University Press, 2021), chap. 1.

76. " 'Evergreen' Digs into Underground Appeal, Finds 'Sold Out' Types Really Dig Its Copy," *Advertising* Age, July 25, 1966, quoted in Glass, *Counter-Culture Colophon*, 131.
77. Charles Reich, *The Greening of America: How the Youth Revolution is Trying to Make America Livable* (New York: Random House, 1970). Reich's argument was first excerpted in a mammoth *New Yorker* article, covering most of the magazine's September 26, 1970, issue.
78. "Metzger Modernizing Dumas' 'Camille,' " *Variety*, November 27, 1968.
79. Vance Packard, *The Status Seekers* (New York: Pocket Books, 1971).
80. Jordan S. Carroll, *Reading the Obscene: Transgressive Editors and the Class Politics of US Literature* (Stanford, CA: Stanford University Press, 2021), 4. Useful to understanding this cohort is Pierre Bourdieu's analysis of those individuals of high cultural and educational capital who are nonetheless alienated from the "legitimate" or traditional culture associated with their middle-class status. Such individuals, Bourdieu argues, are characterized by an investment in "alternative" forms of cultural capital such as cinema, jazz, as well as those "productions of the 'counter-culture' . . . which offer the [works] of the intellectual avant-garde in journalistic form." Pierre Bourdieu, *Distinction: A Social Critique of the Judgement of Taste*, trans. Richard Nice (Cambridge, MA: Harvard University Press, 1984), 84–85. The examples Bourdieu gives of such "journalistic" forms here are naturally French, but tellingly include the leftist intellectual weekly *Le nouvel observateur* (founded in 1964), the scurrilous satirical magazine *Charlie Hebdo* (founded 1970), and the sex and politics journal *Sexpol* (founded 1975).
81. See, for example, *Playboy* founder Hugh Hefner's description of himself in a 1957 editorial: "He likes jazz, foreign films, Ivy League clothes, gin and tonic and pretty girls—the same sort of things that *Playboy* readers like," quoted in Elizabeth Fraterrigo, *Playboy and the Making of the Good Life in Modern America* (New York: Oxford University Press, 2009), 60.
82. Ehrenreich, *Hearts of Men*, 113.
83. "Audubon to Produce New 'Carmen' Film in Europe," *Box Office*, October 17, 1966.
84. "New York Sound Stage," *Variety*, October 26, 1966. Metzger would more accurately have named his film *Carmen 18*. Previous film adaptations of Mérimée's novella number at least seventeen, including films made in Argentina, Belgium, France, Germany, Hong Kong, Italy, Spain, and the United States: *Carmen* (DeMille, 1915), *Carmen* (Walsh, 1915), *A Burlesque on Carmen* (Chaplin, 1915), *Carmen* (Lubitsch, 1918), *Een Carmen van het Noorden* (Binger, 1919), *Carmen* (Feyder, 1926), *The Loves of Carmen* (Walsh, 1927), *Carmen*

(Lewis, 1932), *Andalusische Nächte* (Maisch, 1938), *Carmen* (Amadori, 1943), *Carmen* (Christian-Jaque, 1944), *The Loves of Carmen* (Vidor, 1948), *Carmen* (Scotese, 1953), *Carmen, la de Ronda* (Demichli, 1959), *Carmen Jones* (Preminger, 1954), *The Wild Wild Rose* (Wong, 1960), and *Carmen di Trastevere* (Gallone, 1962).

85. The new title was first announced in "New York Sound Track," *Variety*, August 9, 1967, two months before the film's October 10 New York premiere.
86. "Sex Can Be Dull, Sez Radley Metzger, So He Produced an Action Pic," *Variety*, December 28, 1966; "Audubon to Film French Novel in Two Versions," *International Film Arts News*, April 1967, Radley Metzger clippings file, NYPL.
87. Metzger quoted in Nathaniel Thompson, "Film Notes" in *Carmen, Baby* DVD (First Run Features, 1999)
88. Testa, "Soft-Shaft Opportunism," 46.
89. The trope is also evident in a number of censored scenes from *The Alley Cats*. This footage, which does not appear among the "Alternate Nude Scenes" in First Run Features' 2006 DVD release, was preserved by Metzger on a video copy that I acquired from the posthumous sale of the contents of his New Jersey storage unit in 2020. (See this book's acknowledgements for more on that sale.)
90. "Foreign Films: Where It All Began," *Modern Man Deluxe Quarterly* 815 (Spring 1968): 24, in Heterosexual and Miscellaneous Pornography Periodicals, Human Sexuality Collection, Cornell University; "New York Sound Stage," *Variety*, October 5, 1966; " 'Alley Cat' Can Roam Free," *Variety*, October 12, 1966. In a brief discussion in *Playboy* magazine, critics Arthur Knight and Hollis Alpert hypothesized wrongly that *The Dirty Girls* might have been "assembled from two European movies . . . and tied together by an English narration." Arthur Knight and Hollis Alpert, "The History of Sex in Cinema, Part XVI," *Playboy*, June 1967.
91. Schaefer, "I'll Take Sweden," 210.
92. Brown, "Radley Metzger."
93. Corliss, "Radley Metzger."
94. "Carmen, Baby," *Box Office*, October 16, 1967.
95. Brode, "Radley Metzger."
96. Kathleen Carroll, " 'Carmen' Just Porno, Baby," *New York Daily News*, October 11, 1967, *Carmen, Baby* clippings file, NYPL.
97. " 'Carmen, Baby' in a Modern Setting," *Morning Telegraph*, October 11, 1967, *Carmen, Baby* clippings file, NYPL.
98. Russell Lynes, "Highbrow, Lowbrow, Middlebrow," *Harper's Magazine*, February 1949. Lynes's essay was impactful enough to merit a response piece in *Life* magazine two months later, including a tongue-in-cheek "In Defense of the Highbrow" by senior writer Winthrop Sargeant. "High-Brow, Low-Brow, Middle-Brow," *Life*, April 11, 1949.
99. Dwight Macdonald, "Masscult and Midcult" (1960), in *Against the American Grain* (New York: Da Capo, 1983), 37.
100. Clement Greenberg, "Avant-Garde and Kitsch," *Partisan Review* 6, no. 5 (Fall 1939): 40.
101. Lynes, "Highbrow, Lowbrow, Middlebrow."
102. See the introduction to this book.
103. Greenberg, "Avant-Garde and Kitsch," 21.
104. Brode, "Radley Metzger."

105. On the art/pornography opposition, see Walter Kendrick, *The Secret Museum: Pornography in Modern Culture* (New York: Viking, 1987), chap. 6.
106. The same applies to the related category of "softcore" cinema—of which Metzger's cinema was an important precursor—which seeks to avoid the taint of "low" pornography by substituting a pictorialist, soft-focus style in place of "hardcore" explicitness. See Jancovich, "Naked Ambitions"; David Andrews, *Soft in the Middle: The Contemporary Softcore Feature in Its Contexts* (Columbus: Ohio State University Press, 2006), 31–37.
107. Vincent Canby, " 'Carmen' Updated," *New York Times*, October 11, 1967, *Carmen, Baby* clippings file, NYPL.
108. "Carmen, Baby," *Box Office*, October 11, 1967.
109. Levka had a small role in Metzger's previous film, *The Alley Cats*, in which she performed a provocative dance number—a talent that Metzger capitalized on again in *Carmen, Baby*.
110. Gorfinkel, "Radley Metzger's 'Elegant Arousal,' " 35 (emphasis in original).
111. Also relevant, in terms of Metzger's formal inventiveness, is the nonlinear approach he originally intended for the film's narrative, in which the main story would be told in flashbacks as a jail-cell confessional. Although filmed, these wraparound scenes were abandoned in the final edit. They survive on video transfers that Metzger made of unused footage, included in the 2020 sale of his New Jersey storage unit.
112. Carroll, " 'Carmen' Just Porno, Baby."
113. Brown, "Radley Metzger."
114. Syd Silverman, "Metzger, Leighton and Sexcess Formula: Audubon's 29 Films All in Black," *Variety*, September 3, 1969.
115. Syd Silverman, "Audubon's Proprietorship Years," *Variety*, September 3, 1969.
116. "New York Sound Track," *Variety*, November 15, 1967.
117. "Daniele Gaubert to Star in New Audubon Film," *Box Office*, October 28, 1968.
118. "Audubon-Metzger to Film 'Camille' in English, Italian," *Variety*, August 20, 1968; "Metzger Modernizing Dumas' 'Camille,' " *Variety*, November 27, 1968; " 'Camille 2000' Completes Production in Rome," *Box Office*, January 20, 1969. The shoot also included two weeks at Porto Ercole for scenes of the central couple's getaway, starting in late November. "New York Sound Track," *Variety*, December 11, 1968.
119. On the film's locations, see Ashley West, "Adult Film Locations—Part 13: *Camille 2000*," *The Rialto Report*, October 28, 2018, https://www.therialtoreport.com/2018/10/28/camille-2000.
120. Corliss, "Radley Metzger."
121. "Camille Turns On," *Playboy*, May 1969.
122. A. H. Weiler, " 'Camille' Updated," *New York Times*, July 17, 1969.
123. DVD commentary, *Camille 2000* (Cult Epics, 2011).
124. "Broadway," *Box Office*, June 30, 1969. Press material for Metzger's follow-up film, *The Lickerish Quartet* (1970), included the rather fantastical claim that Sabbatini's plastic bed had been "publicized in practically every major publication in the world." Press sheet for *The Lickerish Quartet* (1970), author's collection.
125. Jean Laplanche and Jean-Bertrand Pontalis, *Vocabulaire de la psychoanalyse* (Paris: PUF, 1967), 152–57; Robert J. Stoller, *Observing the Erotic Imagination* (New Haven, CT: Yale University Press, 1985), 3–43.

126. Alistair O'Neill, "Taste-Making: Indifference, Interiors and the Unbound Image," in *More Dirty Looks: Gender, Pornography and Power*, 2nd ed., ed. Pamela Church Gibson (London: BFI, 2004), 147.
127. A deleted scene thematizes the panel of mirrors in terms of Marguerite's capriciousness. Marguerite has just made love to Armand's rival, the Count de Varville, who gazes into the mirrors and says: "I see you like this, a dozen faces, all different, and each more beautiful than the next, a myriad of Marguerites clustered here, to be enjoyed. And I wonder, which one is the real Marguerite?" The scene in question was included in the cache of VHS transfers held in Metzger's New Jersey storage unit.
128. Gorfinkel, "Radley Metzger's 'Elegant Arousal,' " 34.
129. Testa, "Soft-Shaft Opportunism," 46–47.
130. Andrew Sarris, "Notes on the Auteur Theory in 1962," *Film Culture* 27 (Winter 1962–63): 1–8.
131. See the introduction to this book.
132. Richard Corliss, "Film: Camille 2000," *Village Voice*, December 11, 1969, *Camille 2000* clippings file, NYPL.
133. Richard Corliss, "Film: Camille 2000."
134. On mainstream critics and sex cinema in the 1960s, see Raymond J. Haberski Jr., "Critics and the Sex Scene," in Schaefer, ed., *Sex Scene*, 383–406.
135. Joel Doerfler, "Radley Metzger: Let 'Em See Skin," *Boston After Dark*, February 9, 1971, Radley Metzger clippings file, NYPL.
136. Richard Corliss, "Film: Cherry & Harry & Raquel," *Village Voice*, June 11, 1970, Radley Metzger clippings file, NYPL. On the "taste of necessity," see Bourdieu, *Distinction*, "Introduction."
137. For critic Bart Testa, for instance, Meyer's "style and spirit were as proudly primitive-American and working-class vulgar as Metzger's was pseudo-Euro-sophisticated and faux-elite," while adult-film archivist Ashley West juxtaposes Meyer's "blue-collar pneumatic Robert Crumb world" with Metzger's "decadent excess, sexual dolce vita, and deliriously jaded abandon." See Testa, "Soft-Shaft Opportunism," n14; Benson Hurst, "Maraschino Cherry," liner notes from *Maraschino Cherry: Platinum Elite Collection* DVD (Distribpix, 2009). "Benson Hurst" is an earlier pseudonym for the equally pseudonymous Ashley West of *The Rialto Report* website.
138. Wanda Hale, " 'Camille' Is Deadly Bore," *New York Daily News*, July 17, 1969, and George Melly, "The Swamps of Porn," *Observer* (UK), October 24, 1971, both from the *Camille 2000* clippings file, NYPL.
139. "Playboy Loves 'Camille 2000,' " *Independent Film Journal*, May 13, 1969.
140. "Ava Leighton's Point: Audubon Lift from Sexploits to Sex-Art Level," *Variety*, August 6, 1969.
141. *Camille 2000* was bested among Audubon's releases that year only by *The Libertine* ($1,034,030). Box-office figures calculated from "U.S. Films' Share-of-Market Profile," *Variety*, May 12, 1971.
142. Don Vaillancourt, "Producing Works of Art or Obscenity?," *Newark Sunday News*, February 28, 1971, Radley Metzger clippings file, NYPL; press sheet for *The Lickerish Quartet*.

143. Lanfranco Rasponi, *The International Nomads: Today's Jet Age Society—Who It Is & How, Why & Where It Functions* (New York: Putnam's, 1966), 20.
144. "Metzger Opens Pubbery," *Variety*, May 28, 1969; "Music Publishing Company Is Formed by Audubon," *Box Office*, June 2, 1969; "Metzger Sets Up Ethel Music," *Variety*, June 4, 1969; "National General Still Leading Merger Parade," *Independent Film Journal*, June 10, 1969.
145. "Audubon Into Books," *Variety*, September 10, 1969; "MGM Interphoto Mating Off; Audubon Forms Book Subsid," *Independent Film Journal*, September 16, 1969.
146. Dell was the paperback imprint of Farrar, Straus and Giroux, which first published a translation of Leduc's novella in 1967. The same translation, by Derek Coltman, was used for the film tie-in.
147. A particularly notable example is offered in the differences between the film and novelization of *Carmen, Baby*. Early in the film, for instance, Carmen performs a seductive "bottle dance," in which she dances around a long-necked, obviously phallic wine bottle. At one point, she crouches down and is shot from the waist up bobbing in time to the music. A series of cutaways to dumbstruck onlookers nonetheless suggests that more is happening here than the film is actually showing (Metzger later described the scene as a "triumph of editorial eroticism"). The book, by contrast, is explicit where the film is coy: "Her eyes closed, her knees flexed, she impaled herself upon the green stalk rising from the globe between her feet. . . . Gradually Carmen began raising and lowering her body, each time increasing her acceptance of the bottle as more and more of the gleaming cylinder disappeared within her." Richard Corliss, "Radley Metzger"; Sebastian Grant, *Carmen, Baby* (New York: Award, 1968), 46.
148. See David Church, "The Naked Page: Adult Film Novelizations and the Sexploitation Market," *byNWR*, 2018, https://www.bynwr.com/articles/the-naked-page.
149. See Glass, *Counter-Culture Colophon*, chap. 5.
150. Larry Michie, "Audubon in SEC Plea Reveals Its Profits, Pic by Pic," *Variety*, August 28, 1969. At the time of filing, Metzger owned 57.4 percent of the company and Leighton 38 percent.
151. See, for instance, "Audubon Outlines Expansion as Public Offering Revealed," *Independent Film Journal*, September 2, 1969; Syd Silverman, "Audubon's Amortization," *Variety*, September 3, 1969; Syd Silverman, "Audubon's Proprietorship Years"; Syd Silverman, "Metzger, Leighton and Sexcess Formula"; Syd Silverman, "That Wow '68," *Variety*, September 3, 1969.
152. Silverman, "Metzger, Leighton and Sexcess Formula." Silverman was a grandson of *Variety*'s founder, Sime Silverman.
153. "Charles to Re-Open," n.s., January 24, 1963, Radley Metzger clippings file, NYPL. Under managers Edwin Stein Jr. and Walter Langsford, the Charles had been one of the most prominent venues for the nascent underground film movement at the start of the 1960s. The theater closed in December 1962 after falling into significant debt, at which point Metzger picked up the lease. See Ben Davis, *Repertory Movie Theaters of New York City: Havens for Revivals, Indies and the Avant-Garde, 1960–1994* (Jefferson, NC: McFarland, 2017), chap. 5.
154. "U.S. Films' Share-of-Market Profile."

155. Syd Silverman, "Capsule Analysis of 27 Companies in 'Variety' Study," *Variety*, May 12, 1971.
156. "Metzger in Munich Shoots Film About Eva Peron Type," *Variety*, October 20, 1971. For the San Francisco opening of *The Zodiac Killer* in 1971, the film's director Tom Hanson set up in-theater "traps" to catch the killer if they attended, including a false ice-cream freezer containing police officers. Audubon picked up the film after its debut sans the gimmicks. See the liner notes for *The Zodiac Killer* Blu-ray (American Film Genre Archive, 2017); "Audubon Distrib of 'Zodiac Killer,' " *Variety*, August 13, 1971.
157. "Audubon-Walker Pact," *Variety*, December 9, 1971.

2. "THE NEXT STEP WILL BE TO SHOW 'IT' "

1. Parker Tyler quoted in David Bordwell, *The Rhapsodes: How 1940s Critics Changed American Film Culture* (Chicago: University of Chicago Press, 2016), 119.
2. Parker Tyler, "Do They or Don't They? Why It Matters So Much," *Evergreen Review* 14, no. 78 (May 1970): 25–27, 68–71.
3. On this trope, see Richard Maltby, " 'A Brief Romantic Interlude': Dick and Jane Go to 3½ Seconds of the Classical Hollywood Cinema," in *Post-Theory: Reconstructing Film Studies*, ed. David Bordwell and Noël Carroll (Madison: University of Wisconsin Press, 1996), 434–59.
4. Tyler, "Do They or Don't They?," 68–69.
5. Tyler, "Do They or Don't They?," 69, 70.
6. Andrew Sarris, "The Nihilism of Nudity—II," *Village Voice*, March 27, 1969, quoted in Raymond J. Haberski Jr., "Critics and the Sex Scene," in *Sex Scene: Media and the Sexual Revolution*, ed. Eric Schaefer (Durham, NC: Duke University Press, 2014), 390. Philosopher Slavoj Žižek has similarly argued that "congruence between the film narrative (the unfolding of the story) and the immediate display of the sexual act, is structurally impossible," insofar as the display of engorged genitalia serves as an actual presence of real sexual arousal that cannot be sequestered solely to the realm of a fictive representation. Slavoj Žižek, *Looking Awry: An Introduction to Jacque Lacan Through Popular Culture* (Cambridge, MA: MIT Press, 1991), 111.
7. Richard Corliss, "The Lickerish Quartet," *Village Voice*, November 12, 1970.
8. Béla Balázs, *Theory of Film: Character and Growth of a New Art*, trans. Edith Bone (London: Dennis Dobson, 1952), 46.
9. Vsevolod Pudovkin, *Film Technique and Film Acting*, trans. Ivor Montagu (London: Vision, 1954), 58 (italics in original).
10. André Bazin, "Marginal Notes on Eroticism in the Cinema," in *What Is Cinema?*, trans. Hugh Gray (Berkeley: University of California Press, 1971), 2:170. Closer to the time of Radley Metzger's burgeoning career, literary historian Steven Marcus's groundbreaking *The Other Victorians: A Study of Sexuality and Pornography in Mid-Nineteenth-Century England* (New York: Basic Books, 1966) included the claim that cinema was what pornography "was all along waiting for," since literary pornography was limited by the "bothersome necessity" of language (208). To this we might add the famous assertion with which Fredric Jameson began his study of postmodern visual culture, *Signatures of the Visible*; namely, that the "visual is *essentially* pornographic," such that "pornographic films are . . .

the potentiation of films in general." Jameson, *Signatures of the Visible* (New York: Routledge, 1992), 1.

11. The examples are chosen advisedly. As Pasi Falk has noted, the manifestations of male sexuality—erection and penetration—cannot be safely contained to the realm of fictive representation, since both are preconditioned by the fact of actual sexual stimulation. Pasi Falk, *The Consuming Body* (London: Sage Publications, 1994), chap. 7, "Pornography and the Representation of Presence." The same is not true, Falk notes, of female sexuality, where the representation of arousal does not equally require actual arousal: the "female partner is able to lie or act" in pornography in a way that is not possible for the male (200). If the problem of male sexuality is that it is "anti-representation," in the sense that male arousal cannot be contained to the realm of the fictive, then the problem of female sexuality is that it is, contrariwise, "anti-presentation," insofar as the absence of evidential signs means that it cannot be given as a fact, but *only* represented. The latter conundrum lies at the heart of Linda Williams's classic study *Hard Core: Power, Pleasure, and the "Frenzy of the Visible"* (Berkeley: University of California Press, 1989).
12. "Lesbo Love Film for Audubon," *Variety*, April 19, 1967. Budgetary information taken from "Audubon-Metzger to Film 'Camille' in English, Italian," *Variety*, August 20, 1968.
13. The film was scheduled for a six-week shoot but was delayed for two weeks following an on-set injury to Persson. "New York Sound Stage," *Variety*, September 20, 1967.
14. On the film's locations, see Ashley West, "Adult Film Locations—Part 16: 'Therese and Isabelle,'" *The Rialto Report*, December 4, 2022, https://www.therialtoreport.com/2022/12/04/therese-and-isabelle-2.
15. The "sizzler from France" tagline was featured in advertisements for *Thérèse and Isabelle* in June and July of 1968: for example, *Variety*, June 12, 1968; *Box Office*, July 8, 1968; *Independent Film Journal*, July 9, 1968. The review of the picture as a "foreign film" is in *Variety*, May 15, 1968.
16. "'Therese' an Honest Peek at Lesbian Relationship, Sez Producer Metzger," *Variety*, December 6, 1967.
17. "Bingo Brandt's 'Class Sex' Cellar as Mate for His One-Theme Rialto," *Variety*, April 10, 1968; "Audubon's 'Therese' Set for Dual World Preem," *Independent Film Journal*, April 27, 1968; "Audubon Launches 'Therese and Isabelle,'" *Independent Film Journal*, May 25, 1968; advertisement for *Thérèse and Isabelle*, *Variety*, June 12, 1968.
18. "U.S. Films' Share-of-Market Profile," *Variety*, May 12, 1971.
19. Bart Testa, "Soft-Shaft Opportunism: Radley Metzger's Erotic Kitsch," *Spectator* 19, no. 2 (Spring–Summer 1999): 49.
20. On Grove Press, see chapter 1 of this book.
21. The quotes are from the front and inside cover of Dell's 1968 tie-in rerelease of Leduc's story.
22. Toni Bentley, "The Legend of Henry Paris," *Playboy*, June 2014.
23. "Therese and Isabelle," *Independent Film Journal*, May 25, 1968. A similar observation was made by *Box Office*, which noted that the "graphic visuals are more than matched by the subtitled narration." "Therese and Isabelle," *Box Office*, May 27, 1968.
24. The voiceover here constitutes a mosaic of disparate quotes from the novel, assembled together with only minor changes. Leduc, *Thérèse and Isabelle*, trans. Derek Coltman (New

York: Farrar, Straus & Giroux, 1966), 4, 7, 10, 11, 20, 27, 28, 54. Where possible, I have kept the punctuation of the original English translation.

25. Testa, "Soft-Shaft Opportunism," 48.
26. The passage is verbatim from Leduc, *Thérèse and Isabelle*, 31–32, with the excision of a single sentence.
27. The passage is adapted from Leduc, *Thérèse and Isabelle*, 100–101. The disjunction between the voiceover narration and the visuals was also noted in the film's review in *Playboy*, which observed that Leduc's "words are compelling" but "seldom relevant to the action *les girls* perform on the screen." "Playboy After Hours," *Playboy*, August 1968.
28. Alberta Gallus, "The Body Into Words: Violette Leduc's *La Folie en tête*," *French Forum* 31, no. 3 (Fall 2006): 123.
29. Violette Leduc, *La folie en tête* (Paris: Gallimard, 1970), 73 (my translation).
30. Leduc, *Thérèse and Isabelle*, 8, 13, 109, 110.
31. The same was not the case with Dell's tie-in rerelease of Leduc's novella, which paired the author's prose with what the front cover boasted of as "revealing motion picture scenes"—specifically, an eight-page photographic insert comprising semi-explicit stills from Metzger's film—as though the film overtly showed what Leduc could only describe.
32. André Bazin, "*Le Journal d'un curé de campagne* and the Stylistics of Robert Bresson," in Bazin, *What Is Cinema?*, 1:128, 136.
33. Wanda Hale, "This Is Out, Not Art," *New York Daily News*, May 15, 1968, *Thérèse and Isabelle* clippings file, NYPL.
34. "Therese and Isabelle," *Variety*, May 15, 1968.
35. Andrew Sarris, no title, *Village Voice*, June 6, 1968, *Thérèse and Isabelle* clippings file, NYPL.
36. Bentley, "The Legend of Henry Paris."
37. "Audubon Into Books," *Variety*, September 10, 1969.
38. Production information on *The Lickerish Quartet* is culled from a variety of sources: Ashley West, "Adult Film Locations—Part 14: The Exploitation Film Castle," *The Rialto Report*, June 30, 2019, https://www.therialtoreport.com/2019/06/30/lickerish-quartet-2/; DVD commentary, *The Lickerish Quartet* (Cult Epics, 2011); and "The Lickerish Quartet," *Variety*, October 14, 1970. According to *Variety*, filming began on October 27 and wrapped in mid-December. "International Sound Stage," *Variety*, October 22, 1969; "Italian Films Shooting," *Variety*, December 10, 1969. The film was originally scheduled for a four-week shoot, but, like *Thérèse and Isabelle*, was extended by two weeks—this time after a flu outbreak waylaid most of the cast and crew.
39. Publicity for *The Lickerish Quartet* no doubt exaggerated in claiming that Venturelli won "global recognition" for her "effective portrayal of the erotic and sensual 'Olympe.' " But she certainly drew attention, with *Screw* magazine declaring her the "sexiest chick in sexploitation film history," and even the staid *New York Times* noting her "decidedly well-endowed" appearance. See *The Lickerish Quartet* pressbook, author's collection; Al Goldstein, "Dirty Diversions: Cocky Camille," *Screw*, August 18, 1969; A. H. Weiler, " 'Camille' Updated," *New York Times*, July 17, 1969. Metzger seems to have had Venturelli in mind at least as early as the writing of the script for *The Lickerish Quartet*, in which her character name is given simply as "S" (for Silvana, presumably). Venturelli's name also appears among the project's earliest announcements. See Radley Metzger and Michael De

Forrest, *Radley Metzger's The Lickerish Quartet* (New York: Audubon Books, 1970), and "Audubon Picks Up Pair of Pix," *Variety*, August 27, 1969. In building a feature around Venturelli, Metzger was repeating what he had already done with Uta Levka, whom he first cast in a film-stealing dance sequence in *The Alley Cats* (1965) and then as lead in his subsequent *Carmen, Baby* (1967); as well as Essy Persson, who went from being star of the Audubon acquisition *I, a Woman* to star of Metzger's self-directed *Thérèse and Isabelle*.

40. DVD commentary, *The Lickerish Quartet.*
41. DVD commentary, *The Lickerish Quartet.*
42. Whether accidentally or not, Metzger in later years falsely claimed that it was in fact Grove that had published *The Lickerish Quartet*'s script. Jay Kay Lorentz, "The Erotic World of Radley Metzger: Interview by Jay Kay Lorentz," *Psychotronic Video* 17 (Winter 1994): 32.
43. I twice had the pleasure of hosting Radley to talk to my class in Cult and Exploitation at Columbia University, in 2013 and 2015: both times he insisted that *The Lickerish Quartet* be the film screened.
44. Here I am following Jacques Rancière's tripartite distinction of the properties of the photographic image in his essay "The Future of the Image," from *The Future of the Image*, trans. Gregory Elliott (London: Verso, 2007), 1–31.
45. Jura's work was praised in *Variety*, which deemed his cinematography the "best seen here since the New York Film Fest unspooled Bertolucci's 'The Conformist.'" "The Lickerish Quartet," *Variety*.
46. Richard Corliss, "Radley Metzger: Aristocrat of the Erotic," *Film Comment*, January–February 1973, 25.
47. Peirce's relevance for film theory was first argued in Peter Wollen's influential *Signs and Meaning in the Cinema* (London: Secker & Warburg, 1969), chap. 3, "The Semiology of the Cinema."
48. André Bazin, "The Ontology of the Photographic Image," in *What Is Cinema?*, 1:9. Other scholars have since made similar claims, such as Laura Marks's description of photography as "a sort of umbilical cord between the thing photographed *then* and our gaze *now*," or Jacques Rancière's reference to the photographic image as "the very emanation of a body . . . a skin detached from its surface." Laura U. Marks, *Touch: Sensuous Theory and Multisensory Media* (Minneapolis: University of Minnesota Press, 2002), 96; Rancière, "The Future of the Image," 9.
49. Judith Crist, "The Lickerish Quartet," *New York*, November 9, 1970; "The Lickerish Quartet," *Variety*.
50. The *Independent Film Journal*'s review of the film, for instance, referred to the mysterious woman's "*Teorema*-like chores," while a profile of the director the following year described the character as being "like the central figure of Pasolini's *Teorema*." "The Lickerish Quartet," *Independent Film Journal*, October 30, 1970; Douglas Brode, "Radley Metzger: Master of the Erotic on Film," *Show*, September 1971, Radley Metzger clipping file, NYPL. More recently—and more unsympathetically—Bart Testa has described *The Lickerish Quartet* as an "unacknowledged remake of Pasolini's *Teorema*." Testa, "Soft-Shaft Opportunism," 52. Metzger's position, meanwhile, was that he deliberately did *not* see

Teorema before filming *The Lickerish Quartet*, lest he be accused of the very plagiarism with which Testa and others have charged him. At a screening of *The Lickerish Quartet* at the Museum of Modern Art on January 26, 1971, Metzger responded to an audience question about the Pasolini film as follows: "I felt that, from what I'd heard about *Teorema*, there were similarities, and I didn't want to have any unconscious influences. So I've never seen the film, and I never saw *Persona* [Bergman, 1966], which I understand could also be considered to have certain similarities, not in effect or technique, but in certain ideas in the picture." "An Evening with Radley Metzger," January 26, 1971, Sound Recordings, MoMA.

51. As Rancière writes, differentiating the image's function as resemblance from its status as art: "There is the simple relationship that produces the likeness of an original: not necessarily its faithful copy, but simply what suffices to stand in for it. And there is the interplay of operations that produces what we call art: or precisely an alteration of resemblance. This alteration can take myriad of forms. It might be the visibility given to brush-strokes that are superfluous when it comes to revealing who is represented by the portrait; an elongation of bodies that expresses their motion at the expense of their proportions; a turn of language that accentuates the expression of a feeling or renders the perception of an idea more complex; a word or a shot in place of the ones that seemed bound to follow; and so on and so forth." Rancière, "The Future of the Image," 6–7.
52. DVD commentary, *The Lickerish Quartet*. I have been unable to trace the Diahann Carroll performance that Metzger remembered.
53. Corliss, "Radley Metzger," 24. Metzger's initial plan to use spinning camera movements is evident from the film's published script: "THE LIBRARY FLOOR: Locked to each other, Man and S [i.e., Silvana Venturelli] roll and turn across the floor, shifting from word to word as the floor seems to revolve beneath them so that the pattern of words changes as tempo increases, the rhythm of the words accelerating along with the mounting tension of the sex act. The series of words: TAKE / HAVE / MAKE / CONJUGATE / COPULATE / FORNICATE / LIE / LAY / SCREW / BALL / SLAM / BANG / FUCK. The words seem to spin larger and faster as the Man and S near the climax." Metzger and DeForrest, *Radley Metzger's The Lickerish Quartet*, 113.
54. DVD commentary, *The Lickerish Quartet*.
55. Corliss, "Radley Metzger," 24.
56. Linda Williams, "Radley Metzger, High Modernist Auteur," paper delivered at the Society of Cinema and Media Studies conference, Seattle, March 16, 2019.
57. Bazin draws this distinction in his essay "The Evolution of the Language of Cinema," in *What Is Cinema?*, 1:23–41. "Faith in reality" refers to those filmmakers who prioritize the medium as a device for recording what it represents; "faith in the image" to those who exploit what the medium can "add . . . to the object there represented," whether by manipulating mise-en-scène, cinematography, or editing (24).
58. "TV-Radio Production Centres in the U.S. and Abroad," *Variety*, November 25, 1970; no title, *New York Daily Mirror*, March 12, 1971, Radley Metzger clippings file, NYPL; "New York Sound Track," *Variety*, March 24, 1971; "New York Sound Track," *Variety*, March 31, 1971; "Colgate Film Awards to Altman, Metzger," *Variety*, April 29, 1971.
59. "Museum to Metzger: 'Roger' on Audubon," *Variety*, November 25, 1970; "Fans, Foes to Quiz Metzger at Museum," *Variety*, December 23, 1970; "An Evening with Radley

Metzger," Museum of Modern Art Program Notes, January 26, 1971, Radley Metzger clippings file, MoMA.

60. The play in question was *The Garden of Earthly Delights* (1967), whose acquisition by Audubon was first reported in *Variety* the previous June. "Audubon Has 'Garden,' " *Variety*, June 10, 1970. Although Metzger originally intended this to be his next film, concerns about certain formal similarities with *The Lickerish Quartet* led him to delay, and finally abandon, the project. As he explained to audience members at the MoMA screening of *The Lickerish Quartet*, "The . . . reason I may not do it next is that it has four people in it, and it's a study of reality and illusion and the erotic. There are so many similarities to this film [i.e., *The Lickerish Quartet*] that I perhaps may do something else in between." "An Evening with Radley Metzger," Sound Recordings, MoMA. On Arrabal, see Thomas John Donahue's study, *The Theater of Fernando Arrabal: A Garden of Earthly Delights* (New York: New York University Press, 1980).
61. Lawrence Levine, *Highbrow/Lowbrow: The Emergence of Cultural Hierarchy in America* (Cambridge, MA: Harvard University Press, 1988), 234.
62. This undated radio show is available to listen at "Radley Metzger 1971," *The Rialto Report*, September 24, 2017, https://www.therialtoreport.com/2017/09/24/radley-metzger-3.
63. Corliss, "Radley Metzger," 25.
64. "Metzger in Munich Shoots Film About Eva Peron Type," *Variety*, October 20, 1971; Howard Kissel, "Radley Metzger from Eros to the C.I.A.," *Women's Wear Daily*, January 8, 1973, Radley Metzger clippings file, MoMA.
65. "Little Mother," *Independent Film Journal*, August 3, 1972.
66. The reviews are quoted in "Washington," *Box Office*, October 17, 1972, and "Pittsburgh," *Box Office*, February 12, 1973.
67. According to *Variety*, principal shooting began on January 14 and lasted into the second week of February. "Metzger in Munich Shoots Film About Eva Peron Type"; "Hollywood Production Pulse," *Variety*, February 9, 1972; "New York Sound Track," *Variety*, February 16, 1972.
68. "Little Mother," *Box Office*, August 21, 1972. The scene in question may well have been influenced by the early Audubon acquisition *La récréation* (1961, released in the United States in 1963 under the title *Playtime*), which includes a scene in which two lovers kiss through a shower curtain.
69. "Little Mother," *Independent Film Journal*.
70. Bazin's writings on television are collected in Dudley Andrew, ed., *André Bazin's New Media* (Berkeley: University of California Press, 2014).
71. Add to this the fact that "liveness" has been significantly transformed by the advent of twenty-first-century streaming services, where it now registers as the ever-present simultaneity of all viewing options.
72. Jane Feuer, "The Concept of Live Television: Ontology as Ideology," in *Regarding Television: Critical Approaches—An Anthology*, ed. E. Ann Kaplan (Los Angeles: AFI, 1983), 12–21. See also Wolfgang Ernst, "Between Real Time and Memory on Demand: Reflections on Television," in Ernst, *Digital Memory and the Archive* (Minneapolis: University of Minnesota Press, 2012), 103–12, which associates the ideology of liveness with television's status as an "information system."

73. Archer Winsten, " 'Little Mother' Opens at Showcase Theaters," *New York Post*, January 6, 1973, *Little Mother* clippings file, MoMA.
74. Pressbook for *Little Mother, Little Mother* clippings file, MoMA.
75. Rex Reed, *New York Daily News*, January 19, 1973, *Little Mother* clippings file, MoMA.
76. "Camille 2000," *Independent Film Journal*, July 22, 1969; Joel Doerfler, no title, *Boston After Dark*, January 19, 1971, *The Lickerish Quartet* clippings file, NYPL; Testa, "Soft-Shaft Opportunism," 46.
77. "An Evening with Radley Metzger," Sound Recordings, MoMA.
78. Linda Williams, "Radley Metzger."
79. Testa, "Soft-Shaft Opportunism," 43.
80. The definition is Linda Williams's, from her *Hard Core*.
81. What we are talking about is something akin to what media theorist Bernhard Siegert has called "cultural techniques," by which he refers to the way in which cultural and symbolic distinctions inhere in and are shaped by material operations and artifacts (here, the materiality of media technologies and their affordances). Bernhard Siegert, *Cultural Techniques: Grids, Filters, Doors, and Other Articulations of the Real*, trans. Geoffrey Winthrop-Young (New York: Fordham University Press, 2015).
82. David Andrews, *Soft in the Middle: The Contemporary Softcore Feature in Its Contexts* (Columbus: Ohio State University Press, 2006), 37–44.

3. "THAT'S NOT HIS REAL NAME"

1. Ashley West, " 'The Private Afternoons of Pamela Mann' (1974): The Birth of 'Henry Paris,' " *The Rialto Report*, April 3, 2017, https://www.therialtoreport.com/2017/04/03/private-afternoons-of-pamela-mann.
2. On *Miller*, see Kimberly A. Harchuck, "Pornography and the First Amendment Right to Free Speech," in *New Views on Pornography: Sexuality, Politics, and the Law*, ed. Lynn Comella and Shira Tarrant (Santa Barbara, CA: Praeger, 2015), 9–36; Whitney Strub, *Obscenity Rules: Roth v. United States and the Long Struggle over Sexual Expression* (Lawrence: University Press of Kansas, 2013), chap. 9; and Jon Lewis, *Hollywood v. Hard Core: How the Struggle Over Censorship Saved the Modern Film Industry* (New York: New York University Press, 2000), chaps. 5 and 6.
3. West, "The Private Afternoons of Pamela Mann."
4. DVD commentary, *The Private Afternoons of Pamela Mann* (Distribpix, 2011).
5. "The Private Afternoons of Pamela Mann," *Independent Film Journal*, January 8, 1975; "Playboy After Hours," *Playboy*, March 1975.
6. "Metzger Too Soft for His Name on Hardcore 'Naked,' " *Variety*, April 30, 1975.
7. Doris Wishman was credited as "Kenyon Wintel" in her hardcore films *Satan Was a Lady* and *Come with Me My Love* (both 1976), while Joe Sarno used a variety of pseudonyms, including "Karl Andersson" in *Touch of Genie* (1974) and "Otis Hamlin" in *The Trouble with Young Stuff* (1977). On Wishman's hardcore work, see Whitney Strub, "Hardcore Wishman," in *ReFocus: The Films of Doris Wishman*, ed. Alicia Kozma and Finley Freibert (Edinburgh: Edinburgh University Press, 2023), 67–77.
8. In this *literary* sense (as opposed the linguistic sense of identically spelled words with different meanings), the concept of the heteronym is often associated with the

Portuguese poet Fernando Pessoa, who used more than seventy in his writings and coined the term.

9. "Who's Who in X-Rated Films," in *Who's Who in X-Rated Film, High Society* magazine supplement, 1977.
10. Richard Corliss, "Radley Metzger: Aristocrat of the Erotic," *Film Comment*, January/February 1973, 19–29; Richard Brown, "Radley Metzger: Auteur of the Erotic," *Today's Filmmaker*, August 1971, Radley Metzger clippings file, MoMA; Douglas Brode, "Radley Metzger: Master of the Erotic on Film," *Show*, September 1971.
11. Ralph Blumenthal, " 'Hard-core' Grows Fashionable—and Very Profitable," *New York Times*, January 21, 1973.
12. In January 1973, *Deep Throat* was cited by Blumenthal as drawing an average of "5,000 people weekly to the New Mature World Theater on West 49th Street," where it was seen by audiences of "celebrities, diplomats, critics, businessmen, women alone and dating couples, few of whom, it might be presumed, would previously have gone to see a film of sexual intercourse, fellatio and cunnilingus." Blumenthal, " 'Hard-core' Grows Fashionable." On Sherpix, see Eric Schaefer, "*School Girl* (Paul Gerber, 1971)," *Porn Studies* 4, no. 3 (2017): 272–79.
13. See David Andrews, *Soft in the Middle: The Contemporary Softcore Feature in Its Contexts* (Columbus: Ohio State University Press, 2006), 4.
14. Burton Wolfe, "King of the Nude Movies," *True*, March 1969, in the Russ Meyer Collection, Human Sexuality Collection, Cornell University. On *I Am Curious (Yellow)*, see Kevin Heffernan, "Prurient (Dis)Interest: The American Release and Reception of *I Am Curious (Yellow)*," in *Sex Scene: Media and the Sexual Revolution*, ed. Eric Schaefer (Durham, NC: Duke University Press, 2014), 105–25.
15. John Amero quoted in Whitney Strub, "*Bacchanale* (John Amero and Len Amero, 1970)," in *Porn Studies* 4, no. 3 (2017): 266.
16. Anderson quoted in "Pittsburgh," *Box Office*, February 12, 1973.
17. Rex Reed, no title, *New York Daily News*, January 19, 1973, *Little Mother* clippings file, MoMA.
18. Steven Marcus, *The Other Victorians: A Study of Sexuality and Pornography in Mid-Nineteenth-Century England* (New York: Basic Books, 1966), 278.
19. This older conception, stretching back millennia into Chinese, Greco-Roman, and Islamic erotic and aesthetic theory, is discussed by Richard Shusterman in his *Ars Erotica: Sex and Somaesthetics in the Classical Arts of Love* (Cambridge: Cambridge University Press, 2021). The modern repudiation of this tradition, Shusterman speculates, was the result of "currents of materialism and libertinism in the seventeenth and eighteenth centuries . . . [that made] it far more difficult to maintain the vision of erotic love as an uplifting spiritual desire" (29).
20. Schlegel cited in Pasi Falk, *The Consuming Body* (London: Sage, 1994), 191.
21. Falk, *The Consuming Body*, 186.
22. Elena Gorfinkel, "Radley Metzger's 'Elegant Arousal': Taste. Aesthetic Distinction and Sexploitation," in *Underground U.S.A.: Filmmaking beyond the Hollywood Canon*, ed. Xavier Mendik and Steven Jay Schneider (New York: Wallflower, 2002), 39.
23. "Bisexual Chic: Anyone Goes," *Newsweek*, May 13, 1974. It would be wrong, though, to historicize "bisexual chic" purely to the 1970s. Bisexuality had been a visible component

of the adult media marketplace throughout the 1960s, not just in exploitation film but in pulp fiction and art cinema as well. See Freibert, "Bad Bis Go to Hell: Bisexuality as Transgressive and Lucrative in Doris Wishman's Roughies," in Kozma and Freibert, eds., *The Films of Doris Wishman*, 78–100.

24. See the conclusion to this book for more in this connection.
25. As Metzger later explained: "[Jerry Douglas] told me that I should go and see *Boys in the Sand*. I ran down to the theater where it was playing, put down my money, and saw the picture. I sat through only half of it. I remember thinking at the time that it was junky—jerky camera work, no dialogue, very amateurish. I know now that my thoughts were based on ignorance. I didn't realize where it fit into the canon of gay porn. It was only later, when I mentioned my take on the film to Cal when we were on location, that I gained perspective on it. Cal explained that most gay porn audiences hadn't even seen anything in color." Metzger quoted in Roger Edmonson, *Boy in the Sand: Casey Donovan, All-American Sex Star* (Los Angeles: Alyson, 1998), 100–101.
26. Corliss, "Radley Metzger," 26. Some of the quotes and observations in this paragraph are adapted from Jamie Hooks's useful essay "*Score* (Radley Metzger, 1973)," *Porn Studies* 4, no. 3 (2017): 289–95. Sexploitation scholar Elena Gorfinkel has also written about the film in "Seduction Time: Radley Metzger's 'Score' and the Utopian Gesture," in *Free to Love: The Cinema of the Sexual Revolution* (Philadelphia: International House, 2014), 44–59.
27. Addison Verrill, "Score," *Variety*, November 14, 1973.
28. Addison Verrill, "Test for 'Right Sell' to Wrong Sex," *Variety*, July 3, 1974.
29. This interpretation of Metzger's motives is suggested by film critic Arthur Knight, who, in his annual *Playboy* review of "Sex in Cinema" for 1975, noted that Metzger had " 'heated up' *Score* after its disappointing initial engagements in a softer version." Knight, "Sex in Cinema—1975," *Playboy*, November 1975.
30. Hook, "*Score*," 294–95.
31. *Variety* reported that the film drew a "potent" $31,000 in its first week at the Cine Malibu and Cinema Village houses—"a wow showing for those small sites"—and subsequent ads claimed a two-week gross of $59,549. "Times Passes Up 'Score'; Good Biz for Audubon 'Bi-Sexual Chic' Sell," *Variety*, August 14, 1974; advertisement for *Score*, *Variety*, August 27, 1974. That the hardcore edit likely drew a gay male audience should not be confused, however, with positive reception. Stuart Byron, a self-described "militant" queer film critic at Boston's alternative weekly, *The Real Paper*, despised the film, complaining about the depiction of the bisexual couple, Jack and Elvira, who "come on like twin Fu Manchus." Stuart Byron, "Score," *The Real Paper*, November 22, 1973, *Score* clippings file, NYPL.
32. DVD commentary, *The Private Afternoons of Pamela Mann*.
33. Stephen Gallagher, "The Libertine," *Filmmaker Magazine*, Summer 1997, 47.
34. DVD commentary, *The Private Afternoons of Pamela Mann*.
35. West, "The Private Afternoons of Pamela Mann."
36. The guidelines for determining obscenity enshrined in the "Miller test" included the stipulation that "the work, taken as a whole, lacks serious literary, artistic, political or scientific value." This criterion created a much lower threshold for unprotected speech,

shifting the definition of obscenity from material that was "utterly without" social value (as per the *Roth* ruling of 1957) to that which simply lacked *serious* value. See Harchuck, "Pornography and the First Amendment." Metzger's satirical jab at First Amendment law was even more extended in the "cool" version of the film that he prepared for jurisdictions with stricter obscenity laws. At no small expense, he filmed Barbara Bourbon reading a comic monologue about censorship and the Constitution and superimposed her head over images of genital penetration. This version of the film is available on the two-disc 2011 Distribpix DVD release but was never actually exhibited.

37. For a similar reading of the film, see Lawrence Cohen's essay "The Erotic Imagination of Pamela Mann" in the booklet for Distribpix's DVD of the film.
38. Linda Williams, *Hard Core: Power, Pleasure, and the "Frenzy of the Visible"* (Berkeley: University of California Press, 1989).
39. See chapter 2 of this book, note 11
40. See chapter 1 of this book.
41. "The Private Afternoons of Pamela Mann," *Variety*, February 25, 1975.
42. Bonelli quoted in the film's trailer, which is included in the 2011 Distribpix DVD. For the film's "best picture" nods, see Al Goldstein, "Dirty Diversions: Delectable Derriere Delight," *Screw*, January 30, 1978, and "Film World's Own Porn Awards," *Adam Film World*, August 1976.
43. "The Private Afternoons of Pamela Mann," *Flick*, August 1975.
44. "The Private Afternoons of Pamela Mann," *Independent Film Journal*.
45. "Modest" is taken from Metzger's DVD commentary, *The Private Afternoons of Pamela Mann*. Even rumored budgetary figures for *Pamela Mann* are missing, although the total cost of the film was likely in the $40,000 to $60,000 range. The film's box-office figures are calculated from *Variety* reports during this period. By way of comparison, porn star Harry Reems estimated in a 1976 interview that most porn films grossed only a quarter million dollars after a year-and-a-half nationwide release. Merrill Miller, "Horny Harry Reems," *Adam Film World*, January 1976.
46. "International Soundtrack," *Variety*, March 23, 1977.
47. DVD commentary, *The Private Afternoons of Pamela Mann*. On *The World of Henry Paris*, see chapter 5 of this book.
48. Publishing information taken from Ashley West, "'Naked Came the Stranger' (1975): The Hoax, The Film," *The Rialto Report*, April 5, 2017, https://www.therialtoreport.com/2017/04/05/naked-came-the-stranger-2/, and Marlene Cimons, "Literary Hoax to X-Rated Movie," *Los Angeles Times*, May 24, 1975.
49. DVD commentary, *Naked Came the Stranger* (Distribpix, 2011).
50. Quoted in Margalit Fox, "Mike McGrady, Known for a Literary Hoax, Dies at 78," *New York Times*, May 14, 2012. The line is also quoted in West, "Naked Came the Stranger."
51. West, "Naked Came the Stranger."
52. A budget of $300,000 is cited in Cimons, "Literary Hoax to X-Rated Movie," while *Adam Film World* claimed $350,000. William Rotsler, "All-Time Favorite Porno Film Hits," *Adam Film World*, January 1976. On the mansion location for *Naked Came the Stranger*, see Ashley West, "Adult Film Locations 6: Naked Came the Stranger (1975)," *The Rialto Report*, July 3, 2016, https://www.therialtoreport.com/2016/07/03/naked-came-the-stranger. The

double-decker bus, meanwhile, was rented from the restaurant Sardi's, where it was ordinarily used to shuttle diners from the Sardi's East location on Fifty-Fourth Street to the city's theater district around Times Square.

53. McGrady quoted in West, "Naked Came the Stranger."
54. "Put-on of a put-on" quoted in trailer to *Naked Came the Stranger*, on the DVD of *The Opening of Misty Beethoven* (Distribpix, 2012). The description of the film as an "all-out spoof" is from Stan Isaacs, "The Movie May Be Stranger Than 'Naked,'" *After Dark*, n.d., posted on http://www.distribpix.com/film/naked-came-stranger/naked-came-stranger-emphemera-gallery. Upon learning that Henry Paris was actually Radley Metzger in disguise, one of the book's original authors commented, "I think he approach[ed] the project in the correct way." Isaacs, "The Movie May Be Stranger Than 'Naked.'"
55. Gérard Genette, *Paratexts: Thresholds of Interpretation*, trans. Jane E. Lewin (Cambridge: Cambridge University Press, 1997 [1987]), 50, 51.
56. The film is discussed in Williams's seminal *Hard Core* under its rerelease title, *The Punishment of Anne* (199–201, 222–25).
57. According to *Variety*, principal photography on the film began in Paris on August 2. "New York Sound Track," *Variety*, August 1, 1973; "New York Sound Track," *Variety*, September 5, 1973.
58. On the film's shoot, see Ashley West, "The Image (1975): The Kook, the Thief, His Wife & His Lover," *The Rialto Report*, April 25, 2021, https://www.therialtoreport.com/2021/04/25/the-image-2.
59. "Broadway," *Box Office*, January 26, 1976; "Broadway," *Box Office*, March 22, 1976.
60. See Loren Glass, *Counter-Culture Colophon: Grove Press, the Evergreen Review, and the Incorporation of the Avant-Garde* (Stanford, CA: Stanford University Press, 2013), chap. 3.
61. Susan Sontag, "The Pornographic Imagination," *Partisan Review* 34 (Spring 1967): 181–212; Andrea Dworkin, *Woman Hating* (New York: Penguin, 1974), chaps. 3 and 4.
62. All quotes in this paragraph are from *The Image* pressbook, *The Image* clippings file, NYPL.
63. The authorship of *Story of O*, meanwhile, remained a genuine mystery for decades, until a 1994 *New Yorker* article revealed the author to be Anne Desclos, assistant to and sometime lover of the influential editor of the *Nouvelle revue française*, Jean Paulhan. John de S. Jorre, "The Unmasking of O," *New Yorker*, August 1, 1994.
64. Jean de Berg, *The Image*, trans. Patsy Southgate (New York: Grove, 1975), back cover.
65. "The Opening of Misty Beethoven," *Independent Film Journal*, May 28, 1976.
66. Elisabeth Ladenson, *Dirt for Art's Sake: Books on Trial from* Madame Bovary *to* Lolita (Ithaca, NY: Cornell University Press, 2007), 234; Sontag, "The Pornographic Imagination," 182.
67. Larry Wichman, "Porn's Most Popular Perversion," *Screw*, April 5, 1976; Frank Thistle, "The Big Bondage Boom," *Adam Film World*, August 1976; Donald Groves, "America Is Bullish on S/M," *High Society*, July 1976; Ray Allen, "S-and-M: Porn's New Brand of Pleasure," *Porno Movie Girls*, 1976.
68. Wichman, "Porn's Most Popular Perversion."
69. Groves, "America Is Bullish on S/M."

70. West, "The Image (1975)."
71. On the concept of "erotic capital," see chapter 1 of this book, note 11.
72. Hardcore's iconography of meat and money shots is famously discussed in Linda Williams *Hard Core*, chap. 3.
73. The book represents the act in question only in terms of its sound—"I heard the stream of water, long held in, hit the dry leaves on the ground with violence"—whereas the film includes a genital closeup of Mendum urinating. De Berg, *The Image*, 47.
74. This was not the only scene cut from home-video releases of Henry Paris films, as porn historian Whitney Strub has shown. VCA's 1989 VHS and 2001 DVD release of *Pamela Mann* removes the staged rape, and some versions of VCA's VHS releases of *Misty Beethoven* eliminate the climactic scene in which Misty uses a strap-on to penetrate a man. Metzger's "openness to polymorphous perversity and non-phallic bodily pleasures," Strub concludes, was "obscured by home video editing, which . . . rendered heterosexuality more rote." Whitney Strub, "Sanitizing the Seventies: Pornography, Home Video, and the Editing of Sexual Memory," *Feminist Media Histories* 5, no. 2 (2019): 29. See also David Church, *Disposable Passions: Vintage Pornography and the Material Legacies of Adult Cinema* (New York: Bloomsbury, 2016), chap. 3, which uses the home video Henry Paris releases to demonstrate the "heterosexual porn industry's selective forgetting of its 'rougher' or more 'taboo' art" (135).
75. DVD commentary, *Score* (Cult Epics, 2010); "L'Image," *Variety*, February 4, 1976; no title, *After Dark*, March 1976, *The Image* clippings file, NYPL.
76. Arthur Knight, "Sex in Cinema 1976," *Playboy*, November 1976.
77. Aside from his appearance in *Pamela Mann*, discussed earlier in this chapter, Stevens also appears as a naked party guest in *Naked Came the Stranger*.
78. Marc Stevens, "Slam, Bam, Thank You, Pam," *Screw*, April 12, 1976.
79. Archer Winsten, "Masochism Reflected in Metzger's 'Image,' " *New York Post*, March 18, 1976, *The Image* clippings file, NYPL.
80. Strub, "Sanitizing the Seventies," 29.
81. "Metzger Rolls Double 'Image'; Soft and Sexy," *Variety*, July 4, 1973; *Cinema Sourcebook* 1, no. 3 (1976): ID54, *The Image* clippings file, NYPL. Synapse Films' 2011 DVD/Blu-ray includes the explicit scenes.
82. West, "The Image (1975)."
83. Corliss, "Radley Metzger," 25, 27.
84. Mikhail Bakhtin, *Rabelais and His World*, trans. Helene Iswolsky (Bloomington: Indiana University Press, 1984 [1968]), 10.
85. Bakhtin, *Rabelais and His World*, 26.
86. DVD commentary, *Barbara Broadcast* (Distribpix, 2013). The trailer and radio spot are included as extras on this DVD.
87. On *The World of Henry Paris*, see chapter 5 of this book.
88. Constance Penley, "Crackers and Whackers: The White Trashing of Porn," in *Porn Studies*, ed. Linda Williams (Durham, NC: Duke University Press, 2004), 320. On the homosocial humor of stag films, whose plots often feature men as the butts of the joke, see Thomas Waugh, "Homosociality in the Classical American Stag Film: Off-Screen, On-Screen," in Williams, ed., *Porn Studies*, 127–41; Thomas Waugh, *Hard to Imagine: Gay Male*

Eroticism in Photography and Film from Their Beginnings to Stonewall (New York: Columbia University Press, 1996), chap. 4; and Williams, *Hard Core*, chap. 3. The relation of porn and humor is elsewhere notably discussed in Laura Helen Marks, " 'That Wasn't Meant to Be Funny': Mirth and the Porn Scholar," *Porn Studies* 5, no. 1 (2018): 20–26; Peter Lehman, "Revelations about Pornography," in Lehman, ed., *Pornography*, 87–98; Nina K. Martin, "Never Laugh at a Man with His Pants Down: The Affective Dynamics of Comedy and Porn," in Lehman, ed., *Pornography*, 189–205; and Laura Kipnis, *Bound and Gagged: Pornography and the Politics of Fantasy in America* (New York: Duke University Press, 1998), chap. 4.

89. Richard Milner, "Sneak Preview," *Stag*, November 1980. Similar opinions are expressed in Arnold Leigh, "Eros at the O'Farrell: Behind the Green Door," *Adam Film World*, April 1973 (which philosophizes that the "reason one finds little laughter in erotic films is probably due to man's ability to laugh at his social self and his reluctance to laugh at his animal self"), and "Quick and Dirty . . . and Fun! New Porn Comedies," *Adam Film World*, May 1988 (which notes that porn "has labored without much success to make audiences laugh with the performers, instead of at them").
90. DVD commentary, *Barbara Broadcast*.
91. Scott Roberts, "The Elegant Erotics of Bob Sumner," *Adam Film World*, July 1981. Sumner also produced Metzger's last Henry Paris film, *Maraschino Cherry*. See chapter 4 of this book.
92. Barney Stewart, "Great Sex Scenes," *Adam Film World*, February 1977. A subsequent article in the same periodical credited *Misty Beethoven* with having established "ribald humor" as the "latest 'in' thing" in hardcore. "Ribald Humor on Screen Is Latest 'In' Thing," *Adam Film World*, August 1977.
93. Joel Kovel, "The Antidialectic of Pornography," in *Men Confront Pornography*, ed. Michael Kimmel (New York: Crown, 1990), 155.
94. The observation was most famously made by Steven Marcus. "To the question 'What time is it in pornotopia?' one is tempted to answer, 'it is always bedtime,' for that is in a literal sense true." *The Other Victorians*, 269.
95. Georges Bataille, *Erotism: Death and Sensuality*, trans. Mary Dalwood (San Francisco: City Lights, 1986 [1957]), 37. Similar to Bataille is the work of sexual-identity theorist Robert Stoller, who also locates eroticism in proximity to taboo, albeit in a more unilaterally sadistic fashion. For Stoller, it is specifically the desire to humiliate—to "hurt, harm, be cruel to, [or] degrade" someone—that constitutes the "essential theme in erotics." Robert J. Stoller, *Observing the Erotic Imagination* (New Haven, CT: Yale University Press, 1985), 3, 7.
96. Sontag, "The Pornographic Imagination," 201, 199.
97. Bataille, *Erotism*, 104; Sontag, "The Pornographic Imagination," 185. Elsewhere Bataille describes what happens when the power of a taboo simply vanishes for those who have transgressed it, leaving them "in a state of permanent disorder" in which they know "only moments of sullen disequilibrium" (*Erotism*, 243). It is this quality of "permanent" disorder that typifies what I here theorize as "Bakhtinian porn."
98. On this distinction, see also Linda Williams, "Skin Flicks on the Racial Border: Pornography, Exploitation, and Interracial Lust," in Williams, ed., *Porn Studies*, 271–308.
99. Church, *Disposable Passion*, 5–6.

100. As such, the film works within Nick Davis's Deleuzian conceptualization of the "desiring-image": images that offer "complex, unresolved visions of *desiring*—not as a fixed state but as a restive gerund." Nick Davis, *The Desiring-Image: Gilles Deleuze and Contemporary Queer Cinema* (New York: Oxford University Press, 2013), 7.
101. Williams, *Hard Core*, 223.
102. "Right away I could tell that it was different from the others. . . . The body was partially cut off by the camera, while before it had always been shown in its entirety. . . . What gave me the final proof were the dark, polished fingernails of those two hands. I remembered that Anne left her fingernails natural. And then something about the whole position, the curve of the arms, every detail of the pose, seemed less abandoned, less pleasurable, and the pubic hair a little darker. . . . [Claire's] face was no longer the same: somewhat flushed, less cold, visibly troubled." De Berg, *The Image*, 70–71.
103. Sontag, "The Pornographic Imagination," 205.
104. Sigmund Freud, " 'A Child Is Being Beaten': A Contribution to the Study of the Origin of Sexual Perversions," in *Sexuality and the Psychology of Love*, ed. Phillip Rieff (New York: Collier, 1963 [1919]), 107–32; Gilles Deleuze, *Masochism: An Interpretation of Coldness and Cruelty*, trans. Jean McNeil (New York: Braziller, 1971). In this respect I disagree with Linda Williams, who reads *The Image* through a Deleuzian lens in her *Hard Core*, 222–25.
105. Kovel, "The Antidialectic of Pornography," 163 (emphasis added).
106. The theme of the mask, Bakhtin writes "is the most complex theme of folk culture. The mask is connected with the joy of change and reincarnation, with gay relativity and with the merry negation of uniformity and similarity." Bakhtin, *Rabelais and His World*, 40.
107. See the introduction to this book.
108. Mark Jancovich, for instance, ties softcore to "the anxious relationship of the new petite bourgeoisie to their bodies," while Laura Kipnis and Constance Penley locate a "white-trash" class politics in the pages of hardcore magazines like *Hustler*. Mark Jancovich, "Naked Ambitions: Pornography, Taste and the Problem of the Middlebrow," *Scope* 20 (2001), https://www.nottingham.ac.uk/scope/documents/2001/june-2001/jancovich.pdf; Kipnis, *Bound and Gagged*, chap. 4; Penley, "Crackers and Whackers."
109. The French philosopher Jacques Rancière has pointed to the flaw in Bourdieu's methodology, which confuses aesthetic taste with familiarity—as though the fact that a factory worker doesn't *know* Bach's *Well-Tempered Clavier* means that they couldn't also *appreciate* it. How much truer must this be at the unrulier level of sexual desire, as if there could be a one-to-one relation linking the materials of sexual arousal to class belonging? Jacques Rancière, *The Philosopher and His Poor*, ed. Andrew Parker (Durham, NC: Duke University Press, 2003), chap. 9, "The Sociologist King." Laura Kipnis acknowledges this kind of critique in her work on the class affiliations of *Hustler* magazine. Pornography's status as a "low-class thing," she contends, does not mean that the lower classes are its only consumers. Rather, insofar as it is a low thing culturally, pornography thereby "takes on all the *associations*" of the lower classes, irrespective of who actually consumes it. Laura Kipnis, "How to Look at Pornography," in Lehman, ed., *Pornography*, 126 (emphasis in original). But Kipnis's argument here warrantlessly inverts Bourdieu's basic premise, as though something gets associated with the lower

classes because it is "culturally" low, rather than the other way round (which is Bourdieu's position).

110. Susanna Paasonen, *Carnal Resonance: Affect and Online Pornography* (Cambridge, MA: MIT Press, 2011), 57, 61.

4. "METZGER'S FUTURISTIC SOCIETY"

1. William Rotsler, *Contemporary Erotic Cinema: A Guide to the Revolution in Movie Making* (New York: Ballantine, 1973), 245.
2. Al Goldstein, "The Brains Behind the Throat: An Interview with Jerry Damiano," *Screw*, July 16, 1973.
3. Rotsler, *Contemporary Erotic Cinema*, 39.
4. Advertisement, *Variety*, January 22, 1975.
5. Larry Wichman, "Porn's Most Popular Perversion," *Screw*, April 5, 1976. Beatty later denied having ever entertained plans to appear in hardcore, whether Hollywood-produced or otherwise, citing "artistic reasons" for his aversion. "Beatty Won't Go Hard," *Adam Film World*, February 1977.
6. Terry Southern, *Blue Movie* (New York: World, 1970). The novel is in fact dedicated to Kubrick.
7. Joyce James, "Is There Sex After Sex Films?," *Erotic Film Guide*, October 1983.
8. "Porno Chic," *Flick*, June 1976.
9. Al Goldstein, "SCREW Interview with Jamie Gillis: The Hamlet of Hard-Core," *Screw*, May 17, 1976.
10. Samuel R. Delany, *Times Square Red, Times Square Blue*, 20th anniversary edition (New York: New York University Press, 2019).
11. DVD commentary, *Barbara Broadcast* (Distribpix, 2013).
12. Jim Holliday, *The Top 100 X-Rated Films of All Time* (Hollywood, CA: WWV, 1982). As late as 1987, over a decade after *Misty*'s release, *Adult Video News* declared that the film continues to "hold up as the all-time adult film classic." Gene Ross, "The Opening of Deep Misty Debbie Jones," *Adult Video News*, September 1987.
13. Holliday, *The Top 100 X-Rated Films of All Time*, 7; Al Goldstein, "Dirty Diversions: Porno Pygmalion," *Screw*, April 5, 1976.
14. Steven Marcus, *The Other Victorians: A Study of Sexuality and Pornography in Mid-Nineteenth Century England* (New York: Basic Books, 1966), chap. 7.
15. Marcus, *The Other Victorians*, 268.
16. Damon Young, *Making Sex Public, and Other Cinematic Fantasies* (Durham, NC: Duke University Press, 2018), 22, 4.
17. Reggie Danzig, "Film," *High Society*, July 1976.
18. DVD commentary, *The Opening of Misty Beethoven* (Distribpix, 2012).
19. Danzig, "Film."
20. DVD commentary, *The Opening of Misty Beethoven*.
21. The Paris shoot was organized by French sexploitation director Max Pécas, who had previously arranged for the location work in Metzger's *The Image* (1976), also shot in Paris. Exteriors for Seymour Love's residence were courtesy of Cobble Close Farm, a New

Jersey country home built in the Norman style from dismantled European estates. See Ashley West, "Adult Film Locations—Part 12: The Misty Beethoven Mansion," *The Rialto Report*, September 9, 2019, https://www.therialtoreport.com/2018/09/09/misty-beethoven-3.

22. Admittedly, Escoffier coins the term to describe not a narrative form of pornography, but the commercial operations of the porn industry itself, which is driven between the twin impulse to "identify new varieties of polymorphous possibilities"—the perverse dynamic—and to find strategies of symbolic containment for their representation. "Pornography," he writes, "both harnesses those perverse desires and generates them." Jeffrey Escoffier, *Sex, Society, and the Making of Pornography: The Pornographic Object of Knowledge* (New Brunswick, NJ: Rutgers University Press, 2021), 25.
23. DVD commentary, *The Opening of Misty Beethoven.*
24. Linda Williams, *Hard Core: Power, Pleasure, and the "Frenzy of the Visible"* (Berkeley: University of California Press, 1989), 140.
25. Linda Williams, "Radley Metzger, High Modernist Auteur," paper delivered at the Society of Cinema and Media Studies conference, Seattle, March 16, 2019.
26. Williams, *Hard Core*, 139–40.
27. The latter practice is commonly known as "pegging," following an online contest by sexuality columnist Dan Savage in 2001 to give it a name. As Ingrid Olsen notes, "Reader voting decided pegging was the most appropriate because, besides peg being a term for an anal penetration device, it is also a woman's name." See Olsen, "*Long Jeanne Silver* (Alex de Renzy, 1977)," *Porn Studies* 4, no. 3 (2017): 329. The scene from *Misty Beethoven* possibly inspired a strikingly similar pegging sequence in the French hardcore film *Mes nuits avec . . . Alice, Penelope, Arnold, Maud et Richard* (aka *Kinky Ladies of Bourbon Street*, 1976), which was in production around the time of *Misty*'s release.
28. "The Opening of Misty Beethoven," *Cinema Sourcebook* 1, no. 5 (1976), *The Opening of Misty Beethoven* clippings file, NYPL; Bordon Scott, "Am I Blue?," *After Dark*, May 1976, *The Opening of Misty Beethoven* clippings file, NYPL.
29. Barney Stewart, "Great Sex Scenes," *Adam Film World*, February 1977.
30. See chapter 3 of this book.
31. My reading of *Misty*'s coda differs, in this respect, from that of Linda Williams, in her celebrated analysis of the film in *Hard Core*. There Williams interprets Seymour and Misty's heterosexual union as the culmination of a trajectory common to the hardcore genre, which typically works to resolve an opposition between male and female protagonists. In the process, Williams notes, *Misty*'s coda also resolves the "problem" of the film's conception of sex as performative virtuosity, offering the more satisfying alternative of sex as a "natural" and "spontaneous" event enacted "for its own sake." Williams, *Hard Core*, 147. My reading of the ending, by contrast, sees it as largely recuperative: the film reins in the perverse dynamic that drives the narrative and in this way makes an ending possible.
32. See, e.g., David Church, *Disposable Passions: Vintage Pornography and the Material Legacies of Adult Cinema* (New York: Bloomsbury Academic, 2016), 181.
33. Herbert Marcuse, *Eros and Civilization: A Philosophical Inquiry Into Freud* (Boston: Beacon Press, 1966), 201. Along similar lines, Lauren Berlant and Michael Warner's influential

1998 essay "Sex in Public" argued for the importance of public sexual culture as a queer "world-making" project that rejects the ideology of private intimacy on which heteronormativity depends. Berlant and Warner, "Sex in Public," *Critical Inquiry* 24, no. 2 (Winter 1998): 547–66.

34. World Theater gross reported in "The Opening of Misty Beethoven," *Cinema Sourcebook*. On *Box Office*'s performance metrics, see chapter 3.
35. "The Opening of Misty Beethoven," *Cinema Sourcebook*; Goldstein, "Dirty Diversions: Porno Pygmalion"; Scott, "Am I Blue?"
36. "Beethoven Honored as Best Adult Film," *Box Office*, July 25, 1977.
37. Thomas Hilton, "The First Annual Erotica Awards," *Adam Film World*, December 1977.
38. DVD commentary, *The Opening of Misty Beethoven.*
39. Production data, here and in the paragraphs that follow, is taken from Ashley West, "Henry Paris vs. Constance Money: Chronology and Correspondence of a Conflict—Part 1," *The Rialto Report*, July 30, 2017, https://www.therialtoreport.com/2017/07/30/misty-beethoven-2.
40. Radley Metzger, "Susan Jensen," undated schedule, in West, "Henry Paris vs. Constance Money—Part 1."
41. As Johnnie Keyes, of *Behind the Green Door* (1972) fame, put it: "Jamie Gillis was a crazy dude, man. Yeah, I think he was a cruel motherfucker." Ashley West, host, "Johnnie Keyes: The Man Behind the Green Door," *The Rialto Report* (podcast), March 13, 2013.
42. Ashley West, host, "Constance Money: The Re-Opening of Misty Beethoven. And Her Father," *The Rialto Report* (podcast), January 25, 2015. Metzger, perhaps predictably, remembered the scene very differently, even going so far as to suggest that Money had almost codirected it: "She had some proficiency in S&M, so she was a big help in assisting me direct it due to her familiarity with all the paraphernalia that went into that scene." DVD commentary, *The Opening of Misty Beethoven.*
43. All quotes from West, "Constance Money."
44. "The New Girls of Porn," *Playboy*, July 1977.
45. Quote taken from memo of meeting between Metzger, Sam Lake, and Bob Sumner, December 14, 1977, in West, "Henry Paris vs. Constance Money—Part 1."
46. Radley Metzger to Jennifer Baker, September 24, 1975, and agreement between Audubon Films and Susan Jensen, October 19, 1975, in West, "Henry Paris vs. Constance Money—Part 1." Susan Jensen was Money's birth name; Jennifer Baker was another pseudonym.
47. Leighton to Susan Jensen, May 24, 1977, in West, "Henry Paris vs. Constance Money—Part 1."
48. *Susan Jensen v. Radley H. Metzger, Audubon Films, Inc., Henry Paris, Ava Leighton, Maturpix, Inc., et al.*, March 9, 1978, 7, in West, "Henry Paris vs. Constance Money—Part 1." Interestingly, just before *Barbara Broadcast*'s release, porn star Marc Stevens wrote an article in which he explicitly lambasted filmmakers for this practice: "What really pisses me off is the fact that big name performers like Georgina Spelvin and C. J. Laing are being exploited. First of all, they got a measly $150 a day for the original two- or three-day shoot, and now their names and performances are being used free, with no royalties

or money consideration whatsoever." Marc Stevens, "Guest Dirty Diversions: In Search of the Holey Tail," *Screw*, April 11, 1977.

49. Ava Leighton to Bob Sumner, July 19, 1976, in West, "Henry Paris vs. Constance Money—Part 1."
50. *Susan Jensen v. Radley H. Metzger, Audubon Films, Inc., Henry Paris, Ava Leighton, Maturpix, Inc., et al.*, May 19, 1978, in Ashley West, "Henry Paris vs. Constance Money: Chronology and Correspondence of a Conflict—Part 2," *The Rialto Report*, August 6, 2017, https://www.therialtoreport.com/2017/08/06/constance-money-2.
51. West, "Henry Paris vs. Constance Money—Part 2."
52. Ava Leighton to Ed Grainger, September 24, 1979, in West, "Henry Paris vs. Constance Money—Part 2."
53. "Interview: Constance Money," *Adult Video News*, September 1983.
54. The child, Annabelle Metzger, was Metzger's only offspring.
55. Mendum quoted in Ashley West, "The Image (1975): The Kook, the Thief, His Wife & His Lover," *The Rialto Report*, April 25, 2021, https://www.therialtoreport.com/2021/04/25/the-image-2.
56. The "conman" description is from an audio tape contained in Metzger's New Jersey storage unit, whose contents I acquired in 2020. See this book's acknowledgments for more on that sale.
57. Loren King, "Before the X Revolution," *Boston Sunday Globe*, February 4, 2001, Radley Metzger clippings file, MoMA; Elena Gorfinkel, *Lewd Looks: American Sexploitation Cinema in the 1960s* (Minneapolis: University of Minnesota Press, 2017), 131.
58. Ron Alexander, "I, A Filmmaker," *Gentlemen's Quarterly* (Winter 1969–70), Radley Metzger clippings file, MoMA. The article is discussed at length in this book's introduction.
59. See chapter 1 of this book for a discussion of this practice.
60. DVD commentary, *The Opening of Misty Beethoven*; DVD commentary, *Barbara Broadcast*.
61. DVD commentary, *Barbara Broadcast*.
62. As Metzger later explained: "[The hotel] had gone bankrupt. We made the deal to shoot there and then they decided to auction off everything in the place. The auctioneer came in and said no shooting would be allowed until night. So, the whole film had to be shot from eight at night until about six a.m." Jay Kay Lorentz, "The Erotic World of Radley Metzger: Interview by Jay Kay Lorentz," *Psychotronic Video* 17 (Winter 1994): 34.
63. On the use of footage from the *Barbara Broadcast* shoot, see the "Gloria Leonard Interview" on the DVD release of *Maraschino Cherry* (VideoXPix, 2009).
64. Larry Wichman, "Guest Dirty Diversions: Best & Worst of '77," *Screw*, January 23, 1978. Despite the films' generally positive reception, one review of *Barbara Broadcast* upbraided its director for failing to maintain the standards of *Misty Beethoven*. See "Winner of Porn Awards Comes Up with Loser," *Adam Film World*, June 1978, 66, whose unnamed author praised Henry Paris as an "Orson Welles-type genius of latter-day adult films" but panned *Barbara Broadcast* as "inferior product" marred by a "total absence of plot." "Back to the old drawing board, Henry!" the review concluded.
65. Marcus, *The Other Victorians*, 274.

66. Reggie Danzig, "Fuckfilms," *High Society*, November 1977.
67. Carl Ruderman, *High Society*'s founder, hired Leonard as publisher in 1977 on the expectation that she would be simply a figurehead. But Leonard took her position seriously and used it as a pulpit to advocate for pornography, in which capacity she also appeared on television talk shows and in campus debates throughout the 1980s and 1990s.
68. Edward Dorey, "Fuckfilms," *High Society*, June 1978.
69. William Rotsler, "Erotic Film Checklist," *Adam Film World*, February 1978.
70. Whitney Strub and Peter Alilunas, "Introduction: Sleazy Honesty," in *ReFocus: The Films of Roberta Findlay*, ed. Alilunas and Strub (Edinburgh: Edinburgh University Press, 2023), 11.
71. Peter Lehman, "Revelations about Pornography," in *Pornography: Film and Culture*, ed. Lehman (New York: Rutgers University Press, 2006), 92.
72. Mark Adamsbaum, "Guest Dirty Diversions: Nympho-Lesbo-Pervo-Weirdo," *Screw*, September 19, 1977.
73. Barry L. Sher, "Flick Interview with Filmmaker Gerard Damiano," *Flick*, August 1975.
74. Al Goldstein, "Cream of the Crotch," *Screw*, January 8, 1979.
75. "X-Rated," *Playboy*, November 1977.
76. Marc Stevens, "Fed Up 'n' Fucked Out: Marc 'Mr. 10½' Stevens Explains Why Today's Porn Scene Leaves Him Limp," *Screw*, February 20, 1978.
77. Fredric Jameson, *Archaeologies of the Future: The Desire Called Utopia and Other Science Fictions* (New York: Verso, 2005), 190.
78. Williams, *Hard Core*, 174 (emphasis added).
79. Williams, *Hard Core*, 178.
80. Jim Holliday, *Only the Best: Jim Holliday's Adult Video Almanac and Trivia Treasury* (Van Nuys, CA: Cal Vista Direct, 1986), 214.
81. Mark Adamsbaum, "Guest Dirty Diversions: Sizzling Your Senses," *Screw*, August 8, 1977.
82. See, for example, Vincent L. Barnett, " 'The Most Profitable Film Ever Made': *Deep Throat* (1972), Organized Crime, and the $600 Million Gross," *Porn Studies* 5 no. 2 (2018): 131–51. "In case it is doubted that LCN [La Casa Nostra] syndicates controlled the distribution of much of U.S. porn in the golden age, more than 80 individuals associated with porn were killed by LCN between 1969 and 1979, often in order to prevent information leakage" (135).
83. Delany, *Times Square Red, Times Square Blue*, 77–78.
84. See Nathan Abrams, "Triple EXthnics," *Jewish Quarterly* 51, no. 4 (2004): 27–30.
85. DVD commentary, *Barbara Broadcast*. See chapter 3 of this book.
86. On black female performers in the porno chic era, see Mireille Miller-Young, *A Taste for Brown Sugar: Black Women in Pornography* (Durham, NC: Duke University Press, 2014), chap. 3; Jennifer C. Nash, *The Black Body in Ecstasy: Reading Race, Reading Pornography* (Durham, NC: Duke University Press, 2014), chaps. 2 and 3.
87. There are notable exceptions of course—most famously, Johnnie Keyes's scene with Marilyn Chambers in the Mitchell Brothers' *Behind the Green Door*—but it would not be until the 1980s that interracial scenes became an established generic trope.
88. Mikhail Bakhtin, *Rabelais and His World* (Bloomington: Indiana University Press, 1984), 10–11. On *The World of Henry Paris*, see chapter 5 of this book.
89. "X-Rated," *Playboy*, April 1978.

90. A more recent variant comes courtesy of British comedian Jimmy Carr: "You can get STD's from a toilet seat, interestingly. But only if you sit down before the other guy's got up."
91. The title of Poole's film, in turn, is a play on the title of the off-Broadway play and subsequent film adaptation, *The Boys in the Band* (1968/1970).
92. Jameson, *Archaeologies of the Future*, 197–98.
93. The phrase "world-making project" is from Berlant and Warner, "Sex in Public," 558.
94. The "cool" cut of the film includes a voiceover from Barbara herself, which actually fills out more narrative context for the film's action. This cut is available as an extra feature on Distribpix's 2013 DVD release of the film.
95. The point I am making here is similar to one made by Jake Gerli in an analysis of hardcore director Chuck Vincent's films: "Sexual utopias are either never achieved or, if they are, they are realized in passing as part of a scrambled chronology that does not celebrate them as teleological solutions to sexual problems." From Gerli, "The Gay Sex Clerk: Chuck Vincent's Straight Pornography," in *Porn Studies*, ed. Linda Williams (Durham, NC: Duke University Press, 2004), 201.

5. "CULT PORN IDOL GONE STRAIGHT?"

1. Borges, "Borges and I," in *Labyrinths: Selected Stories and Other Writings* (New York: New Directions, 1964), 246.
2. Roland Barthes, "The Death of the Author," in *Image-Music-Text*, trans. Stephen Heath (New York: Hill & Wang, 1977), 142–48; Michel Foucault, "What Is an Author?," in *Language, Counter-Memory, Practice: Selected Essays and Interviews*, ed. Donald Bouchard (Ithaca, NY: Cornell University Press, 1977), 113–38.
3. Figures cited in Chuck Kleinhans, "The Change from Film to Video Pornography: Implications for Analysis," in *Pornography: Film and Culture*, ed. Peter Lehman (New Brunswick, NJ: Rutgers University Press, 2006), 156.
4. Kleinhans, "The Change from Film to Video Pornography," 156–57.
5. Peter Alilunas, *Smutty Little Movies: The Creation and Regulation of Adult Video* (Berkeley: University of California Press, 2016), 23.
6. See chapter 4 of this book.
7. Gérard Genette, *Paratexts: Thresholds of Interpretation*, trans. Jane E. Lewin (Cambridge: Cambridge University Press, 1997 [1987]), 39.
8. Genette, *Paratexts*, 52.
9. "International Soundtrack," *Variety*, October 20, 1976.
10. "Spawning Ground for Top Directors," *Variety*, June 15, 1977; "Here Come the Clones: Old Friends Return in Remake Fever," *Life*, January 1979, *The Cat and the Canary* clippings file, NYPL.
11. Gavin Millar, "Cinema," *The Listener*, February 19, 1981.
12. On hardcore filmmakers' transition into horror during this period, see Johnny Walker, "By the Numbers: Roberta Findlay, Home Video, and the Horror Genre," in *ReFocus: The Films of Roberta Findlay*, ed. Peter Alilunas and Whitney Strub (Edinburgh: Edinburgh University Press, 2023), 160–76. An earlier example would be the noted horror auteur Wes Craven, who had worked on a number of hardcore features before his infamous horror debut *Last House on the Left* in 1972.

13. Information on rights taken from film historian Tom Weaver's interviews with the film's producer, Richard Gordon, published in Weaver, *The Horror Hits of Richard Gordon* (Albany, GA: Bear Manor Media, 2014), 198.
14. Weaver, *The Horror Hits*, 193, 197. Metzger had earlier paid tribute to his friendship with Gordon by featuring the latter's *Secrets of Sex* (1970) on television in a scene from *Naked Came the Stranger* (1975).
15. "Carol Lynley," *New York Post*, September 14, 1977, *The Cat and the Canary* clippings file, NYPL.
16. "Filming Outside U.S.," *Variety*, January 7, 1977; " 'Cat and Canary' Fund," *Variety*, December 6, 1978; Weaver, *The Horror Hits*, 209.
17. "Cinema Shares Will Distribute Metzger's 'Cat,' " *Variety*, August 16, 1978.
18. Advertisement for *The Cat and the Canary*, *Variety*, February 14, 1979.
19. Jay Kay Lorentz, "The Erotic World of Radley Metzger," *Psychotronic Video*, Winter 1994, 35. What made the legal dispute so "horrendous" was that, in a last-ditch effort to avoid breach of contract, Cinema Shares released the film for a single-day booking in a Fort Lauderdale theater at the end of December. In consequence, the case marked a "rare instance," as *Variety* put it, "of attempting to legally define what constitutes a best-efforts 'theatrical release' as the term is used in standard distribution contracts." Stephen Klain, "Domestic Release Issue Underlines Audubon Films vs. CSI," *Variety*, August 16, 1979.
20. Peter Ustinov would reprise his *Death on the Nile* role as Hercule Poirot in the 1982 *Evil under the Sun*, but that film was a commercial failure, and Christie adaptations thereafter continued mainly as made-for-television films.
21. W. K. Everson, "The Cat and the Canary," *Films in Review*, January 1979; " 'Pond' Making Waves at 75G, K.C.; 'Seduction' Creates $30,000," *Variety*, January 27, 1982.
22. Lorentz, "The Erotic World of Radley Metzger," 35.
23. *The Cat and the Canary* was number ten in the week beginning March 12 and number eight in the week beginning March 19. See "Italy's Top Ten," *Screen International*, March 24 and March 31, 1979.
24. Weaver, *The Horror Hits*, 209. Unlike any of Metzger's previous films, *The Cat and the Canary* enjoyed a long shelf-life on television, particularly in the United Kingdom, where it was close kin to the countless Hammer horror films on late-night syndication. In 1994, Metzger described the film as a "leader in . . . syndication packages," quipping that he had "actually been living off that picture for eight or nine years." Lorentz, "The Erotic World of Radley Metzger," 35.
25. Weaver, *The Horror Hits*, 203.
26. See chapter 2 of this book.
27. Linda Williams, "Radley Metzger, High Modernist Auteur," paper delivered at the Society for Cinema and Media Studies Conference, Seattle, March 16, 2019.
28. André Bazin, "The Ontology of the Photographic Image," in *What Is Cinema?*, trans. Hugh Gray (Berkeley: University of California Press, 1967), 1:9. The analogy of the cinematic image to Ancient Egyptian burial practices was not original to Bazin, albeit that he provided its most famous expression. See Antonia Lant, "The Curse of the Pharoah, or How Cinema Contracted Egyptomania," *October* 59 (Winter 1992): 86–112.
29. Lorentz, "The Erotic World of Radley Metzger," 35.

30. Bill Greeley, "There's No 'X' in HBO," *Variety*, July 14, 1976.
31. David Andrews, *Soft in the Middle: The Contemporary Softcore Feature in Its Contexts* (Columbus: Ohio State University, 2006), 2.
32. See Luke Stadel, "Cable, Pornography, and the Reinvention of Television, 1982–1989," *Cinema Journal* 53, no. 3 (Spring 2014): 59.
33. "Metzger of Audubon: Day Will Come When TV Night Audiences See His Pix," *Variety*, January 14, 1970.
34. "Escapade Plans to Take It Off for Pay-Cable," *Variety*, July 30, 1981.
35. On the history of the Playboy Channel, see Stadel, "Cable, Pornography," and Peter Alilunas, "Playboy TV: Contradictions, Confusion, and Post-network Pornography," in *From Networks to Netflix: A Guide to Changing Channels*, ed. Derek Johnson (New York: Routledge, 2018), 365–73.
36. "Playboy Video," *Playboy*, December 1982.
37. In January 1984, *Erotic Film Guide* reported that Chuck Vincent had signed a multipicture deal with Playboy, lamenting that the channel's softcore policy meant that adult film was losing "one of the master makers of fuck 'n' suck fare." "Show Biz," *Erotic Film Guide*, January 1984.
38. "Playboy, MGM/UA Link," *Variety*, November 30, 1983.
39. Metzger quoted in liner notes for *The Princess and the Call Girl* DVD (First Run Features, 2006).
40. "The Princess and the Call Girl," *Variety*, May 23, 1984.
41. John Motavalli, "Playboy and the Erotic Dilemma," *Cablevision*, December 15, 1986, quoted in Stadel, "Cable, Pornography," 62.
42. Vincent did, however, continue his new vein of sex comedies through his own production company, Platinum Pictures, with *Hollywood Hot Tubs* (1984), *Wimps* (1986), and *Sex Appeal* (1986).
43. Details on the division of labor between Metzger and Kikoïne are taken from the special feature "Talking about *The Tale of Tiffany Lust*: A Conversation with Director Gérard Kikoïne" on the Blu-ray, *The Tale of Tiffany Lust* (Mélusine, 2023). Metzger first got to know Kikoïne through Dodd, from whom Metzger acquired the rights to two films on which Kikoïne had worked as editor, *Le sexe qui parle* (a.k.a. *Pussy Talk*, 1975) and *Mes nuits avec . . . Alice, Penelope, Arnold, Maud et Richard* (a.k.a. *Kinky Ladies of Bourbon Street*, 1976]), both of which were distributed in the United States through Robert Sumner's Mature Pictures.
44. Production details taken from Ashley West, " 'The Tale of Tiffany Lust' (1981): Henry Paris' Secret Comeback," *The Rialto Report*, December 1, 2019, https://www.therialtoreport.com/2019/12/01/tiffany-lust.
45. Suzanne Feele, "The Tale of Tiffany Lust," *Adult Cinema Review*, September 1981.
46. West, "The Tale of Tiffany Lust."
47. It is not known why Metzger chose these specific names, but "Peter Wolfe" is likely a reference to adult magazine publisher Peter Wolff.
48. The adult periodical *Stag* made particular note of *Tiffany Lust*'s "wonderfully funny scenes" and quoted passages of the film's dialog at length. Richard Milner, "Sneak Preview," *Stag*, August 1981.

49. Metzger quoted in Ashley West, " 'The Sins of Ilsa' (1985): The Untold Story of Radley Metzger's Unreleased Last Film," *The Rialto Report*, June 23, 2019, https://www.therialtoreport.com/2019/06/23/sins-of-ilsa. Production details in the following paragraphs are taken from the same source. The film analysis, however, is my own, based on a video recording acquired from the contents of Metzger's New Jersey storage unit in 2020. (See this book's acknowledgments for more on that sale.)
50. Metzger quoted in West, "The Sins of Ilsa." The *Ilsa* series began with the 1975 film, *Ilsa, She Wolf of the SS*, depicting a sadistic female Nazi (played by Dyanne Thorne) conducting medical experiments in a concentration camp, and continued with two official sequels: *Ilsa, Harem Keeper of the Oil Sheiks* (1976) and *Ilsa, the Tigress of Siberia* (1977). Early poster mockups for Metzger's film display a variety of potential titles, including *Young Ilsa*.
51. Genette, *Paratexts*, 48.
52. Footage for the two short films was largely shot in Ava Leighton's apartment, which Metzger had previously used as Pamela Mann's home in *The Private Afternoons of Pamela Mann* (1974). As explained earlier, Metzger at some point acquired U.S. distribution rights to *Le sexe qui parle*. However, it is not clear whether this occurred before or after filming the short with Harnois.
53. In his interviews with Ashley West, Metzger explained his decision to pass on Harnois: "She had a strong French accent, and I wasn't convinced she could handle the dialogue. I could have dubbed her lines, but I also thought that she had the air of a sweet, young girl, which wasn't a perfect fit for the role of a prostitute." West, "The Sins of Ilsa."
54. Linda Williams, "Film Bodies: Gender, Genre, and Excess," *Film Quarterly* 44, no. 4 (Summer 1991): 2–13.
55. West, "The Sins of Ilsa."
56. A title search on the website Newspaperarchive.com shows that the film played every week in March of that year, and at least once more in April of 1988. The listed cast members and capsule plot descriptions are unmistakably of the film that Metzger had prepared as *Sins of Ilsa* (e.g., "A young journalist researching New York's sex industry becomes intimately involved with an erotic performer" and "Woman reporter follows erotic star from Times Square to Paris"). *Yuma Sun*, March 14, 1987, and *Bluefield Daily Telegraph*, April 8, 1988.
57. Constance Penley, "Crackers and Whackers: The White Trashing of Porn," in *Porn Studies*, ed. Linda Williams (Durham, NC: Duke University Press, 2004), 309–31.
58. "The World of Henry Paris," *Adult Video News*, April 1986.
59. *Adam Film World*, July 1987.
60. She also managed to combine her career in adult film with patron membership of the Variety Club children's charity and a trusteeship at New York's B'nai B'rith, where she was among the first cohort of women admitted in 1974. See "Raves for New York (Yes!) Conclude Variety Convention," *Independent Film Journal*, May 11, 1972, and "Cinema B'nai B'rith Admits Gladys, Ruth, Ava, Making History," *Variety*, March 20, 1974. She was elected East Coast vice president of the Adult Film Association of America in 1980 and joined its board of directors three years later. See "Women Front That Adult Film Assn.," *Variety*, March 19, 1980; "New Board of Directors," *The AFAA Bulletin*, March 1983.

61. Metzger quoted in Steve Gallagher, " 'This Is Softcore': The History of Radley Metzger," *Filmmaker Magazine*, August 7, 2014, https://filmmakermagazine.com/87041-this-is-softcore-the-history-of-radley-metzger.
62. David Church, *Disposable Passions: Vintage Pornography and the Material Legacies of Adult Cinema* (New York: Bloomsbury, 2016), 109.
63. The term "New Queer Cinema" was coined by B. Ruby Rich in a 1992 *Sight & Sound* essay. Rich, "New Queer Cinema," *Sight and Sound* 80 (1992): 31–34.
64. Erik Jackson, "What's the *Score*?," *Time Out New York*, n.d. (ca. February 1997), *Score* clippings file, NYPL.
65. Stephen Gallagher, "The Libertine: Stephen Gallagher on *Score*'s Radley Metzger," *Filmmaker Magazine*, Summer 1997, 46–47; Gary Morris, "Seduction Is Universal: Thoughts on Radley Metzger," *Bright Lights Film Journal*, April 1, 1998, https://brightlightsfilm.com/seduction-universal-thoughts-radley-metzger.
66. Not included in the orthonymic titles released in 1999 were *The Princess and the Call Girl* (which wouldn't see DVD release until 2006, through First Run Features) and *The Image* (first released in 2011, through Synapse Films).
67. Morris, "Seduction Is Universal."
68. Jackson, "What's the *Score*?" (emphasis in original).
69. Whitney Strub, "Sanitizing the Seventies: Pornography, Home Video, and the Editing of Sexual Memory," *Feminist Media Histories* 5, no. 2 (2019): 26.
70. Elena Gorfinkel, "Radley Metzger's 'Elegant Arousal': Taste, Aesthetic Distinction and Sexploitation," in *Underground U.S.A.: Filmmaking Beyond the Hollywood Canon*, ed. Xavier Mendik and Steven Jay Schneider (London: Wallflower, 2003), 39.
71. Verrill died on September 14, 1977, at the hands of Paul Bateson, who was suspected of a series of murders of other gay men in the city.
72. A discussion of the Strand's 1978 film festival begins Marc Francis Newman's PhD thesis, "Deviant Programming: Curating Queer Spectatorial Possibilities in U.S. Art House Cinemas, 1968–1989," University of California, Santa Cruz, 2018.
73. Jackson, "What's the *Score*?"
74. Jacques Boyreau, *Sexytime: The Post-Porn Rise of the Pornoisseur* (Seattle: Fantagraphics, 2012).
75. Erik Piepenburg, "Smut, Refreshed for a New Generation," *New York Times*, January 23, 2014.
76. Ashley West, " 'The Heat of the Midnight Sun': The Untold Story of Radley Metzger's Last Film Project," *The Rialto Report*, April 9, 2017, https://www.therialtoreport.com/2017/04/09/henry-paris.
77. Church, *Disposable Passions*, 198.
78. See, for example, the claims made in the afterword to Carl Wilson's *Let's Talk About Love: Why Other People Have Such Bad Taste*, expanded edition (New York: Bloomsbury, 2014), in which Wilson and other writers update and reflect upon his classic study of Céline Dion, *Let's Talk About Love: A Journey to the End of Taste* (New York: Continuum, 2007).
79. For a useful summary of various arguments about taste and algorithmic culture, see Mattias Frey, *Netflix Recommends: Algorithms, Film Choice, and the History of Taste* (Berkeley: University of California Press, 2021).

80. Richard A. Peterson and Roger M. Kern, "Changing Highbrow Taste: From Snob to Omnivore," *American Sociological Review* 61, no. 5 (October 1996): 900–907.
81. Bart Testa, "Soft-Shaft Opportunism: Radley Metzger's Erotic Kitsch," *Spectator* 19, no. 2 (Spring–Summer 1999): 44.
82. See Church, *Disposable Passions*, 51.

INDEX